America Goes to War

The American Social Experience
SERIES

General Editor:
JAMES KIRBY MARTIN

Editors:
PAULA S. FASS, STEVEN H. MINTZ, CARL PRINCE,
JAMES W. REED & PETER N. STEARNS

1. *The March to the Sea and Beyond: Sherman's Troops in the Savannah and Carolinas Campaigns*
JOSEPH T. GLATTHAAR

2. *Childbearing in American Society: 1650–1850*
CATHERINE M. SCHOLTEN

3. *The Origins of Behaviorism: American Psychology, 1870–1920*
JOHN M. O'DONNELL

4. *New York City Cartmen, 1667–1850*
GRAHAM RUSSELL HODGES

5. *From Equal Suffrage to Equal Rights: Alice Paul and the National Woman's Party, 1910–1928*
CHRISTINE A. LUNARDINI

6. *Mr. Jefferson's Army: Political and Social Reform of the Military Establishment, 1801–1809*
THEODORE J. CRACKEL

7. *"A Peculiar People": Slave Religion and Community-Culture among the Gullahs*
MARGARET WASHINGTON CREEL

8. *"A Mixed Multitude": The Struggle for Toleration in Colonial Pennsylvania*
SALLY SCHWARTZ

9. *Women, Work, and Fertility, 1900–1986*
SUSAN HOUSEHOLDER VAN HORN

10. Liberty, Virtue, and Progress: Northerners and Their War for the Union
EARL J. HESS

11. Lewis M. Terman: Pioneer in Psychological Testing
HENRY L. MINTON

12. Schools as Sorters: Lewis M. Terman, Applied Psychology, and the Intelligence Testing Movement, 1890–1930
PAUL DAVIS CHAPMAN

13. Free Love: Marriage and Middle-Class Radicalism in America, 1825–1860
JOHN C. SPURLOCK

14. Jealousy: The Evolution of an Emotion in American History
PETER N. STEARNS

15. The Nurturing Neighborhood: The Brownsville Boys Club and Jewish Community in Urban America, 1940–1990
GERALD SORIN

16. War in America to 1775: Before Yankee Doodle
JOHN MORGAN DEDERER

17. An American Vision: Far Western Landscape and National Culture, 1820–1920
ANNE FARRAR HYDE

18. Frederick Law Olmsted: The Passion of a Public Artist
MELVIN KALFUS

19. Medical Malpractice in Nineteenth-Century America: Origins and Legacy
KENNETH ALLEN DE VILLE

20. Dancing in Chains: The Youth of William Dean Howells
RODNEY D. OLSEN

21. Breaking the Bonds: Marital Discord in Pennsylvania, 1730–1830
MERRIL D. SMITH

22. In the Web of Class: Delinquents and Reformers in Boston, 1810s–1930s
ERIC C. SCHNEIDER

23. Army of Manifest Destiny: The American Soldier in the Mexican War, 1846–1848
JAMES M. MCCAFFREY

24. The Dutch-American Farm
DAVID STEVEN COHEN

25. Independent Intellectuals in the United States, 1910–1945
STEVEN BIEL

26. The Modern Christmas in America: A Cultural History of Gift Giving
WILLIAM B. WAITS

27. The First Sexual Revolution: The Emergence of Male Heterosexuality in Modern America
KEVIN WHITE

28. Bad Habits: Drinking, Smoking, Taking Drugs, Gambling, Sexual Misbehavior, and Swearing in American History
JOHN BURNHAM

29. General Richard Montgomery and the American Revolution: From Redcoat to Rebel
HAL T. SHELTON

30. From Congregation Town to Industrial City: Culture and Social Change in a Southern Community
MICHAEL SHIRLEY

31. The Social Dynamics of Progressive Reform: Atlantic City, 1854–1920
MARTIN PAULSSON

32. America Goes to War: A Social History of the Continental Army
CHARLES PATRICK NEIMEYER

America Goes to War

A Social History of the Continental Army

CHARLES PATRICK NEIMEYER

NEW YORK UNIVERSITY PRESS
New York and London

NEW YORK UNIVERSITY PRESS
New York and London

Library of Congress Cataloging-in-Publication Data
Neimeyer, Charles Patrick, 1954–
America goes to war : a social history of the Continental Army / Charles Patrick Neimeyer.
p. cm.—(The American social experience series ; 33)
Includes bibliographical references (p.).
ISBN 0-8147-5780-4
1. United States. Continental Army. 2. United States—History—Revolution, 1775–1783—Social aspects. I. Title. II. Series.
E259.N45 1996
973.3'1—dc20 95-4406
CIP

New York University Press books are printed on acid-free paper, and their binding materials are chosen for strength and durability.

Manufactured in the United States of America

10 9 8 7 6 5 4 3 2 1

To the Neimeyers—
Janet, Kelli, Patrick, Christopher—
and to Sam

Contents

Illustrations

All illustrations appear following page 88.

Paper Topic

The American Revolution and the Colonial Military American Tradition

Prof Bill Spain

Cdr Eric Brown, USCG

A Theoretical and Contextual Analysis of the Leadership of a Few, Select Leaders of the Revolution

I would like to research the cultural context, societal assumptions, & finally, the behaviors of leadership of a couple of select leaders. I am considering looking at Washington and Franklin, and perhaps one other (Sam Adams or Patrick Henry). I'd like to reserve the flexibility to change these actors as the semester continues and my research progresses. I plan to place founding father challenges/actions in the context of the current beliefs of the evolution of leadership & management thought. Finally, I would compare and contrast aspects of their leadership with current organizational behavior and leadership theories.

IRIQUOIS Confederacy. week 8

Phillip Scott - Battles

Eric Brown - Aftermath.

Preface

During the early months of the Revolution, when the issue of manning and maintaining a national army dominated the thoughts of many in and out of Congress, John Adams declared flatly that "we must all be soldiers." What he meant was that all true patriots against British repression should demonstrate their loyalty by becoming armed soldiers in the cause of freedom. Yet while Adams himself had several opportunities to act upon his declaration, he never did. When Congress asked him to perform a modestly risky mission to Canada in 1776, he refused to go, claiming that his command of the French language was inadequate. (Curiously, this did not affect his subsequent missions as diplomatic minister to the French Court.)[1] General Charles Lee even suggested that Congress pass laws that *obliged* every citizen to serve at least one term as a soldier.[2] Yet soon after the fighting began, Lee loudly complained to Congress of the quality of soldiers recruited for the army. Adams and Lee, like many others of their revolutionary generation, talked one way but acted another.

Adams and others of his background and class never served as soldiers because by the time of the Revolution, defense had ceased to be a function of the entire community. The myth of the classless, independence-minded farmer or hard-working artisan-turned-soldier has been a long-standing legend that is difficult to overcome.[3] Contrary to popular lore and some modern commentators, the well-to-do and "yeoman farmers" seemed to prefer staying at home rather than rushing to the front lines after the *rage militare* of the first campaign had worn off. Seizing on the idea that an army of citizen-soldiers represented true republican virtue, later generations of historians skewed the history of the Continental army, ascribing the characteristics of the first year of the war to the war as a whole.[4]

In this book I hope to separate fact from the fire-eating rhetoric of the rebel elite, and to show who served in the army during the Revolution, and why. I will demonstrate that those who served in the army as long-termed Continental soldiers were not those whom historians have traditionally associated with the defense of liberty. Rather, I will argue that Adams and others of his class and political persuasion came to rely increasingly on those *not* connected to the communities that enlisted them for national service; these groups included African Americans, ethnic minorities, and "free white men on the move."[5] These were precisely the sort of people least able to resist the blandishments of a recruiting party and most willing to part temporarily with their civil liberties in exchange for a steady wage.

Willing to serve—though not for an indefinite period of time—these groups struggled against attempts by congressional elites to force them to enlist for the duration of an open-ended war. By the later years of the war, the common enlisted man would view the Continental Congress as arbitrary and capricious, just as Parliament had been to colonial elites. Using even greater means of repression as the war ground on, Continental officers attempted to keep the army together by force. The soldiers reacted by employing means of resistance long used by others in the armed services in the eighteenth century: insubordination, desertion, and mutiny.

Resistance within the army against the various acts of Congress paralleled the rebellion of colonial elites against the repressive policies of Parliament and crown and culminated in the great Continental army mutinies of 1781–83. Little scholarship has been devoted to cataclysmic events such as the various Continental army mutinies that occurred during the last three years of the war. Perhaps, as Revolutionary War historian John Shy has suggested, this is because the "bedrock facts of the American Revolutionary struggle, especially after the euphoric first year, are not pretty."[6]

This book demonstrates that our understanding of the traditional republican fears of the tyranny of a standing army needs some revision. We know that from the mid-seventeenth century on, Whig writers extolled the virtues of the citizen-soldier. They were strongly influenced by memories of Oliver Cromwell's "New Model Army." Cromwell's army swept away the supporters of a tyrannical king (Charles I) but used methods that showed little concern for human rights. The New Model Army, more loyal to Cromwell than to England, served as an example of the dangers posed by standing armies to liberty. Unlike Cromwell's New Model Army, however, the Continental army was not feared by Whiggish elites because of its supposed loyalty to the commander in chief, George Washington. Rather, new evidence suggests that the conduct of the army during the latter years of the war made colonial elites (including Continental army officers) increasingly afraid of the revolutionary tendencies of an *armed* lower class army only slightly connected to the communities that enlisted them.[7] Moreover, while Whig writers consistently extolled the virtues of a propertied citizen-soldiery, they neglected to consider the ramifications of a soldiery that considered its own military labor as a form of property and their struggle to preserve it from expropriation by Congress.

The desperate search for military workers to serve the Continental army as long-termed soldiers caused colonial elites to reconsider the value of racial and ethnic minorities who came to be increasingly attracted to the bounties offered by Congress and state governments. Alexander Hamilton and John Laurens, members of George Washington's staff during the war, both thought that the large African American population of North America was an asset too valuable to be ignored. Various New England states formed units composed entirely of African Americans. The mid-Atlantic states had complete battalions of Irish and German immigrants. The states of Massachusetts and South Carolina employed whole tribes of Native Americans as soldiers.[8] This book will demonstrate how these groups were affected by army service.

Many people, institutions, and archives provided invaluable assistance in the preparation and research for this book. I owe much to the strong hand of my mentor, Marcus Rediker of Georgetown University. His keen eye for detail and sage criticism made this book a far better product in the end. David Fowler and the entire staff of the David Library of the American Revolution allowed me free rein of their vast archive of Revolutionary War material, and I cannot express enough my true appreciation of their invaluable assistance in nearly every phase of research for the book. Mark Lender of Kean College was especially helpful in providing some background for the direction of the research. James Kirby Martin's work has probably influenced me the most. His clear understanding of the importance of studying the army from "the bottom up" enabled me to discover insights into the composition of the Continental soldiery that I had failed to see before. Martin also provided invaluable criticism in earlier drafts of this book; his advice and wisdom were greatly appreciated. I would like to give special thanks to Niko Pfund, my editor at New York University Press. His support and positive attitude toward the entire project definitely made it much more enjoyable.

My strongest measure of thanks and appreciation is extended to my family. First, I would like to thank my parents for preparing the way. My father, now long deceased, left me with the gift of perseverance. My mother provided me (and still does) with the capacity to see beyond the surface of events and come to a deeper understanding of things. My wife Janet, my daughter Kelli, and my sons Patrick and Christopher sacrificed quality time together, vacations, and travel opportunities so that I could spend time in research libraries and archives for the past five years. Janet was an invaluable proofreader and soulmate who encouraged me every step of the way. Without her support and that of my family, this book would not have been possible.

Prologue

Two men in blue, members of a German baron's military recruiting party, noticed Candide, a wandering young man down on his luck, sitting in a corner of a tavern. "Now there's a well-made fellow," said one to the other, and they quickly moved in on their prey. Striking up a conversation after offering to buy the destitute lad food and drink, they asked Candide whether or not he was "an admirer of the king?" "Good heavens no," said Candide, "I have never seen him." Disregarding his answer, the recruiters asked Candide if he would at least drink a toast, compliments of them, to the king's health. Seeing no harm in that, Candide emptied his glass. "That's enough," cried the recruiters, "you are now his support, defender . . . and hero in the bargain. Go where glory awaits you." With that, the recruiters clapped Candide in irons and hauled him off toward the army barracks.[1]

At the barracks, Candide was quickly taught to "right turn, left turn, slope arms, order arms, how to aim and fire." He was "given thirty strokes of the cat" when he moved too slowly. The next day, he received only twenty strokes, which made him think he was making progress as a soldier. The following day, he received only ten and "was thought a prodigy by his comrades." Soon afterward, Candide decided to exercise his belief in "free will." Thinking that "it was a common privilege to man and beast to use [their] legs when [they] wanted," he deserted his regiment. His free will and privileged legs took him only six miles. Recaptured, he was thrown into a dungeon with four other "six-foot heroes." Given the choice at his court-martial of running the gauntlet of his regiment thirty-six times or "twelve bullets in the brain," Candide chose the former.[2]

Candide's experiences were not so different from those of practically any soldier in an eighteenth-century standing army. The pay was low, the mortality high, the military justice severe. Moreover, there existed a yawning social gap between the soldiers who labored and their officers who managed. Alexander Hamilton, future secretary of the U.S. Treasury and member of Washington's personal staff during the Revolutionary War, once wrote that "with sensible officers, soldiers can hardly be too stupid. . . . Let the officers be men of sense and sentiment, and the nearer the soldiers approach to machines perhaps the better."[3] What Hamilton ultimately wanted were mindless automatons that did not complain when they were not fed or properly discharged, and did not leave the field until victorious or dead—something that men of his own class and background were unwilling to do. He wanted men without passion or history. During the Revolution, he got neither.

Eighteenth-century colonial American soldiers had more in common with their European counterparts than they did with a "true" citizen army. However, American soldiers differed from their European cousins in at least one respect—they usually had set term limits for the amount of service they were willing to provide the state. European armies consisted of formations of men whose terms of enlistment—if such terms existed at all—were quite long compared to those of Americans. During the eighteenth century, it was not unusual for British soldiers to enlist for twenty years or more in a particular regiment. Russian soldiers were conscripted into the czar's army for twenty-five years, and their families mourned their departure for service as if they had already died.[4]

Concentrating on the poorer segments of society, eighteenth-century recruiters on both sides of the Atlantic tried to induce those without property to enlist as long-termed soldiers. The states of South Carolina and Maryland, for instance, passed laws that induced the indigent to serve in the Continental forces: "Every vagrant or man above 18 years of age, able bodied, and having no family, fixed battalion, or visible means of subsistence" was subject to impressment into military service. In order to attract the lower sorts into the ranks, many states granted immunity from prosecution for debts less than fifty dollars. By 1776 Congress passed laws that required new recruits to serve "for the duration of the war," which meant they were required to serve until a peace was concluded, meaning they served for virtually an unlimited term like Russian conscripts.[5]

It was not surprising that Congress was notoriously unable to get enough American citizens to serve more than six months. Manpower had to be shared with the rural agricultural and urban industrial sectors of the economy, which led to a chronic shortage of regular army soldiers throughout the war. Higher bounties and other entreaties were offered, but they never effectively provided Washington's army with the desired number of soldiers. However, the shortage of labor also had the side-effect of enabling these military wage laborers with a rare opportunity to bargain for better conditions and benefits.

Starting out as a diverse, disparate group of individuals, the Continental soldiers were quickly transformed from unskilled or itinerant laborers to a waged (and armed) group of military workers who sought to protect their valued skills from being expropriated by Congress. As the war progressed, the military manpower that kept the Revolution going became aware of its own importance in winning independence. The great Continental army mutinies of 1780 and 1781, for instance, were just two expressions of this consciousness. The soldiers demanded and, in many cases, received just compensation for their military efforts and sacrifices. However, they were usually only successful when they collectively threatened established authority with violence such as mass mutinies, or with work stoppages such as desertion or refusal to reenlist.

Yet, as we shall see, there were some members of the colonial community who wanted desperately to join the army, at least for a temporary period of time. Unemployed (and unskilled) immigrants took their places in the Continental ranks along with out-of-work native agricultural laborers, transients, and free (and unfree) African Americans. Malcolm Blair, an Irish indentured shoemaker, had run away from his master, Andrew Summers, during the spring of 1776 in Philadelphia. Crossing the Schuylkill River, he was last seen headed in the direction of the Continental army. Summers logically surmised that the army was an ideal refuge for runaways such as Blair. He stated in an advertisement that he thought Blair "might try to get into the army," because in addition to his skills as a shoemaker, "he could beat the drum very well."[6]

A Cosmopolitan Community

The Continental army had trans-Atlantic roots. Thomas Paine remarked in *Common Sense* that "Europe, not England" should be considered "the parent-country of America." John Adams stated in a similar way that a complete history of the American Revolution would be a "history of mankind during that epoch."[7] Paine's and Adams's comments are a significant departure from the traditional historiography of the Revolutionary era. By bursting the political confines of early American history, they make the Revolution appear to be something more than a disagreement between kindred relations. Rather, they contend the rebellion was a European, or at least an "Atlantic" phenomenon. Moreover, they require contemporary historians to widen their scope of inquiry into the revolutionary aspects of all Atlantic cultures and even into the subcultures that existed within the British empire itself. By doing so, we can begin to see that the American Revolution was perhaps a rebellion within a broader cycle of rebellion going on in the eighteenth-century world, in which a large number of Atlantic peoples with various political and cultural sensitivities took part.[8]

In 1776, all the colonies became communities of increased ethnic and racial diversity. The sights, smells, and clamor of at least a dozen different nations and tongues in the larger American ports would have led visitors to conclude that they were in a truly cosmopolitan land. Enclaves of immigrants dotted the frontiers. German and Irish redemptioners sullenly lined port city wharves waiting to be "redeemed" by a farmer or merchant. Convicts, slaves, and various non-British peoples clung to ways that were alien to those descended from English immigrants. It was a multicultural society of turmoil and contrast.[9] These same groups were the usual targets for colonial recruiters.

The use of foreigners, convicts, and other repressed groups as long-termed, waged soldiers was a common European practice. The Spanish army, for instance, customarily owed its soldiers part of their wages and even thought that withholding pay would prevent desertion. One commander remarked that "it is a good thing to owe them something." The people of Antwerp, however, probably disagreed with him. In 1576, unpaid Spanish soldiers looted the city when they found out their wages were not forthcoming. This "Spanish Fury" caused the death of more than six thousand civilians.[10]

In eighteenth-century America, the employment of long-termed soldiers hinged similarly on a wage-based enlistment contract and attracted or coerced a significant number of foreigners into the ranks of the army. Sought after for their value as long-termed soldiers, African Americans, immigrants, free white transients, and even deserters from the opposing army appeared in the Continental ranks in larger numbers than commonly thought.[11]

Pay, Discipline, and Resistance

Because America decided to employ a wage-based military force to win its freedom, many colonial elites were shocked to learn that the enlisted man's ideas about freedom and "liberty" were vastly different from their own. Soldiers whose sole possession was often only their own body strongly reacted to governmental attempts to commandeer them. However, their struggle went beyond merely avoiding the expropriation of their own labor—they also fought to establish a "moral economy." Men went off to war knowing that American soldiers were not only to be paid, but were also entitled to a set ration of food and an annual suit of clothes. Furthermore, colonial American soldiers were not like their British or Russian counterparts—they served for distinctly limited terms, and they believed that most of colonial society recognized these Americanized traditions of armed service. Violations of customary rights became, as we shall see, a tremendous source of tension between the soldiers and the army command.[12] The struggle between Continental army officers and their men needs to be viewed in the same sort of light. Why were the men mutinying? What were their grievances, and why did so few officers share the common soldier's point of view?

Arrangement of Chapters

The chapters in this book are arranged topically. Chapter 1 analyzes the social backgrounds of the enlisted ranks who were recruited in three distinct geographical regions—New England, the mid-Atlantic states, and the South—showing how men were recruited from each area and why they agreed to the terms of enlistment.

Chapters 2 and 3 contain discussions of the Continental appeal to the foreign born. These chapters use enlistment and pension records to show that large segments of the Continental army were not born in the United States, which means that these soldiers could not have been, as traditional historiography would have it, citizen-soldiers who left their farms or businesses to defend hearth and home. What advantage did service in the army provide immigrants? How did their participation reveal the larger implications of social struggles that were not merely American but Atlantic in nature?

Chapter 4 reviews the issue of race and the army. What effect did the turmoil of eight years of war have on the thousands of slaves and free blacks who entered the struggle? Were the British in fact liberators, as Lord Dunmore styled himself? How did the Continental army, which fought the forces of "political slavery," treat the thousands of blacks it employed? How was the African American community affected by service in the Continental army?

No discussion of race and the army would be complete without some mention of the continuing struggle between Native Americans and the resurgent Anglo-American communities on the Revolutionary war frontier, as is done in chapter 5. This is the shortest chapter, because very few Indians served terms as waged Continental soldiers or even as redcoats. Rather, Native American tribes were viewed by both sides as wartime allies rather than as reinforcements for the regular ranks. We learn which tribes found it in their interest to ally themselves with the Continental forces. How did military service and the war as a whole affect the future of the few tribes that did become allies?

Chapter 6 extends the discussion of soldierly motivation. Continental soldiers were not automatons in a military machine, as Alexander Hamilton had hoped they would be. Rather, they were actively engaged in a struggle with their officers to control their workplace, the army camp. This chapter highlights the contractual nature of the bargain struck between individuals and the government upon recruitment. Most scholars now agree that Washington wanted an army that was similar in character to the British standing force he opposed; he wanted, above all, docile, obedient, and disciplined soldiers. When the men resisted, he attributed their behavior to the "leveling tendencies" of the "lower sorts" or the reactions of an exceedingly "dirty and nasty" people.[13]

Chapter 7 analyzes the ways in which Continental soldiers resisted their officers and government in an attempt to maintain their right to sell their labor as freely as possible. Ethnic soldiers with a broad experience of resistance organized and led mutinies and revolts, yet these were not the only forms of rebellion. Soldiers also engaged in insubordination, desertion, and work stoppages. Scattered, isolated resistance took on a more collective nature as the war lengthened and as soldiers were held in the military against their contracts and wills. Recognizing the desperate need of Congress for military manpower and knowing that absolutely *no one* was waiting in the civilian community to replace them, the soldiers used scarce military labor to bargain collectively and to extract concessions from the government.[14]

All the chapters are closely associated with one another in scope and purpose. The evidence revealed that the presence of large numbers of non-white and non-Anglican groups that participated in the conflict caused the war to be more Atlantic than strictly North American. How these groups were pulled to and fro is important, because it ultimately allowed them to gain some social concessions from traditional colonial power structures either during or at the end of the war. It is quite obvious, for instance, that if the war had never taken place, the number of free African Americans within the colonies around 1783 would have been much smaller. At the very least, the turmoil of war changed the status quo for many of these unempowered groups.

An argument should be made against the mythified view of the Continental soldier. There is a need to recover his real history—his hopes and fears, his origins, motivations, and actions. Noting the experience of the majority of men who comprised the army—the poor, the illiterate, the outcasts of a colonial society long stratified into classes—we see that the Continental army was motivated and manned primarily by those not connected to property or settled community. But this very characteristic also served to make the army more revolutionary than its creators had intended. In 1780, Joseph Plumb Martin aptly described the feelings of many in the army: "We therefore still kept upon our parade in groups, venting our spleen at our country and government, then at our officers, and then at ourselves for our imbecility in staying there and starving in detail for an ungrateful people who did not care what became of us, so they could enjoy themselves while we were keeping a cruel enemy from them."[15] This is a worm's-eye view of the Continental army.

CHAPTER ONE

Few Had the Appearance of Soldiers: The Social Origins of the Continental Line

In 1776, Captain Alexander Graydon was sent into the Pennsylvania hinterlands on a recruiting trip for the Continental army. Finding no one willing to sign the terms of enlistment, he slipped across the Maryland border, hoping, he stated, "that [he] might find some seamen or longshoremen there, out of employ."[1] His efforts yielded only one recruit, a man deemed so valueless by his community that a local wag informed Graydon that the recruit "would do to stop a bullet as well as a better man, as he was truly a worthless dog."[2] Graydon later wrote that his problems with recruitment served "in some degree to correct the error of those who seem to conceive the year 1776 to have been a season of almost universal patriotic enthusiasm." Louis Duportail, a French volunteer and chief engineer of the Continental army, noticed the same trend. "There is a hundred times more enthusiasm for this Revolution in any Paris cafe than in all the colonies together."[3] While both officers probably exaggerated the extent of patriotic decline, their assertions run counter to traditional historical accounts concerning the Continental army and those who comprised it.

While patriotism and political activism as motivating forces cannot be rejected in all cases, huge amounts of evidence point to an American army closely akin to its European cousins. That meant those who served long terms as soldiers were usually not those best connected to the communities that recruited them. Soldiers were obtained by any means available; their officers certainly did not consider their men to be avenging killer-angels hell-bent on defending liberty for all.

What inspired the Whiggish elite was not always the same as what motivated the average enlisted man. Thus officers like Anthony Wayne sometimes referred to their men as "Food for Worms . . . , miserable sharp looking Caitiffs, hungry lean fac'd Villains." Other officers lamented that their men were "the sweepings of the York streets," or "a wretched motley Crew."[4] Senior officers, including George Washington, feared their own men. Washington was especially wary of foreigners who were attracted (as many were) to the large state and congressional bounties offered for service. He demanded that only natives form his headquarters guard. Joseph Galloway, General William Howe's intelligence chief, once estimated that three-fourths of the Continental deserters who came into British-occupied Philadelphia were foreigners. Henry Lee went so far as to label the Pennsylvania battalions "the Line of Ireland." Southern states used convicts as soldiers and were happy to get them. Prisoners of war were courted by both sides, and Washington unsuccessfully admonished his recruiters to stop accepting them. Nathanael Greene thought that the Carolina militia that opposed Cornwallis "were the worst in the world" and questioned whether the few who did not desert were not more interested in plunder than in what he deemed to be their patriotic duty.[5] These observations were certainly not indicative of a patriot or classical "republican army." Why were these officers so vehement in their condemnation of the men they commanded? If service connoted an implicit patriotism, why were Continental army recruits feared by their own officers? To answer these crucial questions, we must examine the colonial military tradition and the social origins of the American Continental soldier.

The Colonial Military Tradition

Long before the Revolution, the Virginia Assembly used to require that every male who was fit to carry a weapon to bring it to Sunday services so that he could participate afterward in militia drill. This law made sense since a sudden attack from Indians was considered a plausible occurrence. It appeared with the passage of time, however, that growing economic demands and a recession of an active Indian threat caused a distinction to develop between those who served long terms as soldiers and those engaged in commercial and economic enterprise. The comments of Lieutenant Governor William Bull of South Carolina to the British Board of Trade underscored the dilemma of propertied citizens rather well. Bull reported that although he thought the local militia was an effective force, their participation in extended military activities was "Inconsistent with a Domestick or Country Life."[6]

Struggles between European powers in North America forced the English colonial militias out of their principal role of fighting the local Indian threat and sometimes employed them against French or Spanish interests hundreds and, on occasion, thousands of miles from their homes. There were few compelling reasons for men of business (commercial or agricultural) to leave their secure locales for some far-flung battlefield. George Burrington, a prewar royal governor, was even instructed "to take especial care that neither the frequency nor the unreasonableness of remote marches, musterings,. & trainings be an unnecessary impediment to the affairs of the inhabitants."[7] Before Burrington's instructions, a report sent to the royal government suggested that the entire militia system be abolished because

> we learn from Experience that in a free Country [the militia] is of little use. The people in the Plantations are so few in proportion to the lands they possess, that servants being scarce, and slaves so excessively dear, the men generally under a necessity there to work hard themselves in order to provide the Common necessities of Life for their Families, so that they cannot spare a day's time without great loss to their Interest . . . wherefore a militia there would become . . . burthensome to poor people. . . . But besides it may be questioned how far it would consist with good Policy to accustom all the able Men in the Colonies to be well exercised in Arms.[8]

Those in power did not fear a standing army as much as they feared that those who were held in repression might one fine day turn their guns and training on their oppressors. Rather, militias worked best in local defensive situations. Despite a 1746 law that allowed the North Carolina militia to come to the aid of the authorities of Virginia and South Carolina, they were not required to do so. Fines were levied only if militiamen failed to aid in the defense of North Carolina. When some North Carolina militia companies received orders to march against the Cherokees in 1759, they refused to move because it meant leaving the colony. Governor Arthur Dobbs informed William Pitt that 420 out of the 500 men recruited to fight the Cherokees eventually deserted.[9]

Over time, colonial governments revised the requirements for vested citizens to serve and increased the number of exemptions to "Persons of Estates" so that in practice "no Man of an Estate is under any Obligation to Muster, and even the Overseers of the Rich are likewise exempted; the whole Burthen lyes upon the poorest sort of people."[10] While the number of exemptions varied from time and place according to the military exigencies of each colony, the new system favored the most powerful members of the community and squarely placed the burden of serving on the least powerful.

A comparison between the North Carolina Militia Act of 1774 and the original Carolina militia law (drafted by John Locke in 1669) reveals this transition. Whereas Locke's original law required "all inhabitants and freemen of Carolina, above 17 years of age and under 60" to bear arms, the 1774 law exempted many categories of freeholders such as clergymen, overseers, millers, judges, commissioners, lawyers, river pilots, constables, and so on (persons deemed necessary to run the community in both war and peace) from service. Furthermore, since Carolina had so few whites compared to blacks, no overseer of more than five taxable slaves was required to perform military service. Indeed, overseers in this category who thought it was their patriotic duty to participate in colonial military affairs were fined 40 shillings.[11]

Exemptions expanded at such a rate that only one-half of the able-bodied white males in a typical North Carolina county attended muster drills in 1772.[12] The well-to-do who declined to serve could afford to pay the militia fine, which was modest in any case. People who fell into the exempted categories were, by no means, always rich or even members of the upper class (overseers, for example, were not particularly well-to-do), but they did have one thing in common: all were connected in some way with the commercial or legal functioning of the community.

Changes in the militia system were, by the latter half of the eighteenth century, inevitable. The colonies had grown too complex for the situation to be otherwise. Because the militias tended to be motivated only when their parochial interests were threatened, and large numbers of citizens were exempted by the community anyway, colonial recruiters turned to those groups of men who "fell outside" the class of people required normally to do a turn or two in the militia. These were Native Americans, mulattos, African Americans, white indentured servants, and "free white men on the move," sometimes known as itinerant laborers. These were also men who, if given the opportunity, were most willing to part temporarily with their civil liberties—if they were accorded any to begin with—in exchange for the steady wage of a soldier. They were precisely the same people against whom the militia system tended to discriminate. "In actuality," a principle function of the militia often "turned out to be protecting the propertied and the privileged in colonial society from the unpropertied and unprivileged."[13] Recruiting thus tended to avoid circumstances that put the privileged community at risk from those they wanted to control. Long-term soldiering, therefore, fell to those not connected to the community or militia structure but disadvantaged enough to be lured away from low-paying jobs.

"The lower sort" was allowed to carry weapons most often when the theater of conflict was far from the local community. By their removal as soldiers in a distant campaign, itinerants, indigents, immigrants, racial outcasts, and others considered "surplus population" by the propertied during wartime served two purposes. First, the unpropertied fulfilled the political and military obligation of a community to provide soldiers without having to draft men of means. Second, using the lower sorts as soldiers on distant campaigns removed a potentially threatening source of discontent from one's own area. Moreover, the very real prospect that the poorer sorts and *not* the propertied would face death or mutilation on the battlefield must have played into the picture as well. An example of this system at work occurred in New York in 1711. On this occasion, soldiers were easily recruited by the New York Assembly for an expedition against Canada. They voted to provide "350 Christian volunteers, 150 Long Island Indians, and 100 Palatine Germans." One hundred additional Germans were eventually added to man frontier posts. Germans and Indians had been long exempt from militia duty, and some had been arrested earlier for disorderly conduct by local constabularies. Nevertheless, the New York Assembly went to these groups first when soldiers were required for a long, distant campaign.[14] These same groups eventually formed ethnic buffer communities between Native American tribes and Anglo-American communities in the East.

Likewise, during the Seven Years' War, Virginia sent men most easily spared from the economic infrastructure. George Washington complained in 1754 that these men were "loose, Idle Persons [who were] quite destitute of House and Home." General James Abercromby thought that the soldiers who formed his army were the "rif-raf of the continent," homeless men who came from parts unknown to him.[15] Those called "rif-raf" by Abercromby became "patriots" to colonial recruiters.

Who were these "loose people" described by Washington and Abercromby? Did the pattern observed in colonial militias also appear when the Continental army was formed? Common soldiers in the eighteenth century, regardless of the army for which they fought, generally came from the lowest strata of society. Descriptions of eighteenth-century soldiers included "the sweeping from jails, ginmills, and poorhouses, oafs from farms beguiled into 'taking the King's shilling,' adventurers and unfortunates who might find a home" in a regiment.[16] While this thesis was supported by the comments of Continental officers, an in-depth analysis by at least one recent scholar revealed that the social structure of some eighteenth-century military organizations was more complex than previously supposed. For instance, new evidence has revealed that "the majority of British conscripts and German mercenaries (who formed the bulk of the British expeditionary force sent to quell the rebellion) did not come from the permanent substratum of the poor, but were members of the working classes who were temporarily unemployed or permanently displaced, and thus represented the less productive, but by no means useless, elements of society."[17] Was the same true for Continental recruits as well?

Two overarching and interrelated prewar social trends help to explain the origins of the Continental army: an expanding population and immigration. During the eighteenth century, British North America had experienced a tenfold increase in population (from 250,000 in 1700 to 2.5 million in 1775). The colonies, especially the middle and southern regions, had absorbed a great many immigrants after 1700. Some scholars have estimated that from 1720 to 1770, most colonial counties increased their population densities by a factor of three. As the larger and denser population pressed against the local land supply, the result was an exhaustion of available, undivided, cultivatable land. An ensuing land shortage caused an increase in the concentration of wealth as large landowners and speculators sold at high prices. Those who lacked land or the capital to purchase it were denied basic economic opportunities. Thus many a man who came of age in 1770 faced the hard choice of migrating or accepting either a nonagricultural trade or lower standard of living. Land availability shrank in some older New England towns to extraordinarily low levels. "A degree of social polarization," noted historian Kenneth Lockridge, "accompanied the concentration of wealth. For a time the proportion of men labeled 'gentlemen' increased faster than ever before, as did the proportion of men accepting poor relief, both proportions continuing to grow until the Revolution."[18] Like a rubber band stretched at both ends, the ranks of rich and poor increased as the Revolution approached.

In Kent, Connecticut, for instance, where prewar economic opportunity was once bright, the situation was "darkened" by the time of the Revolution "by the pressure of population . . . against a limited land supply."[19] An early eighteenth-century anonymous writer who called himself "Amicus Patriae" noted that "many of our old towns are too full of inhabitants for husbandry; many of them living upon small shares of land. . . . And also many of our people are slow in marrying for want of settlements."[20]

In fact, a popular prewar trend among New England youth was for young men to work for their families until their late teens, then for themselves, until about age twenty-six when they either married or moved on. Payment for services was usually rendered "in kind," which meant that young male family members were hired out by their fathers to fulfill a debt or establish credit. Hard currency rarely exchanged hands. For a father to provide inheritance for all his children, he had the choice of dividing up his small holdings into even smaller portions (which ran the chance of "spoiling the whole" and lowering the standard of living for everyone) or he could hire out his children as labor to earn enough money or credit to purchase holdings for all. The ability of fathers to hire out sons was "indispensable to the functioning of the family economy." What was also created by this system was a pool of temporarily poor young men waiting for some sort of familial release, inheritance, or time to build up enough capital to purchase a small holding for themselves.[21] Mostly unskilled, these young laborers were exactly the type of men who might be attracted to the hard currency and steady wages offered by an army recruiter.

Immigration was a second powerful prewar social factor and added to the problem of land shortage. It increased the number of "loose people" moving here and there in search of employment. An estimated 700,000 immigrants arrived in North America from the beginning of British settlement to 1760. This figure suggests that a yearly average of 4,500 people arrived to increase the continental swell. Between 1760 and 1775, American shores were flooded by immigrants. Approximately "221,500 arrivals" occurred during this fifteen-year period, the largest portion coming from the British Isles. The 40,000 Scots who emigrated, for instance, constituted "three percent of the entire population of Scotland."

The 55,000 Irish who left Ireland for the colonies accounted for 2.3 percent of their home population. The British and Irish contributions, however, represented only part of the emigration equation from Europe. During the same years, "at least 12,000 German-speaking immigrants entered the port of Philadelphia." At the same time, more than 84,500 enslaved Africans arrived on North American shores.[22] All told, "an average of 15,000 people were arriving annually, which is triple the average of years before 1760 and close to the total estimated population of the town of Boston in this period."[23]

In prewar Philadelphia, a considerable degree of geographic mobility was evident in the lives of the city's laboring immigrant poor. James Cooper, a resident of the city, took in his Scottish-born nephew Tacey, a deserter from the British navy. Tacey, a sailor since the age of eight, "made his escape to the American Army" and later served with the Continental navy. After the war, Tacey worked near the city docks as a mariner and later headed out to newly opened lands in Kentucky.[24] James Brown, a dispossessed Irish weaver, gave further evidence of the great mobility of the "lower sort." Emigrating to a small town near Lancaster, Pennsylvania, after disembarking at Philadelphia during the late 1760s, Brown decided to try his luck in Danbury, Connecticut, in a linen factory. When the British burned the factory at the beginning of the war, he returned to Pennsylvania, out of work, with no prospect of employment in sight. A Continental recruiting officer convinced him that his best employment opportunity lay in the army. Before leaving for service, Brown moved his wife and family to Philadelphia, where they could be near friends while he was away. He eventually came home from the army, moved back to Danbury, and resumed his factory job. He died in Ontario County, New York, in 1815.[25] Later chapters will examine immigration during the Revolutionary era in greater detail. It is important at this juncture, however, to note how immigrants added to the masses of people in America in search of a living wage.

Social Origins of the Enlisted Men

The best way to determine the social forces that affected the formation of the Continental army is to divide up the states into three distinct geographic regions—New England, the mid-Atlantic, and the South—to determine how each area recruited and organized its potential military manpower. Each region used its own approaches for supplying men to the army, but the outcomes were remarkably similar. Ultimately, a complex pattern of recruitment becomes visible in which age, class, and social status played significant roles in determining who would serve in the army.

In New England, where population density was relatively high, there is evidence that those who made up a portion of the army at least for one term of service were part of an amorphous group of temporarily unemployed young men. An analysis of 396 Massachusetts soldiers revealed that their average age at the time of enlistment was twenty-three. Of this number, however, almost 42 percent were under twenty-one years of age at enlistment time, and 68 percent were younger than twenty-six, the average age when most young men from New England married. Only 24 percent of these men were in the 26 to 40 age bracket.[26]

Most of this Massachusetts cohort (88 percent) was native to the state. More than 91 percent claimed to have been born in America. Of the eight soldiers who claimed foreign birth, three were from England, two from Ireland, and one each from Scotland, Nova Scotia, and Jamaica. However, the 1782 muster records revealed that native soldiers enlisted from all parts of the state of Massachusetts, including Maine, and did not necessarily represent the town in which they signed the terms of enlistment.[27] Moreover, records from the Fourth and Ninth Massachusetts Regiments showed that the soldiers came from the lowest socioeconomic strata of New England society. Over 277 men listed a prewar occupation in their enlistment records. One hundred forty-eight of them claimed to have been engaged in an agrarian-related field before enlisting. Yet less than 10 percent of these men can be found in postwar tax records as owners of any sizable parcels of real estate. Stephen Brown, of Rehoboth, Massachusetts, and formerly a private in the Fourth Massachusetts Regiment, was worth only $72.75 five years before his death in 1825. Bristol Bennett, an African American who served in the army, was worth only $7.10 at age sixty-three. When he died in 1835, Bennett's effects had to be sold to cover the cost of his funeral. It was not enough, so he was buried in a pauper's grave. Another African American soldier from Massachusetts, Joseph Green, was convicted of grand larceny and hanged in Worcester only three years after his discharge from the army—a sad end to one who toiled in the defense of liberty.[28]

An examination of the enlistment records of two New England towns that provided long-termed soldiers for the army showed the same general recruiting patterns found in the Fourth and Ninth Massachusetts Regiments. The town of Peterborough, New Hampshire, for instance, had a population of 549 in 1775. Of this number, about 170 men were credited as having served in some capacity in the armed forces. Yet the vast majority did not enlist beyond a single campaign or one year's service. Some men enlisted for three days and never served again. Few of these Peterborough soldiers could be termed "yeomen soldiers"; rather, the large majority were "an unusually poor, obscure group of men, even by the rustic standards of Peterborough."[29]

It was not uncommon for more mature and settled well-to-do townsmen who were listed on the militia roles to pool their money to procure a "down-and-outer" for three years' service. This practice served more than one purpose. First, any two militiamen who hired another man for long-term service were usually excused from all military responsibility for as long as their man served in the army. Second, the hometown of the recruit's "employers" received credit for having provided a soldier. Thus, a drifter who heard of someone hiring a substitute in a neighboring town or county might find himself seated in a strange village tavern and "hired" to fulfill a different town's quota or someone else's military obligation. Sometimes men like Samuel Baker of Bolton, Massachusetts, conformed to the time-honored practice of hiring out their sons to the army just as they had hired them out to neighbors to fulfill a debt or social obligation. Others sent servants or black slaves in their stead.[30]

The men furnished by the town fathers of Peterborough were for the most part young, but a few were exceptionally old. The ages of town recruits varied from ten-year-old John Scott, son of Captain William Scott, to the captain's sixty-nine-year-old uncle. The majority of the men, however, averaged about twenty years old.[31] Common soldiers were men like John Alexander, James Gordon, Samuel Lee, and Michael Silk, all of whom represented the town in the enlistment records but left no other documentary trace of their existence. They owned no property, paid no taxes, and did not vote. They served, some deserted, and a few died. Those who did not die in service did not return to Peterborough after the war.[32] If not for their service records, these men would have been unknown to history.

Concord, Massachusetts, sent men like Ezekial Brown, a former inmate of the debtor's prison, "with little or nothing to lose" according to his own account, into the army. Brown was unable to participate in the fight at Concord Bridge and probably heard the "shot heard round the world" from the window of the town's debtor prison. Brown was like many other landless sons of Massachusetts. His family drifted about Middlesex County in search of work in the years leading up to war. "Warned out" of Concord, he was able to prove his worth as a scrivener and was eventually allowed to settle there by the town fathers. Due to the vagaries of the marketplace, however, Brown soon lost all he owned and ended up back in debt with nothing to show for nearly ten years of labor. Nor was Brown the only disadvantaged man Concord sent into the ranks. In this state of few blacks, at least 8 percent of the men Concord sent into the Continental army were African Americans bought as substitutes by the well-to-do who did not wish to leave their businesses. By 1780, only eight men out of sixteen who had signed up to fulfill Concord's Continental quota "had any known connection to the town."[33]

Where enlistment records existed and soldiers listed their age and prewar occupations (the evidence is fragmentary), the data revealed that the majority of New England recruits were, like the enlistees of Peterborough and Concord, young, landless, and unskilled. The conspicuousness of youth was also common in earlier wars. Younger transients "were often ex-servants who sought jobs in a variety of towns." Without capital to buy land or skill to earn a steady wage as an artisan, they drifted about commercial towns like Beverly, Salem, and Newburyport seeking employment where it could be found. One-fifth of the privates from Essex County who served in the Seven Years' War had been servants.[34]

Massachusetts was not the only northern state that recruited the young and indigent. An examination of the army records of fifty-four men of the First New York Regiment revealed that 72 percent of recruits were in their teens or early twenties when they enlisted. Almost a fifth of the enlistees of the four New York regiments in the northern army were teen-aged boys who were formerly part of "the strolling poor," that is, transients who drifted from town to town in search of employment. They listed a variety of occupations, but most common was that of farmer or laborer. Some of the men were simply classified as "unemployed."[35]

Moving from New England and New York toward the middle states, we find that New Jersey's economic structure was similar to that of other states north of Maryland. There, "the richest tenth of the Revolutionary taxpayers alone held about 45 percent" of all the wealth of the state—a figure similar to other northern states of the period. Moreover, within the middle third of taxpayers, the average person within this group held roughly "six times less wealth than his counterpart" in the upper brackets. Over "20 percent of the taxable populace was propertyless."[36] Moreover, New Jersey tax lists of 1778–80, analyzed by age, "show that a significant number of landless or marginal men were young." An analysis of six New Jersey towns revealed that the "yeoman farmer" of revolutionary yore was largely a myth. The proportion of men who held insufficient land for farming "varied from 55.5 percent in Piscataway to 76.2 percent in Shrewsbury."[37]

Data on 710 enlisted soldiers of the New Jersey Brigade reveal that its soldiers "reflected the disparities of the civilian world"; a man's wealth determined the likelihood of his serving as a Continental soldier. Fully "90 percent of the privates and noncommissioned officers came from the poorest two-thirds of the [tax] ratable population (61 percent from the poorest third, 29 percent from the middle third)." Nearly one-half of the brigade owned no taxable property at all. While "some 30 percent of the general taxpayers owned farms of 100 acres or more, only nine percent of the soldiery had similar holdings." A mere 20 percent of the troops held even modest assets of twenty-five- to thirty-acre farms. Few soldiers came from families that owned slaves (always a good indication of accumulation of capital). None of the soldiers seemed to be involved in manufacture: not one soldier, for instance, listed any holdings in "fishing, iron-working, or other non-agricultural" ventures. More than 146 (34 percent) of the soldiers did not come from the towns in which they were recruited. Only 41 percent of the soldiers within the brigade can be identified as having *ever* been a resident of the townships they represented in the army. Some were like John Evans, a black soldier who listed Reading, Pennsylvania, as his home of record, though there is no evidence that he ever lived there. Two soldiers, Privates James Sarge and William Gallaspe, were ostensibly recruits from local New Jersey townships, yet the town records contained no tax or genealogical records of them or their families. Like the soldiers from Peterborough, New Hampshire, many soldiers who represented New Jersey in the ranks drifted into the army, served or deserted, or both, and then disappeared quickly from the historical record.[38]

The brigade had other similar social characteristics as well. More than half were under the age of twenty-one at the time of enlistment. The young were recruiting targets because they had little to lose and certainly no wealth, business, or influence that kept them tied to their communities. In fact, one recruiter stated outright that youths were generally sought because "they have little, and some no property." Their apparent rootlessness, their very lack of connection to communities, made them "very proper for the Service." Only fifty-three Jerseymen listed their prewar civilian occupations, if in fact they ever had been anything other than unskilled laborers. Only eight of the fifty-three claimed to be farmers. The largest occupation listed was laborer (18), followed by shoemakers (9), tailors and coopers (3 each), carpenters (2), weavers (2), and eight other miscellaneous, less-skilled occupations. Of the entire roster of troops about whom tax data were available "only 31 percent came from families with enough land to farm."[39] The paucity of skill coupled with the youthfulness of the recruits suggests that the young men had not had enough time to establish a trade but had already cut their familial ties, leaving them free to join the army when the opportunity arose. Moreover, the soldier's lack of taxable wealth suggests that the New Jersey Brigade was manned principally by the lower classes.

In sum, the peopling of the New Jersey Brigade owed much to the class structure of the state. Its rank and file reflected those who composed most of the populace at large and who were most likely to end up in the army as long-term soldiers—the very same poor, dispossessed, drifting, or "loose" people described by Washington in 1754. A 1778 muster roll from Middlesex County underscored the trend toward using those who needed the army's money. All twenty-eight men listed were hirelings, that is, substitutes for those with money who wanted to avoid Continental service. The "common denominator" of the Jersey soldiers was their lower-class origin.[40]

In neighboring Pennsylvania, the preference for young boys and men remained consistent. A total of 1,068 Pennsylvania recruits listed their ages upon enlistment, ranging from as young as ten and as old as seventy. The largest percentage of these extremely young soldiers were not fifers or drummers but common soldiers. It was not unusual for senior officers to employ youngsters as waiters (personal servants) and then list them as regular soldiers so that they would draw a full soldier's ration.[41]

At least 122 soldiers (11 percent) of the total number within the sample joined the army at age seventeen and under. Taken altogether, there was a marked preference for soldiers in the younger age brackets, due to their accessibility and lack of connection to a community. Almost three-fourths of the men listed their age as being between seventeen and thirty-two; 55 percent were in their twenties. At twenty-five, the average Pennsylvanian was slightly older than his comrades to the north, but the presence of more than a few "grandfathers" may have skewed the sample.

It is important to note that all but one of the men aged fifty-seven or older enlisted after 1780, when the shortage of available recruits was greatest.[42]

Pennsylvania troops differed from New England's in one respect. A substantial portion of the Pennsylvania soldiers were foreign-born. Of the 582 Pennsylvania soldiers who listed their place of birth, two out of three admitted they were not native to the United States. The sample upon which the point is based is small compared to the larger number of soldiers who listed no birthplace at all; nonetheless, the pattern remained consistent for every Pennsylvania unit in which place of birth was recorded.[43] Because Pennsylvania had been a major clearinghouse for prewar immigrants, it is not surprising that so many of the foreign-born ended up in its ranks.

Prewar occupations of recruits are available for 273 Pennsylvania enlisted men. Ninety-two men (34 percent) were farmers, the most common category. The next-closest category was shoemaker (23), followed by weaver (19), blacksmith and carpenter (12 apiece), then by various descriptions that included a great number of individual "laborers," one clerk, and a schoolmaster. In all, almost 64 percent of the Pennsylvanians who listed prewar occupations claimed to be tradesmen or laborers of some sort. While an occasional vintner or silk dyer could be found in the lists (skills that paid considerably higher wages), they were the rare exceptions.[44] Again, while the sample is not large compared to the number of soldiers recruited, the data remain consistent throughout individual units whenever a significant number of the men listed their occupations. In sum, the Pennsylvania line also reflected the society that formed it. The typical Pennsylvania soldier was young, although slightly older than his comrades to the north. The average Pennsylvania soldier was probably not born in the state, nor even the United States.[45]

Passing from the mid-Atlantic states to the Upper South, we find that the social origins of the soldiers were similar, though with a few minor variations. A study of a list of recruits raised by General William Smallwood revealed that the median enlistment age of his Marylanders was younger than the Pennsylvanians and closer to the New Jersey troops at twenty-one years of age. Again, like the soldiers from New Jersey, few of these southern men owned enough wealth to appear on the taxable lists. Many had been unskilled laborers of some sort prior to their enlistment; few had little more than the clothes on their backs. A Baltimore company of 102 men listed "no farmers at all" and 35 percent as laborers.

In largely agricultural Delaware, sixteen of twenty-four recruits listed "farmer" as their prewar occupation. While two out of three Delaware soldiers may have claimed an agrarian occupation, the term "farmer" could be misleading, for only one soldier out of eight Marylanders from Somerset County who claimed to have been farmers left any record of property ownership. The median value of property owned by Smallwood's soldiers was a mere £45, which testified to their poverty, although this condition was common to more than 33 percent of all families in 1783 Maryland.[46]

Smallwood's recruits were similar to those raised in Pennsylvania in another respect: many were not born in the United States. Although enlisted late in the war, the foreign born comprised 40.1 percent of the recruits, despite instructions from the Maryland General Assembly to avoid enlisting foreigners if at all possible. At an average age of twenty-nine, these men were older than their native counterparts, whose median age was twenty-one. The majority of the foreigners were recruited in urban Baltimore or in rural areas adjacent to the city. Only 90 of 308 (29 percent) soldiers claimed that they came from Maryland. Ten came from Pennsylvania, Virginia, or New Jersey. The rest of the 308 merely listed "America" as their place of birth. Only nine foreign-born recruits were identified as having families on the 1783 tax assessment list. Furthermore, fourteen of Smallwood's recruits had been recorded earlier in a book of convicts at Annapolis between the years 1771 and 1775.[47]

Although Smallwood's Marylanders were recruited late in the war, the pattern of enlisting foreign-born men and young boys seemed to prevail in other southern units that had been recruited earlier. A muster roll of men recruited by Captain James Bowie for a 1776 Flying Camp (a pool of soldiers recruited for a specific emergency or a single campaign) revealed trends similar to those in Smallwood's roster. Sixteen of sixty soldiers listed (27 percent) were foreigners. Another 1776 list of men enrolled by Captain James Young revealed that fifty-two of ninety men (60 percent) were foreign-born. All the native soldiers listed "America" as their place of birth. They may have enlisted in Maryland, but that did not mean they were actually native to the state. A roll of men "furnished by the Classes of Prince George's County for filling up the Old Regiments, 1780," listed fourteen of twenty-five men (56 percent) as foreign-born. Not including a thirty-five-year-old native named Thomas Walls, the average age of the American-born was eighteen, while the foreign-born were nine years older.[48] Many immigrants had come to America bound as indentured servants, served their time, and joined the army at a more advanced age.

An examination of the muster records of the First Company of Matrosses (artillerymen) revealed not only a large foreign-born presence within the unit, but the average native-born Matross, like his comrades in Bowie's Flying Camp and the Prince George's County recruits, was also only about twenty-one years old. The foreign-born, as in other Maryland units, were older by a substantial margin (twenty-seven) than their native comrades. Of the 102 total enlisted in the unit, sixty-four (53 percent) were foreign-born. Moreover, the natives within the unit were a real hodgepodge of American youth. Only eighteen (17 percent) claimed to be from Maryland. Another thirteen claimed Pennsylvania as home. At least two men came from as far away as South Carolina, while five hailed from Nova Scotia. "Laborer" was the most frequently listed occupation, as declared by nearly half (46 percent) of the entire unit. No recruit listed farmer or any other agrarian occupation. Most were apparently urban laborers.[49]

In sum, Maryland soldiers were like the rest of the army: young, poor, and largely landless. Very few of Smallwood's men appear on the 1783 Tax Assessment. Most had recently emigrated to the area or were hired laborers in other men's households. General Smallwood, who knew his base of recruitment, explained to the Maryland General Assembly that he would not be able to raise as many troops as he had hoped because the Assembly had delayed in sending him bounty money. Most free laborers in Maryland had long since committed themselves to local farmers for the year's work and would not be available for army service until after the fall harvest.[50]

Maryland counted on the "lower sort" for its soldiers so thoroughly that its legislators wrote laws to require their service. Any able-bodied man who was judged by a court to be a vagabond was forced to serve at least nine months in the Continental army. If these men elected to remain in the army for at least three years or the duration of the war, they received the standard bounty offered to everyone else. And yet the issue provoked a debate within the Assembly; some worried that the law would drive out of Maryland's able-bodied vagrants who might otherwise become substitutes for drafted militiamen.[51]

Just over the Potomac River in Virginia, class was also a factor in recruiting. Leven Powell, an unsuccessful aspirant for a commission in the army, remarked that the best offices went to the "best people," but

Powell himself apparently was not one of them. The field officers appointed in the first regiments in Virginia were not part of the lower or even middle class. Even junior officers frequently took a slave with them to camp.[52]

Like their brother soldiers to the north, the Virginia Continentals were young. A survey of 419 Virginia pension records indicated that more than 90 percent of the private soldiers were under twenty-five years of age at their time of enlistment. The median age of new recruits "was only 20 years and at least 21 recruits were mere boys of 14 or 15 years of age." Few of these young men owned land, but most claimed to be farmers or were sons of poor tenant farmers. The social profile of the men varied little over time. The mean age of the soldiers in 1776 remained the same in 1781. That the army did not age, despite the length of the war, suggested that the ranks turned over at a high rate and were replenished year after year by youthful and probably penniless cohorts.[53] Few of these men served more than one term. At Valley Forge, for instance, only forty men out of one thousand signed up for another term, despite the promise by Governor Patrick Henry of an additional twenty dollars above the reenlistment bounty offered by Congress.[54]

Unlike soldiers in New Jersey, Pennsylvania, and Maryland, however, the majority of the Virginia recruits surveyed (82 percent) were born in the state. Of that number, half still lived in the county in which they had been born when they enlisted. Only five men were identified as foreign-born. Due to geographic size and the tendency for southern settlements to be more dispersed than those to the north, the Virginians were apparently less mobile. Few of the recruits, however, resided east of the fall line. The heaviest concentrations of recruits came from the piedmont and the Shenandoah Valley. These two areas held those people who fled the wealthier Tidewater region once it had been consolidated by the gentry into large plantations.[55]

Again, the status of people recruited as soldiers was revealed by the extreme aspersions cast upon them by senior military leaders. Charles Lee openly despised his men and referred to Virginia recruits as "riff raff—dirty, mutinous, and disaffected."[56] Lee's comments were nearly identical to those made by General Abercromby a generation earlier, "riff-raff, loose, and idle people."

Virginia's soldiers may have been sedentary before the war, but they certainly were not afterward. Few veterans stayed in the Old Dominion after they were discharged, leading again to the conclusion that they were similar in circumstances to the "loose people" described by Washington in 1754. Records that any of these soldiers acquired land were nearly nonexistent. The vast majority claimed to be farmers but were most likely itinerant laborers or tenant farmers on someone else's estate. Of 658 soldiers surveyed, almost half (325) moved out of the state immediately after the war.[57] The soldiers' willingness to move (perhaps to bounty lands in the Ohio area) indicates that they did not have much to return to after completing their service.

Virginia veterans returning from the war were highly mobile. Private Martin Amos, for instance, was recruited from his Albemarle County home at the age of sixteen. After his discharge, he moved west into Kanawha County (now West Virginia), from there into the Ohio country, then back to Mason County, Virginia (now West Virginia), and finally ended up in Gallia County, Ohio. Another comrade, Daniel Barrow, was recruited in Brunswick County, where he had been born in 1757. After the war he moved from Virginia to North Carolina, then on to Knox County, Tennessee, then Wayne County, Kentucky, and finally to Jackson County, Illinois.[58] Both Amos and Barrow were young when they marched off to war. As teenagers they had probably led marginal existences as sons of tenant farmers or laborers. They had had little time in their short lives to accumulate wealth and no prospects of an inheritance. Army service probably gave them steady employment. The bounties they earned were likely the largest amount of cash they had ever seen.

In conclusion, it is apparent that the social origins of the majority of men who comprised the Continental army (where records can be found) were lower class. In every geographic area except Virginia, the large number of "out-of-towners" within the ranks testified to the mobility of these "loose people" or "free [and unfree] men on the move." Looking for work and sustenance and encountering a recruiting party, they found themselves joining the ranks with others unable to resist the demand for their service. The New Jersey regular, for instance, was neither "a yeoman nor a middle class soldier—just as New Jersey was not a predominately yeoman society."[59] The same can now be said of Concord, Massachusetts; Peterborough, New Hampshire; and Prince George's County, Maryland.

Men of means avoided service by hiring replacements such as Joseph Plumb Martin, an out-of-work farm laborer. Martin, having little prospect for work, saw a stint in the army as a logical choice. He "endeavored," in his words, to get "as much for his skin as he could," willing "to become a scapegoat" to the highest bidder on recruiting day. Compare, for a moment, Private Martin's comments with those of a true yeoman farmer from New York: "My situation in life was that of a farmer in respectable circumstances and rather above that which furnished the usual recruits for the regular army."[60]

The high number of racial and ethnic minorities present in the Continental ranks deserves further investigation. The middle colonies in particular seemed to have heavily recruited foreign-born soldiers. Place of birth did not appear to be a factor in recruiting. A New Jersey militia colonel commented in 1777 that he thought the Jersey Brigade was comprised "mostly" of foreigners, who probably were, in turn, either deserters from the British army or immigrants.[61] The colonel's comment was an exaggeration but nonetheless does shed some light on who ultimately ended up in the ranks. By the end of the war in Maryland, for instance, it is hard to see how the state could have fielded troops for the army without recruiting foreign-born soldiers because they comprised nearly half the men enlisted in the line. The typical foreigners in American service were Irish or German, but occasionally they were Canadian, French, Swiss, and even now and then Scandinavian. Following chapters will develop this hypothesis more fully.

What ultimately sustained the army was the sheer volume of Americans who were *temporarily* willing, like Joseph Plumb Martin, to become "scapegoats" so others might stay at home. In the New Jersey line, one soldier in five was in the ranks because he had become a substitute for another man of better means. The huge volume of National Pension Files (there were more than 80,000 claims) testified that a substantial portion of American males (both black and white) must have served a term in the army. But only a tiny portion of the population performed truly extended military service. Thus the origins of the army may have been cloaked in idealistic rhetoric because the true facts about the Continental army were perhaps "painful and embarrassing."[62] Like their civilian counterparts in the lower classes, the youthful Continental soldiers drank, swore, fought, and gambled in camp and on the march. They were a class apart from their officers and were feared by them nearly as much as the British. They were, however, willing to work for pay as soldiers when others would not, taking their chances, frequently dying in the "glorious cause" extolled by later generations of historians who celebrated a mythified sort of fighting man.

CHAPTER TWO

The Most Audacious Rascals Existing: The Irish in the Continental Army

Probably in no part of Europe was the effect of the American revolt and British policy more deeply debated, written about, or considered than in Ireland. For many Americans, Ireland was a kindred spirit and an entity separate from Great Britain; it was another land held in subjugation and oppression. Stories carried to America by emigrants strengthened the connection between the two colonies. The British, on the other hand, viewed Ireland "with the assurance of a landowner speaking of the remote corners of his estate."[1]

Past historiography on Irish participation in the American Revolution has confined itself to arguments about the extent of Irish enlistment in the Continental army or the most patriotic ethnic subgroup (Celtic or Scotch-Irish). Numerous historians of generations past have commented on the revolutionary fervor of Irish immigrants. The Scotch-Irish, in particular, were credited by many observers as being active in the Continental army. David Ramsey, an eyewitness to the Revolution, remarked, for instance, that "the Irish in America, with a few exceptions, were attached to Independence." He noted that many soldiers in the Pennsylvania line were of Irish descent, but he was careful to reveal that "they were mostly Presbyterians, and therefore mostly Whigs."[2] Horace Walpole and even George III were under the impression that the whole war was "little more than an uprising of rabble-rousing Presbyterians, largely Scotch-Irish: a sort of latter-day Cromwellian outburst against the due civil, ecclesiastical, and political order of a sensible and free British empire."[3] Few of these eyewitnesses to the Revolution attempted to support their impressions with hard evidence.

However, more recent scholarship has demonstrated that the Revolution did indeed have the trans-Atlantic roots suspected by Ramsay, Walpole, and George III. A number of path-breaking studies have concluded that the American Revolution was just one rebellion in a cycle of revolt that took place throughout the Atlantic community during the eighteenth century. These revolts were led by a wide variety of groups: sailors, slaves, artisans, farmers, and waged urban workers.[4]

There is substantial evidence that the American and Irish revolutionary movements were connected in a number of ways. Irishmen closely followed events unfolding in America through the *Freeman's Journal*, edited by the Irish radical, Charles Lucas. Letters from Irishmen to the *Journal* raised questions about the rights of Englishmen when they became colonists. The Stamp Act was strongly debated in its pages. Lucas even ran a series of articles on the subversion of civil authority by military forces quartered among the Americans. Following the Boston Massacre, he asked James Bowdoin and Joseph Warren, two future prominent leaders of the American rebellion, "What redress do you expect for grievances in America, which [had been long] grown familiar in England, and almost the established sole mode of government in Ireland?" Lucas equated "oppression" in America with "the heavy Yoke of Tyranny" in Ireland.[5]

Ireland, in fact, had been a hotbed of discontent for a number of years preceding the American Revolution. In County Antrim alone, more than 30,000 cottagers had been evicted due to the collapse of the weaving industry and high rents demanded by landlords. A handloom weaving collapse in Cork in 1769, a potato and grain failure from 1765 to 1767, and a linen industry depression all served to cause a great number of desperate Irishmen to be bound for America as servants. Disturbances in Munster in the 1760s broke out intermittently in Cork, Kilkenny, Limerick, Tipparary, and Waterford. Agrarian disorders manifested themselves in the Whiteboy movement and among the "Levellers" who rode about the countryside at night blowing horns, pulling down fences, and attacking British tax officials.[6]

Ireland was a natural point of reference for the Americans to draw from and an obvious quarter from which to expect allies.[7] It was also morally advantageous for Americans to appear as citizens of the world. By presenting their grievances against the British with an international, even universal rhetoric, the Americans portrayed the struggle in terms that would strike the most fear in the hearts of the British administration and generate the greatest solidarity from other parts of the world. When news of celebrations of the Sons of Liberty in Boston reached Ireland, toasts were raised to "the Sons of Liberty throughout the world." Joseph Warren practically burst with anticipation when he contemplated withholding flax seed from Ireland that "might well throw a million people of Ireland out of bread." "We consider," he wrote a few days later, "that a suspension of trade through the continent with Great Britain, Ireland and the West Indies, as the grand machine that will deliver us."[8] Warren's logic, of course, was that food riots in Ireland would force the British to see their military weakness in keeping a number of colonies in subjugation and require them to cut their losses before they lost them all.

There is evidence that some of the Irish recognized a parallel between their own situation and that of America. After noting that 152 ships had departed with 37,000 passengers for America, an Irish observer added in a letter to Dublin's *Freeman's Journal:* "Read this, Ye! Men in Power, and relieve this oppressed, sinking and Betrayed nation. . . . Repeal the Boston Port Bill. . . . Restore to the Middlesex Freeholders [Wilke's usurped constituents] their Birth-rights. Restore the Charter of Boston."[9] When one Irish reader was apprised of the intention of the British to quarter troops in the homes of American colonists, he asked whether it would not lead the British to eventually do the same thing in Ireland. Was it "part of their plan," he asked, "of Humiliation nearer to home?" By "tamely submitting to fix such shackles on . . . America would [it] not shew that we ourselves are ripe for the same humiliation?"[10]

Many Irishmen did not wait for the British to entirely "fix their shackles" and used their feet to depart the Emerald Isle. Emigration was rapidly depopulating large parts of the country. Lord Hillsborough, a secretary of state for colonial affairs during the years before the Revolution, was particularly "afraid of dispeopling Ireland." As an owner of a huge Irish estate with thousands of tenant farmers, he strongly opposed settlement of western lands with immigrants, especially Protestants, who provided a measure of security against the Roman Catholic majority in Ireland. Hillsborough surmised that remote colonies established far from imperial power and control were difficult to keep "in just subordination to and dependence upon this kingdom," and that these settlements would become a magnet for emigration from Ireland and Scotland.[11] He was more correct than he ever imagined.

In North America, Ambrose Serle, Lord Dartmouth's agent in America and a civilian observer attached to General Howe's army during the war, also feared the large amounts of emigration and thought that the Irish exodus, "both voluntary and involuntary . . . have been really alarming and inconsiderately allowed." Serle was fearful that the emigrants, who he thought were mostly "Scotch-Irish, Presbyterians in Religion, disposed absolutely to the present faction against the government, and many of them now principal agitators in these Confusions." He estimated that since 1771, 33,000 had emigrated to America.[12]

Irish emigration to America occurred generally in four distinct waves: 1717–18, 1727–28, 1740–41, and 1771–73. In each case, economic decline, political or religious discrimination, and oppression by landlords of Irish estates were cited as the principal reasons. It was during the last period, however, that the largest exodus of immigrants ever to leave Ireland took place. Two trends are revealed as well. The emigration from Ireland in the years immediately preceding the Revolutionary War was large, and it was mostly Protestant.[13]

Arthur Young undertook a "tour of Ireland" during the height of the 1770s' "America craze." He was interested in finding out why the Irish were fleeing to America. Young also observed, without realizing it, a growing Irish resistance to the home government and described the increasingly violent way they expressed their dissatisfaction.[14] He found that "the spirit of emigrating appeared to be confined to two circumstances: the Presbyterian religion, and the [collapse] of the linen manufacture." Young thought that "the Catholics never went, they seem not only tied to the country but also to the parish where their ancestors lived."[15]

Young was correct about the social conditions but wrong about the level of Catholic emigration. While it was true that Irish-Catholic emigration occurred at a lower rate during the 1770s, the number of involuntary emigrations were not considered. During the years 1770 and 1775, at least 10,000 Irish Catholic convicts were transported to Maryland and Virginia.[16] Historian David Noel Doyle noted that many Irish who left their homeland in the 1770s may have started out as Catholics but were not too fervent about their religion. Knowing the anti-papal cant of the majority of the American colonial settlements, these men, upon arrival, simply stopped practicing Catholicism, married lower-class Protestant women, or did not admit to practicing any religion at all.[17]

The potential problem posed by large numbers of disaffected immigrants was not ignored by the British military. The bishop of Derry wrote to Lord Dartmouth in 1775 attributing much of "the rebellious spirit" in the central colonies in America to the emigration from Ireland "of near thirty three thousand fanatical and hungry republicans in the course of a very few years."[18] Thomas Gage commented to Lord Dartmouth in September 1775 that "emigrants from Ireland have arrived also at Philadelphia, where we are informed Arms were immediately put in their hands upon their landing."[19]

Evidence suggests that the Irish emigrants possessed strong separatist sentiments before the Revolution even began. Charles Smith, a British merchant, wrote Lord Dartmouth in 1773 informing him that his business required him to travel throughout the colonies every two or three years. "Everywhere," he observed, were "dispositions which savors too much of rebellion." "These rebellious sentiments," he noted, "were especially prevalent in the back settlements particularly of Pennsylvania. Some 8,000 to 10,000 people were imported there from Ireland in one year. These settlements are composed of an uncultivated banditti on whom lawless publications take great effect. Can the event be any other in a few years to throw off their dependence? They are ripe for it."[20]

The existence of backcountry dissatisfaction caused a few members of Congress to attempt to ally the Scotch-Irish Presbyterians to the patriot movement before British emissaries got to them. In November 1775, Congress sent Elihu Spencer and Alexander McWhorter, "two eminent divines," at an extraordinary salary of forty dollars a month, "to go amongst the [Scotch-Irish] and Regulators and inform them of the nature of the dispute between Great Britain and the Colonies."[21] The ministers appealed directly to them in terms they understood. Comparing the tax on tea to the imposition of the hearth tax in Ireland, they reminded the immigrants that if they deserted the cause of liberty their ministers could have "no fellowship" with them and that no more missionaries would be sent to their remote settlements. Linking previous revolutionary activity in Ireland with the situation in American, four Philadelphia Presbyterian ministers told their congregations that if the patriot movement was wrong in its conduct then "our forefathers that fought for liberty at Londonderry and Enniskillen in King James' time were wrong."[22]

Wrong or not, many contemporary observers thought that the Continental army's composition had little to do with American indignation. Rather, a substantial part of the army appeared to be predominated by a polyglot mixture of disaffected Irish Americans. Captain Johann Heinrichs of the Hessian Jaeger Corps wrote a friend in 1776 that people should "not call the war an American Rebellion, [for] it is nothing more than an Irish-Scotch Presbyterian Rebellion."[23] British Captain Joshua Pell described the American forces as "chiefly composed of Irish Redemptioners and Convicts, the most audacious rascals existing." Captain Frederick MacKenzie, an officer in the Royal Welsh Fuzileers, wrote in his diary after the Long Island Campaign of 1776 that "the chief strength of the Rebel Army at present consists of Natives of Europe, particularly Irishmen: many of their regiments are composed principally of these men."[24] Lieutenant William Feilding wrote that the rebel army "was said to be half Irish & Scotch, but far more of the former than the latter, chiefly Emigrants who settled in this Province since the last war."[25]

Dr. John Berkenhout, on a trip from New York to Philadelphia, wrote in 1778 that the American army consisted predominately of "Irish transports." Berkenhout traveled, however, through the middle colonies where Irish immigration was strong and the ranks of the soldiery most likely reflected the colonies' ethnicity. There is no evidence that New England troops, for example, had large Irish elements within their ranks other than British army deserters and a few native Irish redemptioners who resided in the area. In general, New England was not conducive to emigration on the scale of the middle states or even the Southern states. Nevertheless, Berkenhout offered his opinion that Washington's troops were "a contemptible body of vagrants, deserters, and thieves."[26]

Most of the above commentators probably overstated the involvement of the Irish presence in the Continental army, nor were they all deserters, vagrants, or thieves. As Irish historian David Noel Doyle wryly commented, it was probably easier for the British to think they were killing debauched Irishmen and Presbyterians rather than fellow English-descended Anglicans. What was important to note, however, was that all these officers suspected that Irish-born emigrants were being heavily recruited by the Continental army.

Indeed, the Scotch-Irish were in the forefront of those who, early on, declared for independence. As a result of the outbreak of fighting at Lexington and Concord, a number of declarations and manifestos appeared among their settlements on the frontier. One group of Pennsylvania Scotch-Irish issued the "Westmoreland Declaration" in May 1775, fifteen months *before* the Continental Congress got around to declaring independence. In this document, the residents of Hanna's Town protested "the oppressive acts of Great Britain" and expressed their willingness to "oppose these with their lives and fortunes." Forming themselves into militia companies, they organized a battalion of associators under Colonel John Proctor and declared that although "they did not desire any innovation," they would join any concerted plan for the defense of America.[27] The Fair-Play settlers of the Susquehanna Valley issued the "Pine Creek Declaration."[28] These Scotch-Irish settlers were squatters on the estates of wealthy absentee landlords. Having made some improvements to the land, they formed their own fiercely independent community and signaled their willingness to support the patriot cause. The community members hailed the patriot movement by voicing their approval and endorsed it in a manner similar to the Westmoreland Declaration. A portion of the Tory-infested Carolina back-country even set forth the "Mecklenberg Resolves," a manifesto that supported the cause of liberty but also included references to old regulator grievances concerning rules for lawyers, sheriffs, and court officials.[29]

Not only was Congress anxious to gain the loyalties of these Irish emigrants but sought, in July 1775, to "tamper" with the Irish homeland as well. Issuing "An Address to the People of Ireland," and listing, among other things, a number of their own grievances against the crown, Congress sought to find in the Irish a common ground and moral justification for taking up arms against the mother country. "We know that you are not without your grievances," concluded the authors of the address. "We sympathize with you in your distress, and are pleased to find that the design of subjugating us, has persuaded the administration to dispense to Ireland, some vagrant rays of ministerial sunshine. . . . In the rich pastures of Ireland, many hungry parricides have been fed, and grown strong to labour in its destruction."[30]

Americans insisted on seeing Ireland as the nation most nearly sharing the same colonial experience. Even George III thought that the Irish might draw some sort of parallel between their own situation and that of the Americans. "Should America succeed," thought the king, "the West Indies must follow them, not independence, but for its own interest be dependent on North America; Ireland would soon follow the same plan and be a separate state." A type of domino theory was alive and well in eighteenth-century Britain.[31]

Officers of the British army had their own fears. Captain Mackenzie of the Welsh Fuzileers was very concerned that the Irish were likely candidates for enlistment in the Continental army. Anglo-Americans, thought Mackenzie, had been isolated from the turmoil of eighteenth-century Europe and were too soft for army service. The Irish, on the other hand, were used to the hard hand of warfare and were "in general much better able to go through the fatigues of a campaign, and live in the manner they presently do, than the Americans." Moreover, he noted that the Irish were willing to enlist for the low wages and rations offered by Congress, and that "the prospect of acquiring some property, and becoming men of some consequence" was a powerful motivator toward their recruitment. Mackenzie thought that "the leaders of the Rebellion hold up to them these flattering prospects, and at the same time magnify the dangers they are exposed to if conquered. . . . Among so many ignorant people these things have great weight."[32]

Not only were the Irish used to the hard hand of war but the one wielded by the British as well. Arthur Lee sent a dispatch from Cork noting the number of Irish captives forcibly rounded up for transportation to the colonies as soldiers for the British army: "Chained to ringbolts and fed with bread and water; several of them suffered this torture" before finally agreeing to sign the terms of enlistment. Newspapers revealed what happened to many of the impressed soldiers once they reached the colonies. Listed under the heading "Men run from His Majesty's ships in Boston Harbor" were the names of twenty-one impressed Irish recruits.[33] Two Irish soldiers who ended up in the Continental army as a result of this practice were Thomas Kincaid and Thomas Doyle. Deserting the British army upon landing at Boston, Kincaid joined the patriot army and was eventually promoted to sergeant during the war. Thomas Doyle was with the British troops that cut down the patriot militiamen on Lexington Green. Deserting to the rebel cause, he caught a bullet in the British assault on Breed's Hill and was bayoneted to death by his former comrades.[34]

Recruiting the Irish for the Continental Army

There is substantial evidence that Irish immigrants were highly sought after as long-termed recruits for the Continental army. George Washington thought that if Congress did not provide native-born Americans to fill the ranks, then "we must look for Reinforcements to other places than our own states."[35] "Other places" obviously meant engaging for America the rich pool of immigrant manpower recently arrived from Europe.

The Irish, in fact, led the way in providing recruits for the army. So strong was the Irish presence in some units that Ambrose Serle observed that the Continental army drew the greatest portion of its strength from the number of "transported [Irish] felons" sent to the colonies in the early 1770s. "Great numbers of Irish emigrants," declared Serle, were in the army for "mere subsistence."[36] Private Daniel Barber styled the Pennsylvania and Maryland lines "Catholic troops," due to the large number of Irish soldiers within the ranks. Barber thought it was marvelous that the troops got along so well with the Presbyterian forces of New England.[37]

An examination of Continental army muster reports confirmed Lee's and Serle's assertions. In relatively homogeneous New England, few records listed the soldiers' place of birth. Occasionally, Ireland-born soldiers were recruited through newspaper ads, but nearly 100 percent of the actual muster records made no mention of the actual nativity of New England's Continental soldiers. Because of the records, there is no way precisely to determine the actual level of Irish-born men in the New England units. However, the records did reveal hundreds of Irish surnames. Between 10 and 20 percent of every New England regiment had such soldiers. In New York, the pattern was the same. In Orange and Ulster counties, however, which by their very names indicated that they were settled by northern Irish, more Irish enlistees listed their place of birth in the muster reports. A July 1775 muster roll for these two counties revealed that thirty of one hundred men, or 30 percent, had been born in Ireland.[38]

In fact, the Irish presence in the Continental ranks seems to correspond to areas where prewar emigration was encouraged or allowed. The mid-Atlantic states have long been recognized by scholars as prewar clearinghouses for emigration. Pennsylvania regiments, in particular, contained large numbers of Irish immigrants. In the 1st Pennsylvania regiment, for example, 315 of 680 enlistees (46 percent) were Irish. Another 218 soldiers suspiciously claimed "America" as their place of birth. Four companies of the 7th Pennsylvania regiment, a unit of nearly 800 soldiers, reported that 75 of 100 men from four companies claimed Ireland as their place of birth. The muster rolls of the 11th Pennsylvania recorded the birthplaces of 201 recruits; of this number, 45 percent (90 of 201) were Irish. This regiment appeared to be an especially diverse group. Recruited in 1778, its Irish enlistees ranged from teen-aged drummer boys to a sixty-year-old private and former saddler named James Todd.[39] An April 1779 muster report for the Pennsylvania State Regiment of Artillery revealed that 65 of its 205-man complement (32 percent), including its commanding officer Thomas Procter, had been born in Ireland. In fact, only 42 men (20 percent) of the entire unit were from Pennsylvania.[40]

Muster records from Maryland, another well-known nexus for immigrants and transported convicts from Ireland, revealed the same trend. The Maryland 1st Company of Matrosses (artillery) muster rolls compiled from 24 January 1776 to 19 February 1776 showed that Irishmen comprised 45 percent of the entire 101-man unit. Moreover, only 18 soldiers actually came from Maryland.[41] A review of lists of men recruited as soldiers and as substitutes for American-born men drafted by the militia for Continental service also contained significant numbers of Irish-born enlistees. Men recruited in Anne Arundel County, Maryland, from 31 December 1777 to 18 November 1778 showed that 29 out of a total of 50 recruits listed their place of birth; of this number, 20 were Irish (70 percent).[42] A roster of men of Captain Bowie's Maryland militia company enlisted as part of the "Flying Camp" intended for Continental service showed that even militia units utilized Irish-born soldiers if they were intended for long service away from home. The August 1776 muster records showed that more than one-third of 90 men who listed their birthplace upon enlistment were from Ireland. Of the 80 men Thomas Ewing had recruited for the "Flying Camp" in 1776, nearly half had been born in Ireland. In a Delaware company in Colonel David Hall's regiment, a unit associated closely with the Maryland troops throughout the war, nearly half of this 28-man unit listed Ireland as their place of birth.[43]

The trend toward recruiting Irish soldiers continued throughout the war in Maryland. In 1782, the state was faced with a possible British seaborne invasion. The task of organizing a renewed recruiting effort fell to General William Smallwood. Smallwood's instructions contained the usual offer of an enhanced bounty, together with an admonition from the Maryland General Assembly to scrutinize foreign volunteers closely, because "many of this class of men make a practice of enlisting with no other view but to go off with the [bounty] money."[44] Smallwood must not have looked too closely, because immigrants comprised nearly half of the 308-man complement. Over 80 percent of this half of Smallwood's Marylanders claimed Ireland as their birthplace. Fifty-nine others, like their brother soldiers in Pennsylvania, merely listed "America" as their place of birth.[45] Most of the Irish enlistees (65.8 percent) were urban laborers who resided in or near the city of Baltimore or the surrounding farmlands of Baltimore, Anne Arundel, or Harford counties.[46]

South of the mid-Atlantic centers of immigration, however, evidence of Irishmen in Continental units becomes more fragmentary. Still, there were units in southern regiments that had large numbers of Irish enlistees. In the case of General Daniel Morgan's Virginia riflemen, recruited on the frontier, 162 of his total complement of 418 men were Ireland-born. Fragmentary evidence indicated that South Carolina recruited some Irish enlistees as well. Two companies organized in 1775, the Charleston Volunteer Company of Rangers and Captain Heatley's Company of South Carolina Rangers, were each nearly half Irish. Forty percent of the 500-man 1st Regiment of Provincial Troops of South Carolina were Irish.[47]

In sum, the evidence indicates that the Irish were spread liberally in all the Continental lines but were most prevalent in the brigades and companies of the middle states. Though the fragmentary surviving enlistment records make it nearly impossible to come up with the exact number of Irish soldiers who served in each unit, we can make a rough estimation.

The military strength of Washington's army fluctuated greatly throughout the war. Using the year 1777 as a benchmark, the army consisted of thirty-eight regiments totaling 8,378 rank-and-file soldiers. Because of an army reorganization undertaken by Congress in late 1776, a larger burden was placed on the middle states to provide long-termed troops for the army. This phenomenon occurred because the most southern states (Georgia and South Carolina) were allowed to keep their regiments at home as a defense against possible British seaborne invasions or slave insurrections. Of the nine regiments sent to Washington's army from North Carolina, only two had more than two hundred full-time soldiers. Virginia sent fifteen undersized regiments. New York and New England's Continental quotas were generally reduced because their soldiers had served a campaign longer than those of other states. It fell to the middle states (New Jersey, Pennsylvania, Delaware, and Maryland) to provide the bulk of the post-1776 Continental recruits. Delaware, due to its minuscule population, merely continued to fill the vacancies in its one existing regiment. Maryland's quota was raised to eight regiments; Pennsylvania provided thirteen, and New Jersey added four. The Pennsylvania line, however, was the largest single military organization in Washington's army.[48] Taken as a whole, the middle states contributed nearly half of the total force of the main Continental army in 1777 and 1778. The Irish presence within these middle-state regiments averaged, according to existing records, around 45 percent of their entire strength. When this number is compared to the total rank and file of Washington's army, it becomes conceivable that roughly one out of every four Continental soldiers was of Irish descent.[49]

Because the Continental army relied so heavily on the Irish for long-termed soldiers, Washington felt his army was especially vulnerable to desertion and "tampering" by the enemy. The use of Irish soldiers was so widespread by 1777 that when Washington attempted to form his headquarters guard, he told Colonel Alexander Spotswood that he was "satisfied there can be no absolute security for the fidelity of this class of people, but yet I think it most likely to be found in those who have family connections in the country." Washington wanted only natives for his headquarters guard, "and some men of property, if you have them." He did not get them. At no time during the war did the muster rolls of his guard ever reveal a roster entirely free of at least some Irish-born soldiers.[50]

General Charles Lee also had an extraordinarily low opinion of the abundance of Irish soldiers, even when they stocked his own ranks. He ordered his deputy adjutant "not to take any natives of Great Britain, or Ireland, as recruits, unless they have been some time residents in this country, and have wives and children. . . . As this Sir, is a matter of no small importance."[51] Lee's orders were ignored by recruiting officers, however, as he later complained to Washington that "the men are good, some Irish rascals excepted." He referred to the ethnic elements in the American ranks as "banditti" and thought that the "spirit of desertion in the back Country Troops [was] alarmingly great." Lee stated that recruiting officers had "injudiciously" filled their quotas with "Old Countrymen and particularly the Irish" and they had "much contaminated the [native] troops."[52] The "contamination" to which Lee referred was the restiveness that many Irish soldiers seemed to demonstrate within the Continental army. Contentious and prone to desert, Irish Continental soldiers demanded tangible gains for their service. Not connected, necessarily, to the patriot cause by ideology, the Irish soldiers were apt to use their feet when things were not to their liking.

The evidence suggests that Irish soldiers did, in fact, desert the army at a higher rate than the American-born. A review of the *Maryland Gazette* from May 1777 to December 1777 found that 58 percent (eleven of nineteen) of the advertisements for deserted soldiers mentioned that they were Irish.[53] The advertisements in the *Pennsylvania Journal and Weekly Advertiser* revealed the same pattern of desertion for Pennsylvania's Irish-born soldiery. Discounting repeat advertisements for the return of soldiers, runaway servants, and slaves, the *Journal* listed 112 deserters from various Pennsylvania companies and recruiting officers. Of that number, 33 percent of those advertised were Irish soldiers.[54]

Nearly every edition of wartime colonial newspapers advertised for a number of soldiers identified by their officers as deserters. The following advertisements were typical of attempts by company officers to get their men back:

> —DESERTED from Captain John McGowan's Company of the Sixth Pennsylvania Regiment the following persons, viz.: JAMES WALLACE, born in Ireland, aged thirty years, five feet six or seven inches high, smooth in complexion, brown hair, usually resides in Derry Township, Lancaster County. Francis McClusky, born in Ireland, about the same age and size, smooth complexion, light brown hair, and worked for some time at Captain William Old's forge.[55]

> —THREE HUNDRED DOLLARS REWARD: Deserted from the 13th Pennsylvania Regiment, the following persons, viz.: JOHN MELVAIN, born in Ireland, five feet ten inches high, sandy complexion, very talkative and drunken; resided in East Nottingham, Chester County.[56]

The reason for the high desertion rate is not hard to deduce. Having had little time to establish themselves in the communities that recruited them, Irish soldiers were hard to identify and blended into the colonial populace with little effort. Because of the deserter advertisements, however, we can get a general picture of the average Irish soldier who served in the Continental army. The advertisements or entries in orderly books not only gave the soldiers' physical description but included their manner of speech, such as, "speaks little English," or "has the brogue on his tongue."[57] Most of them had been in the country less than seven years. While a few were listed as having deserted earlier in the war, the largest number (75 percent) had enlisted and deserted toward the middle and end. Most were described as generally shorter (five feet, five inches) than the average Continental army recruit, who measured five feet, seven inches. Most likely, poor diets had contributed to the Irish soldiers' shorter stature.[58]

Henry Broderick, a German officer in the British army, confirmed that by 1777 large numbers of Irishmen were moving between the armies at a high rate. Moreover, because many men ran off with their army rifles and their congressional- or crown-issued clothing, the loss of such soldiers increased the cost of financing the war effort on both sides.[59] However,

Stephen Kemble, a British army officer, thought that deserters had a tendency to overstate the case for Irish desertion from the Continental army. He noted that "several Deserters lately from the Rebels, with their Arms, report, as all deserters do, that most of the Irish . . . will leave them [the Americans] on our taking the field."[60]

The British, of course, were not immune to the allure of America on their own soldiers. By 1779 they were having difficulty keeping their units filled due to losses incurred over four years of fighting. Sending recruiting parties to Ireland was viewed by some British generals as a highly dangerous policy. General Pattison, in a letter to Colonel Cleaveland, a recruiting officer in Britain, wrote: "If they don't send me out sufficient Drafts, how will it be possible to carry on the Service of the ensuing campaign—As to recruiting in Ireland, I can only say, Necessity has no Law—I most certainly should give the Preference to raising our Men in England or Scotland if possible."[61] After the arrival of fifty-seven of his new Irish-born recruits in New York later that year, Pattison changed his mind. He lamented to Cleaveland that he wished the "Fifty-seven . . . were again in the Bogs from whence they sprang [meaning Ireland]—hard Times indeed & great must be the scarcity of Men when the Royal Artillery is obliged to take such Reptiles." Pattison wanted no more Irishmen recruited for his battalion because he rightly worried that they would desert to the Americans at their first opportunity. "I have more already than I could wish from that Country," stated the General, "and I am informed by Capt. Chapman that 49 of the Men enlisted there have Deserted."[62] Reptiles or not, these Irish soldiers rapidly became the backbone of the lines of the middle states.

Henry Clinton, commander of all British forces in North America, seemed to be especially concerned about the Continental army's Irish element. He stated in a letter to George Germain that he was determined to "try all Means which should appear to be likely to draw off from the American Army, the Number of Europeans which constituted its principal Force." "The Emigrants from Ireland," he declared, "were in general to be looked upon as our most serious Antagonists. They had fled from the real or fancied oppression of their Landlords; Thro' Dread of prosecution for the Riots which their Idea of that Oppression had occasioned, they had transplanted themselves into a Country where they could live without Apprehension."[63] Clinton speculated that "it would be a powerful temptation to the Irish, [if he were] authorized to hold forth to them His Majesty's Pardon for all Crimes heretofore committed by them in

Ireland, except Murder." Clinton thought that the "prospect of returning home without Apprehension to their Families" for many of the single, male immigrants "might have considerable influence" among the Irish and "could produce no evil to the State."[64] While there is some evidence that Lord Rawdon was able to recruit a small unit of Irish-Americans to fight for the crown, there was no indication that his "pardon" had any effect on Irish soldiers in the Continental army.[65]

The British, however, had to walk a fine line in offering enticements for getting the Irish to join, because they risked offending the native loyalists who first joined their provincial corps. To get around this problem, Clinton decided to "work upon the national attachment of the Irish by inviting them into a regiment whose officers should be all from that country." Muster returns beginning in August 1778 and continuing until September 1781 show that unit strength ebbed and flowed from a low of 240 men in 1778 to a high of 612 in March 1779. By 1780, the Irish American volunteers were back down to just 286 men and ended up at the end of the war with 398.[66]

Desertion, no doubt, was the chief cause of the fluctuation, although Clinton himself did not think so. The Irish employed by the British were involved in only two major engagements, both of them British victories. Disease and battle-related deaths may have taken their toll, but certainly not half of their total strength. The fluctuations in numbers confirmed that the immigrants who served the British had no real loyalty to the crown and served only when it suited their interests. Ebenezer Buck, a civilian observer of the Continental army, noted that so many men deserted both armies that he "believed we [the Americans] keep about even with them."[67]

The ebb and flow of Irishmen into both sides of the conflict led an unknown writer to note in Captain Robert Kirkwood's orderly book that the British army was in reality "a Motley Collection of Forreigners, in a Land wholly unknown to them, cut off from their Native Country." Kirkwood's author observed that "we [the Americans] shall find among themselves a Reinforcement to our army. The Irish, who are incorporated into their forces, will through shame of their Country's Cause Deserted by them . . . leave the English." The author noted that the Scotch and Hessians will probably "follow the example of their Countrymen [and desert the British also]."[68]

Irish soldiers appeared to be everywhere. Their presence was so prevalent that General Charles Lee remarked toward the end of the war that the American rebellion was "nothing more than a Mac-ocracy, meaning that the Revolution was dominated by the Scotch-Irish."[69] The renowned Tory, Joseph Galloway, evidently agreed with Lee. Appearing before Parliament in 1779, he declared that "about one-half of the Rebel Army was Irish and only a quarter of it American."[70] Even though it was an exaggeration, Galloway's remark indicated that the Irish presence in the Continental ranks was a strong one.

The revolutionary generation of America was, as Owen Edwards once remarked, among the first to come to terms with the idea of Irish nationality. The translator of the journals of the Marquis de Chastellux, a French officer in Rochambeau's army, noted that while Englishmen and Scotsmen were regarded with jealousy or distrust in America, the Irishman, "the instant he sets foot on American ground becomes, ipso facto, an American; this was uniformly the case during the whole of the late war." This was because the Irishman was "supposed to have a sympathy of suffering" due to oppression extant in 1770s Ireland. Thus, "his sincerity was never called into question."[71]

The reasons that Irishmen joined the army were as varied as the individuals themselves, though the Irish did have legitimate grievances against the crown. The sheer volume of emigration in the early 1770s was an obvious indication of their dissatisfaction at home. Moreover, if they were fleeing oppression and high rents, as Arthur Young surmised, then, given their situation, they could hardly do any worse in the colonies. Service might bring "connections, land-grants in the West (a traditional bounty, renewed during the Révolution), perhaps on demobilization a manly swagger and a wife to replace the down-look noted in so many descriptions of colonial Irishmen."[72]

Perhaps the Irish chose the Americans because of their antipathy toward the British. Alexander Graydon, a Continental army officer, thought that "as to the genuine sons of Hibernia, it was enough for them to know that England was the antagonist. Irishmen, like the mettlesome coursers of Phaethon, only required reining in."[73] "Coursers of Phaethon" (or unruly horses) seems to be an appropriate appellation. The Irish soldier formed a substantial part of the British, American, and even French forces during the Revolution.[74]

There is little doubt that political leaders in Ireland and America felt they had a common cause. Demands made by the Irish during the war, particularly on the issues of free trade and tolerance of *Roman* Catholicism, were inextricably connected to the prewar turmoil in Ireland and the wartime events in America. Charles Lucas, a friend of America in Ireland and editor of the radical Irish newspaper *The Freeman's Journal*, kept alive the feeling of commonality between the two countries. Wolfe Tone, the Irish revolutionary of the 1790s, quoted Thomas Paine in support of political reform in Ireland. Tone argued that America was a shining example of a country that had overcome religious and sectarian strife and wished that Ireland might have its own version of the American Revolution. Revolutionary ideas, manpower in the form of emigrants, and the common struggle for economic and political emancipation thus flowed back and forth across the Atlantic. At the end of the war, the Yankee Club of County Tyrone sent Washington a letter of congratulations on the achievement of American independence. Washington replied that he hoped that Ireland had received some benefit from the American struggle.[75] For Ireland, however, it was a struggle that has not yet ended.

CHAPTER THREE

A True Pell-Mell of Human Souls: The Germans in the Continental Army

On a hot July day in 1775, John Adams and several other members of Congress commiserated about the recruitment of men for the Continental army. An idea came to Adams, however, when a German citizen of Pennsylvania walked through the front doors of Independence Hall. Wearing the full uniform of a Prussian "deaths-head" Hussar, the German soldier "appeared like an apparition." "He was the most warlike person" Adams had ever seen. After proclaiming that he could raise fifty other men just like himself, the German strode out the doors of Congress determined to recruit some of his countrymen for Continental service. Adams later remarked to a fellow member of Congress that he thought that the Continental army should make use of the "multitude" of Germans who had immigrated to the colonies during the years leading up to the Revolution. Admitting that he "was not fond of raising many Soldiers out of New England," Adams decided that "by engaging their own (German) Gentlemen and Peasants they shall rivet their People to the public Cause."[1]

Recent scholarship on colonial history has demonstrated that British America was not simply an English but rather a multicultural society. Far from being a homogeneous monolith, colonial society comprised many divergent races and ethnic groups. For some, the war was an opportunity for social and economic mobility. Others may have been inspired by the rhetoric of colonial revolutionaries. It appears, however, that revolutionary fervor had little to do with the reasons why certain ethnic groups chose to enter the struggle or remain neutral. More often, their decisions were a matter of survival or a way to even a score with an old enemy. This chapter will show how American and British recruiters vied with each over a source of military labor they could not ignore.

Ethnic Germans, the largest non-Anglo-Saxon ethnic group to emigrate from Europe in the prewar years, enlisted in both armies during the Revolution. Pietistic religious sects like the Dunkers, Mennonites, and Moravians tried to remain neutral. When a loyalist captain inquired in 1776 whether the Moravians were inclined to "join the other party," he was informed that "it does not accord with [their] character as Brethren to mix in such political affairs, we are children of peace, and wish peace with all men; whatever God lays upon us we bear."[2] Most Germans, however, were not members of pacifist sects. The Lutheran and Reformed clergy, who led those who constituted 90 percent of the German population, "were virtually unanimous in their support of the movement for American Independence." They often harangued captive Hessian prisoners of war and attempted to convince them to abandon the British and join the Continental army.[3]

The Germans and America

The large prewar German population of America convinced many that this ethnic bloc was a resource too valuable to overlook. From the beginning of colonial settlement to the year 1760, at least 700,000 immigrants from various nations had arrived in North America. By 1760, however, American shores were flooded by newcomers fleeing famine, war, and pestilence in Europe. Germans affected by the War of the Austrian Succession and the ravages of the Sun-King arrived in record numbers. It has been estimated that nearly 58,000 Germans had come to Philadelphia alone. By the mid-eighteenth century, at least seventeen Philadelphia merchant houses were actively engaged in the German immigrant trade, which accounted for 96.6 percent of all German immigrants to Philadelphia after 1763.[4] At least eighty-eight immigrant ships carrying between 120 and 200 souls each arrived at the port of Philadelphia after the Seven Years' War.[5]

Germans seemed to be especially drawn to the colony of Pennsylvania due to high demand for servants and the relative religious freedom afforded them by the state government. As early as 1677, William

Penn had toured German principalities to recruit immigrants and indentured servants for his colony of Pennsylvania. Offering religious toleration to sects that were not tolerated in their homeland, Pennsylvania attracted numerous denominations. Thirteen Mennonite families, for instance, founded Germantown, Pennsylvania, in 1683; many other denominations followed. In 1742, Heinrich Muhlenberg, founder of a large and prominent family, arrived to organize the Lutheran church in Pennsylvania. By 1745, there were an estimated 45,000 Germans in Pennsylvania. By 1776, the Germans comprised nearly one-third of Pennsylvania's entire pre-war population. Germans also emigrated to New York. They established Neuberg—now known as Newburgh—New York, in 1709. Arriving as indentured servants, many eventually moved into the Mohawk valley (the frontier at that time).[6] Taken together, it is estimated that New York and Pennsylvania alone held about 225,000 Germans by 1775.[7]

The Germans left their homelands for a variety of reasons, though economic motivation and relief from the ravages of contending armies seemed to predominate. The Palatines had suffered greatly from the devastation visited upon them during the Thirty Years' War. During the War of the Spanish Succession, Queen Anne of Great Britain had allowed 10,000 Palatine refugees to settle in England. Finding it difficult to assimilate into the English culture and coming under increasing native resentment, the London government sent them to the colonies. More than 3,800 went to Ireland, the rest to New York and North Carolina. Roughly one in four died en route or immediately after landing in America. Other immediate causes for mass migration from the Palatine were related to a hard winter in 1709–10, restoration of Catholicism as the official religion of the region, and floods.[8] War taxes, robberies, and war reparations contributed as well.

In general, eighteenth-century immigrants avoided New England and the southern plantation districts. Not only was less land available for newcomers there, but the local inhabitants were reputed to be unfriendly to non-English people. Thus the primary destination for most Germans and other eighteenth-century immigrant groups were the middle colonies. The Germans favored Pennsylvania over New York due to its more lenient religious policy, access to fertile back-country lands, and the proximity of similar, established ethnic enclaves.[9]

Peter Brunnholtz, a German Lutheran pastor in Philadelphia, noted the surge of migration to America from the various Rhineland principalities. The number of those "who arrived alive" during one particularly active month in 1751, stated the pastor, "was 1,049." Brunnholtz observed that a group of people called "Newlanders" habitually went out into the Württemberg district of Germany and persuaded the people "to come into this country and that everyone would be as rich as noblemen, and etc."[10] "These deceivers," he declared, "have this profit in it, that they with their merchandise are brought in free, and in addition, for every head they bring to Amsterdam or Rotterdam, they receive a certain sum from the merchants . . . while [the immigrants] are packed into the ships as if they were herring."[11] Brunnholtz recommended that German newspapers in America and Europe report such nefarious recruiting methods but lamented that "the farmers don't read the papers, and many indeed would not believe it, as they moreover have a mind to come."[12]

Recruiting Germans for the Army

By 1776 thousands of young German men were working in the urban enclaves and rural countryside of North America. One of these young men was Johann Carl Buettner. The experience of Buettner illustrates vividly how many young German immigrants must have ended up in uniform during the Revolution. It appeared that Buettner had drifted about the towns of Germany during the years before the outbreak of the American war in an attempt to find work as a surgeon's assistant. Having little success, he happened to be near Hamburg one day and was induced by two "Newlander" recruiters to sail to America to find work. Promised by them that he would only have to indenture himself for two years to work off the cost of passage, the gullible Buettner signed on as a "redemptioner" bound for America. Disembarking at the port of Philadelphia, he quickly discovered that the ship's captain demanded that he submit to six years of servitude. When Buettner and six others refused these steep terms, the captain became enraged and threatened to ship the recalcitrants to Barbados, where they might be worked to death before their terms expired. Buettner submitted and ended up working for a New Jersey Quaker farmer who paid $150 to the ship's captain in exchange for his indenture.

After several attempts to run away, Buettner found an opportunity to escape when he learned from several Hessian deserters that the Congress was enlisting German servants in the Continental army, to serve under a former Prussian officer who called himself Baron von Ottendorff. The only stipulation was that the servants get permission to enlist from their masters and that "these masters would receive during their servants term of service a part of their pay."[13] The United States, in turn, promised each redemptioner "13 acres of land free of charge, to be taken possession of as soon as peace was declared."[14] Buettner was thus "persuaded to enter this volunteer corps" although, as he later admitted, he "was less concerned about the freedom of North America than about his own."[15]

Hoping, perhaps, that appeals to ethnic blocs might help to hold the forces of rebellion together, members of Congress and state governments actively courted men like Johann Buettner. North Carolina's delegate to Congress, Joseph Hewes, wrote to James Iredell that the proceedings of Congress regarding independence were "generally approved of here by all ranks of people; the Germans who compose a large part of the inhabitants of this province [North Carolina] are all on our side; the sweets of liberty little known in their own country are here enjoyed by them in its utmost latitude."[16] Iredell urged Congress to take advantage of the military possibilities provided by the large number of ethnic Germans within their midst.

In the minds of colonial elites like John Adams and Charles Carroll of Carrollton, men like Buettner were ideal candidates for service as long-termed soldiers. If members of ethnic groups joined the army, thought Adams, they would keep the burden of serving from "the Natives of the country who were needed for Agriculture, Manufactures, and Commerce." Charles Carroll asked Benjamin Franklin whether or not it would be prudent to "engage 5 or 6 thousand men, Germans, Swiss, or the Irish Brigade?" Informed by others that his proposition was too expensive for the fledgling United States, Carroll had to content himself with those ethnic soldiers already in the country.[17]

To reach out to these soldiers, the Pennsylvania Committee of Safety wisely had every proclamation, alarm, or broadside printed in German as well as English.[18] Agents for Heinrich Miller's German newspaper *Staatesbote* ranged throughout the frontier settlements of Nova Scotia and all the way south to Georgia. Using the printed media to spread the message to ethnic Germans living in the back-country settlements of New York and North Carolina, Miller published in German, in August 1775, "An Appeal . . . to the German Inhabitants in the Provinces of New York and North Carolina." Written by Ludwig Weiss, president of the Pennsylvania-German society, Weiss and Miller had been urged by some members of Congress to publish this broadside so as to counteract British propaganda in New York and North Carolina that was apparently making some Germans less "disposed toward the common cause."[19] Weiss reminded his fellow Germans that their brethren in Pennsylvania had not only established militias of German citizens but also a "select corps of Jagers [riflemen] who are in readiness to march whenever it is required."[20] Weiss thought it was particularly important to remind the New York Germans of the following:

> Little do the Germans in New York government have to gain from turning to certain rich people in the City of New York and Albany who are owners of large plots of ground on which many Germans live as tenants. For it will do the Germans more good in the end if the general freedom of the country is maintained than if they are to live at the mercy of their landlords. . . . At the present time, however, there is no better rule for Germans to follow both in New York and Carolina than to look with suspicion on the counsel (of the landlords) and rather go the way of the common people who earn their way on their own land.[21]

By 1776, Britain had introduced its own German military forces into the conflict in the form of Hessian mercenaries. Congress moved quickly to counteract any thoughts the British might have entertained about recruiting or impressing German-Americans as replacements for dead or deserted Hessians. Pleased with the resolute congressional action, George Washington wrote to the president of Congress that a regiment made up of German-Americans "would go far in counteract[ing] the designs of our Enemies."[22]

Throughout the war, Congress usually respected the prerogative of each state to form its own military units, although some provincial units were eventually incorporated as "Continental" forces. On rare occasions however, Congress recognized the importance of cultural identification with a particular military unit and sanctioned recruiting across political boundaries so that recruiters could take advantage of ethnic solidarities. The establishment of the German Battalion on 25 May 1776 was such an attempt to persuade members of an ethnic group to support the war effort. From a military standpoint, this formation was significant, because the responsibility for recruiting and supporting Continental units in the field was generally left up to the individual states. Thus units recruited across state boundaries were often unevenly supported. This caused tremendous dissatisfaction among the soldiers of the same unit who wit-nessed their comrades getting better pay, clothing, and equipment while sharing the same campfires and conditions of life. Assigned to the Middle Department in June 1776, the German Battalion consisted of five companies from eastern Pennsylvania, two companies from Baltimore County, Maryland, and two companies from Frederick, Maryland.[23] Army recruiters chose these particular areas for an enlistment campaign because of their heavy concentrations of ethnic Germans.

Within weeks after congressional approval specifically to recruit ethnic Germans, the "German Battalion" began to take shape. A review of the initial muster roll of Captain Philip Graybill's Company from Maryland revealed that indeed all of his thirty-four enlistees were German. Congress issued warrants to the Committee of Observation for Baltimore County that appointed Germans to command the companies and ordered the treasurer of the Committee of Safety to pay them a bounty of 160 to 300 dollars each depending on the rank to which they were appointed.[24]

During the early stages of the Revolution, recruiting for the battalion was restricted to those citizens who understood the German language. The reason for this was clear: the officers, noncommissioned officers, and squad-mates were all German immigrants or sons of German immigrants, many of whom barely understood English. A soldier named "James Fox" was ordered to join another unit, because "not being a German or the son of a German [he] could not serve in that Regiment."[25] George Washington expressed his satisfaction with the recruiting of the unit when he reported to Governor Lee that "the German Battalion had enlisted 1,074 men by July 1776."[26]

Another all-German unit that gained prominence during the early months of the war was the one that Johann Buettner joined, the Ottendorf Corps. Not too much is known about this unit except that its commander, Captain von Ottendorff, a German adventurer, allegedly deserted the army about midwar and joined with Benedict Arnold after he also had changed sides. Ottendorff was authorized by Congress on 5 December 1776 to recruit his unit in the German-speaking communities around Philadelphia; the group amounted to approximately five companies of men, all of whom were German.[27] Congress also authorized a second special German unit known as "the Marechaussee Corps." This unit acted as Washington's military police and occasionally as headquarters guard. Mounted on horseback, these men took their place behind the last file of men on the battlefield and cut down any soldier who left the line, deserted on the march, or flinched in the face of the enemy. Commanded by Prussian emigré Bartholomew von Heer, the unit was recruited in the Pennsylvania-German neighborhoods of Berks and Lancaster counties.[28]

After the first year of the war, Peggy Kunze was amazed at the number of German men who had been recruited by the Continental army, although she hinted that not all went willingly. Observing the first Pennsylvania Germans march off to join the new army, she commented that "the Yagers [riflemen] are most all gone. Next Sunday we shall have very few men in our Church, all my neabors are gone. . . . The men must go, or be taken to gail, or tard and fetheard."[29] Although, like the Quakers, some of the more orthodox German sects, such as the Dunkers or Moravians, avoided serving in the armed forces, Congress and the Sons of Liberty made it hard for most Germans to stay neutral. Those who refused service in the militia on religious grounds were forced to pay triple taxes, and those who were not so inclined served or, as Peggy Kunze noted, faced the wrath of the local Committee of Safety.

Pennsylvania and Maryland were not the only states to recognize the value and revolutionary tendencies of the ethnic Germans. When Virginia created six new regiments, it designated one of them the German Regiment (the Eighth Virginia) and directed that the regiment "be made up of Germans and other officers and soldiers (with) Peeter Mulenberg [*sic*], Colonel."[30] Muhlenberg, destined to become one of Washington's general officers, allegedly climbed onto his Woodstock, Virginia, pulpit in January 1776, wearing military garb beneath his ministerial robes. He ordered the beating of drums outside the church doors and soon had three hundred, mostly German, volunteers for Continental service.[31]

The majority of all German Continental army recruits, however, enlisted in Pennsylvania. Pennsylvania Germans played a substantial role in manning their state line. The muster lists of the First through Thirteenth Pennsylvania Regiments revealed that between 10 and 20 percent of their recruits had Germanic surnames. Regiments recruited in the eastern counties of Berks, York, Northhampton, and Lancaster; areas near the cities of Philadelphia or Reading listed even higher levels of 50 percent or more Germans. On average, Pennsylvania's regiments contained 13 percent Germans. The Pennsylvania companies that had been part of the German Battalion were at first 100 percent German. In the Sixth Pennsylvania Battalion, recruited in the German neighborhoods of Berks

County and Reading, more than one in five soldiers had a German surname. In this battalion, Captain Jacob Moser's company was composed entirely of ethnic Germans.[32]

Pennsylvania citizens who observed recruits like those of Captain Moser and others on their way north to join Washington's army at Cambridge heard them reciting a popular folk rhyme as they passed by:

> Kleine Georgel, Kaiser, Koenig,
> Ist fer Gott un uns zu wennich
>
> [Old England's Georgie, emperor, King,
> For God and us is a trivial thing][33]

American recruiters did not neglect other Germans who could be enticed to join the Continental army. With the arrival of Hessian forces, Congress conducted a spirited debate about the possibility of recruiting them or, at the very least, enticing them to desert the British. Washington was in favor of "raising some Companies of our Germans to send among [the Hessians] when they arrive, for exciting a spirit of disaffection and desertion. If a few trusty, sensible fellows could get with them, I should think they would have great weight and influence among the common Soldiery . . . having received no injury, nor cause of Quarrell from us."[34]

Congress quickly appointed a committee of members "to devise a plan for encouraging Hessians, and other foreigners, employed by the King of Great Britain, and sent to America for the purpose of subjugating these states, to quit that iniquitous service."[35] Congress felt that if "the foreigners" became aware of the "practice of these states, [they] would chuse to accept lands, liberty, safety, and a communion of good laws, and mild government, in a country where many of their friends and relations are already happily settled."[36] Therefore, to encourage further Hessian desertion, Congress published a broadside that offered each deserter fifty acres of land and all "foreign mercenaries who chose to leave the British army free exercise of their respective religions, all the rights, privileges, and immunities [that] American citizenship offered."[37] In an effort to win over the Hessians, Congress ordered the broadside disseminated among the "foreign troops."

Copies were forwarded to George Washington at New York. Washington wrote John Hancock that he "was persuaded that [the broadside] would produce Salutary Effects, if it can be properly circulated among them."[38] Washington feared, however, that the circulars would be merely snapped up by Hessian officers and that the troops—the true focus of the broadside—would never get to see it. By August 26, however, Washington announced to Hancock that "the Papers designed for foreign Troops, have been put into several Channels, in order that they might be conveyed to them, and from the Information I had Yesterday, I have reason to believe many have fallen into their hand."[39] It is not clear what "channels" Washington used, but one of them must have been Christopher Ludwick, who would soon become Baker-General of the Army. Benjamin Rush related that Ludwick apparently crossed over to Staten Island where the Hessians were camped and gave them "the most captivating descriptions of the affluence and independence of their former countrymen in the German counties of Pennsylvania."[40]

The Americans tried to entice Hessians into rebel service in two ways. One way, as previously noted, was to persuade the rank and file with offers of property and propaganda about the superiority of American life compared to their lives in Europe. The second way was to encourage Hessian prisoners of war to serve in the Continental forces or work for American entrepreneurs in war-related industries (farms, iron forges, shoemaking, etc.) and thereby directly expose them to the republican institutions of America. But when these means failed, the Americans were not beneath resorting to a third way: simple coercion. Late in the war, some Hessian ironworkers employed by the infamous Jacob Faesch at the Mount Hope foundry complained in a letter to General von Lossberg that "an American Captain, who was a German . . . a Captain Dille . . . came with a detachment of eight men."[41] He offered the prisoners three choices: enlist in the Continental army, pay thirty dollars in Pennsylvania currency for the cost of their provisions during their imprisonment, or return to jail. When the Hessians thought that jail was better than working for Faesch or the Continental army, the captain became enraged and "told them that they were at his disposal."[42] When the men steadfastly refused to enlist, the captain broke his sword over the head of one of the prisoners and stabbed another with the broken end. Carting them off to a jail and confining them without food or water, agents of Jacob Faesch caught up with the party and offered to pay the thirty dollars for the men. Seeing no other way out of their dilemma, the Hessians again agreed to work for Faesch.[43]

Despite the offers of land and gracious living, only sixty-six Hessians (less than 2 percent of the total number of mercenaries in America) deserted in 1776, a remarkably low figure.[44] Eighteenth-century armies normally experienced much higher rates of desertion, but the war at that point was going badly for the colonists, and because German soldiers had never before served at such a great distance from their homes, most chose initially to ignore the American appeals.[45] As we shall see, this low desertion rate changed as the shock of being in a foreign land wore off.

The Americans persevered in their attempts to recruit Hessians away from the British. There were two principal reasons for this policy. First, every Hessian who deserted the British served to hurt the crown doubly. It cost the British time and money to recruit others to fill the deserter's place and increased the armed strength of American ranks at the same time. Second, most American emissaries and agents in Europe knew well that the Hessian soldiers were not mercenaries in the truest sense of the word. Because of a liberal exemption policy that favored resident taxpayers, the German princes impressed any luckless person who happened to be within reach of their recruiting parties.[46] They had tremendous difficulty just getting these soldiers to port for shipment to America.

The poet Johann Gottfried Seume was one who apparently fell into the hands of Hessian recruiters. Seume's memoirs revealed his erstwhile comrades to be "a true pell-mell of human souls." He described various members of his unit as "a runaway student from Jena, a bankrupt merchant from Vienna, a haberdasher from Hannover, a dismissed post writer from Gotha, a monk from Wurzburg, an official from Meinigen, a Prussian Hussar guard, a cashiered Major from the fortress, and others of a similar stamp."[47] A disabled tailor from Cassel admitted to his recruiting officer that he did not come into his unit to be a soldier but rather to "collect debts among the officers."[48]

There were numerous attempts to desert, and there were also a number of recorded mutinies among the soldiery on their way to ports of debarkation to America. The diary of Johann Conrad Dohla of the Anspach-Bayreuth Regiment recorded such an episode. On the morning of 10 March 1776, after being packed aboard ship near one of the Rhineland ports to prevent desertion, the soldiers took things into their own hands, placing long boards from the ships to the land and disembarking their members. Dohla stated that the officers tried to appease the troops with offers of food and wood for their fires but that the "superabundance of wine, which the residents of Ochsenfurth furnished," caused the soldiers to remain defiant. "Each man," stated Dohla, "made it known that he would not go aboard ship again . . . and in their rage and drunkenness, took to their heels." The Jaeger Corps was ordered to stop the escape.

They shot a few of the mutineers in the legs and had the drawbridges of the city raised. Order was finally reestablished but the incident was, according to Dohla, a "source of great antipathy" between the Jaegers and the Anspachers for many years afterward in America.[49]

One reason for the fractious nature of Hessian recruits was that a great many were not even from Hesse. Some of the German soldiers sent over by German princes had been physically seized on the streets of German towns, placed in a uniform, and quickly shipped overseas. Occasionally referred to as "foreigners," these ersatz Hessians had little understanding of how or why they were suddenly in the employ of the Prince of Hesse. Colonel Georg von Schleither from Hannover was even authorized by George III in collusion with the German princes to recruit such men as replacements for depleted British units serving in America. Of his 1,867 "foreign" recruits, 14 percent deserted before they reached the North Sea ports.[50] Quite a few of von Schleither's men were not even German, and others (39 percent) had previous military service in various other countries. Von Schleither's recruits confirmed that "in the eighteenth-century young men moved around in Europe quite a bit, especially within German speaking principalities."[51] Needless to say, von Schleither's recruits were not very effective, and deserted to the Americans at the first opportunity. Thus the average German recruits, through a series of coincidences, found themselves bound for America with little conception of the circumstances of the rebellion other than what their officers had told them. This made them prime targets of the Continental army recruiters.

The first major opportunity to persuade a large single body of Hessians to change sides came when a substantial group of prisoners fell into American hands after Trenton. Before 1777, many Hessians had been convinced by their officers that horrible ends awaited them if they fell into the hands of the rebels. They were told that they would "have their bodies stuck full of pieces of dry wood, and in that manner burnt to death." The Hessians were thus naturally apprehensive of being captured.[52] But after Trenton, 1,046 Hessian prisoners were exposed to the "virtues of the Republic."[53] After 1777, the desertion rate began to increase substantially. Republican virtue, however, often had very little to do with the reasons for Hessian desertion (see fig. 1).

Johannes Reuber, a prisoner from the Trenton engagement, stated that soon after their capture the Hessians were allowed to work for American farmers and were given, in turn, subsistence and a monthly wage.[54]

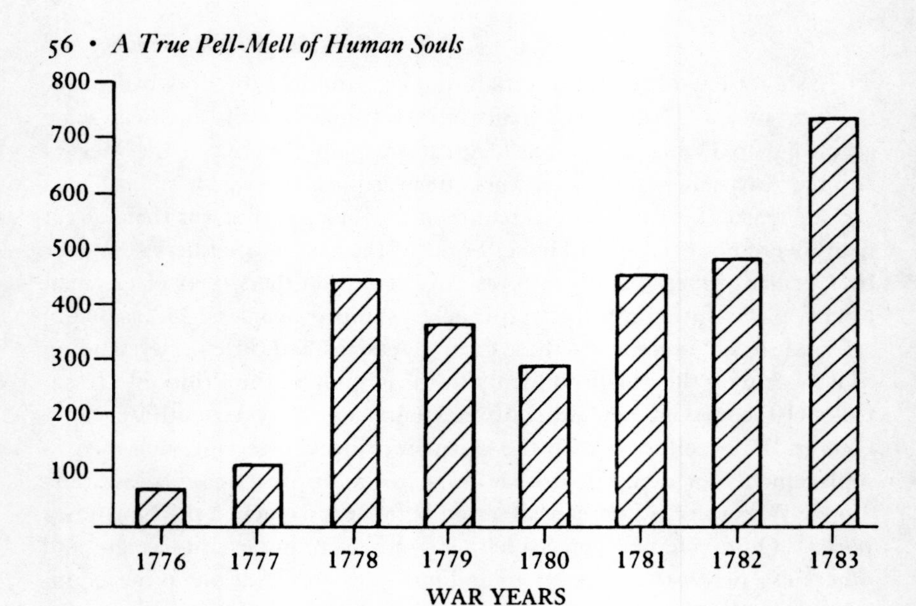

Source: Archivschule Marburg, Istitut Fur Archivwissenschaft, Hessische Truppen Im Amerikanischen Unabhangigketskrieg (HETRINA): Index nach Familiennamen, 5 vols., passim; Elliot W. Hoffman, "German Soldiers in the American Revolution" (ph.D. diss., University of New Hampshire, 1982), appendix 2.

Figure 1. Hesse-Cassell Deserters

British prisoners were not offered this option. Reuber noted that "the English were the enemies and we Hessians were treated much better than they."[55] Hessian quartermasters, who occasionally received passage through American lines, were amazed to see the prisoners passing on horseback. According to Quartermaster Muller, these Hessian prisoners had hired themselves out to the inhabitants and were riding their employers' horses to make their regular Saturday report at the barracks.[56]

In November 1777, General Israel Putnam issued a proclamation in German that gave Hessians more tangible reasons to desert. Putnam stated that the people of the United States were ready to receive the Germans "as brothers and fellow inhabitants." Moreover, Putnam offered "as further encouragement" that, if desired, they would be "carried back to their Fatherland, at public expense" and would pay deserters for their regimental equipment "according to [its] actual worth."[57]

Upon arrival at Winchester, Virginia, the British were imprisoned while the Hessians were given the freedom of the city. "We Hessians could walk around and none of the inhabitants bothered us or treated us as enemies. . . . They all were of the opinion that [we] would never return to the English army and rather remain in America."[58] Reuber noted that even after they were exchanged, many of the prisoners who went to work on the local farms married American women. Even after their exchanges were effected, many deserted again to return to their wives and their former places of employment.[59]

General Knyphausen observed the same thing. American dragoons, sent out into the countryside to collect the prisoners for exchange, had difficulty locating and convincing many to come back. Knyphausen, however, thought this was an American ploy for persuading more Hessians to desert to a manpower-short Continental army. The Americans began to value the Hessians as an alternative and reliable labor force and as bodies to be exchanged for American prisoners of war. After the exchange, Knyphausen admitted that at least 132 prisoners (18 percent of those exchanged) wished to stay with the Americans.[60]

Because of the large number of Hessians who seemed willing to abandon the British, Congress was led to believe by two estranged Hessian officers named Karl Fuher and Karl Kleinschmitt, that, with a little encouragement from the Americans, a corps of deserters could be easily raised among them.[61] The former Hessians claimed they were motivated by a desire "to Shew [their] gratitude for the Friendship [they] received by the Americans during their imprisonment of fifteen months."[62] They further stated that "we can flatter ourselves with great success as a great many have already spoke to us in this City [Philadelphia] and promised to [enlist]." As a final sweetener to their proposal, Fuhrer and Kleinschmitt mentioned that "a great deal of expense" would be saved by recruiting the Hessians, because "all the German troops received new clothing lately and with a little alteration will completely [be] clothed."[63]

On 29 August 1778, Congress resolved to allow the corps to be raised and for them to be called "the German volunteers."[64] Events, however, soon caused Congress to rescind the plan. A deserter attracted to this offer was Lieutenant Charles Juliat. Juliat had run away from his unit near New York in hope of getting a commission in the Continental army. Count Pulaski offered him a place in his largely foreign American legion. Juliat, however, spoiled the deserter corps plan when he decided to redesert back to the other side. Partially responsible for a military debacle at Little Egg Harbor, New Jersey, Juliat's actions changed congressional minds about the German volunteers, convincing them in December 1778 to "lay aside" the plan for raising the German unit. Congress then informed the Board of War to notify Fuhrer and Kleinschmitt that they were to settle their accounts with the auditors at Philadelphia.[65]

Whether Juliat's defection was merely a ploy by British intelligence will probably never be known. Nor was this the first time that Congress had been stung by foreign officers in the employ of the Continental army. Johann Carl Buettner's commanding officer, Major von Ottendorff, had also deserted to the Hessians, later turning up in Benedict Arnold's command after the latter's defection to the British in 1780.

Until the German corps fiasco, congressional appeals to the Hessians did not actually require service in the Continental army but rather promised land and citizenship to the defectors. After the arrival of the French army under Rochambeau, an appeal was made to German soldiers to enlist in the French Royal Deux-Ponts Regiment of Germans.[66] The door was thus kept open for the enlistment of Hessians. Moreover, commanders such as Colonel Charles Armand du Tuffin and Count Casimir Pulaski (until his death in 1779) continued to receive the Germans despite the disapproval of Congress. Congress officially resumed Hessian recruitment in 1782.

Hessian desertion rates rapidly increased by 1778, although not necessarily because of the German volunteer plan. Compared to the first two years of the war, the rate of desertion for 1778 represented a 253 percent increase over the previous rate. All the diaries and journals of the principal Hessian commanders noted the rising rates; all felt compelled to offer reasons for the increasing desertions. Bad food, improper clothing, low pay, and even the weather were cited as the principal causes. At Monmouth Court House, more than four hundred Germans deserted in a week due to the heat, enemy pressure, or a desire to remain in the Pennsylvania area where many had met and married American women.[67]

Friedrich Muenchhausen reported in February 1778 that "the German recruits who have been distributed among the English regiments and who are very dissatisfied are now deserting in rather large numbers."[68] The Hessian headquarters noted similar trends with their own recruits:

> Most of the recruits, mainly foreigners, behave very badly and desert at the first opportunity; therefore we cannot use them on outposts. Many of them may have intended to take advantage of the chance of free passage to this country, and finally to quit Europe. They would have had to work about four years to pay the costs of their crossing.[69]

After 1778, Hessian desertion from Continental army prison camps became common. Frequently shuttled from town to town or hired out to civilian entrepreneurs, the Hessians created something of a spectacle wherever they went. This was especially true of the "Convention army" of prisoners captured at Saratoga. Almost from the beginning of their existence these prisoners were subjected to intensive recruiting by the Continental army and were forced to make winter marches to several prisoner of war camps during the course of the war. Not coincidentally, these camps were located near German-American population centers.[70] By April 1778, 773 Germans abandoned the Convention army prisoner camp. General von Riedesal decided to make an example of one deserter, who was stripped, lashed, and had his Hessian insignia torn from his uniform. Von Riedesal thought that this punishment would deter others from contemplating desertion. To his dismay, however, the Hessian was taken up by American soldiers, reclothed, given money, and paraded about the camp as a "martyr" and "hero" in the cause of liberty. Von Riedesal lamented that "the country now abounds with deserters."[71]

Individual sagas of deserted Hessians abound. One soldier, Johann Kratz, made three trips across the Atlantic in the process of becoming a North American citizen. Abandoning the Convention army in May 1779, Kratz married an American woman, moved to Kentucky, was captured by Indians, and rejoined British forces at Fort Niagara. Repatriated back to Germany in 1783, Kratz deserted the Prince of Hesse a second time. He and a comrade sold their military equipment for the fare across the Atlantic and returned to America; he rejoined his wife and child and finally settled in Ontario, Canada.[72] Two German cousins, George and Carl Zorbach, former Hessian soldiers, sold themselves to an American farmer as indentured servants in late 1782 and remained in America.[73] Two other Hessian soldiers, Johann Eickhof and Johann Wedeking, were released from service and imprisonment when John Thomas, a German-American citizen of Frederick, Maryland, paid the required eighty dollars for their release. Now indentured to Thomas as farm laborers, they eventually married two of his daughters and resisted repatriation.[74]

During June 1782, 350 Hessian prisoners were marched from Reading to Lancaster, Pennsylvania. During the march, 130 (37 percent) of the 350 men were enlisted in the Continental army. Nearly all the rest were indentured out to local farmers, so few made it to Lancaster at all. Johann Leibheit was one of the prisoners who made the trek. Sometime during the march, Leibheit, along with eighty of his comrades, enlisted in the Second Canadian (Congress's Own) Regiment. The unit was originally intended for recruiting disaffected Canadians but had changed over time to include anyone not native to the thirteen states. Moses Hazen, the unit commander, had his subordinate, Anthony Selin, a Swiss adventurer, concentrate on recruiting Hessian prisoners. Upon recruitment, Johann Leibheit became John Lipehite, was eventually discharged, and settled near Pompton, New Jersey, where he lived out the remaining fifty years of his life.[75]

Hessians were recruited not only for the army but also for the navy. A Hessian officer reported that the captured Continental frigate *South Carolina* held on board fifty Hessian prisoners of war of the Convention of Saratoga who had engaged themselves as sailors at Lancaster and Reading.[76] Baron von Lossberg reported to the Landgrave that these men enlisted at the behest of a German minister who advised them that "neither the King of England nor their own Princes would pay for their maintenance, or interest themselves in the least in their fate."[77]

A French officer named Charles Armand de Tuffin sought to fill out a partisan corps formation with some of these convention soldiers until von Riedesal complained to General William Heath, the American commandant, who eventually forbade Armand's recruiters from working the prison camps.[78] Nevertheless, Continental army recruiters, in desperation, tried a myriad of subterfuges to entice Hessians into their service. This included dressing up some of the deserters in fancy uniforms and parading them about the camp in the company of women, or having them ride in coaches while shouting deprecations at their former officers. Congress also printed and distributed handbills throughout the prison camps that offered additional money and land to those who would take service in the Continental forces.[79]

And yet when the Hessian officers attempted to do the same thing to the Americans, they were singularly unsuccessful. Major Baurmeister noted that "the experiences of the provincial battalions were sufficient proof that it [was] useless to enlist the Germans among the rebel prisoners, for as soon as they are fully equipped, they run away."[80] Baurmeister lamented that "the Americans have a knack of attaining their ends by persuasion as well as by money. General Washington's army would have had all its companies full strength if ten pounds sterling had been offered per man."[81] Some Hessian deserters, however, enlisted in the Continental army only to surrender themselves to a British or Hessian outpost at the earliest opportunity, thus sparing themselves a long stay in a notoriously unhealthy prisoner of war camp.

Certain German troops fought as separate units with American forces but had been organized outside the colonies. When the French army arrived in Rhode Island in 1780, it brought with it a polyglot force that was typical of most eighteenth-century armies of the time. This force of about seventy-five hundred men ranged from the Irish regiment, Dillon (sometimes known as the Wild Geese), to French regular and colonial troops (which included some of the later well-known black Haitian revolutionaries), to the German infantry regiment, Royal Deux-Ponts (Zweybrucken).[82] "That German-speaking troops fought with as well as against Americans during the Revolution is sometimes overlooked. . . . It has been estimated that perhaps one-third of Rochambeau's army at Yorktown consisted of German and Swiss troops."[83] Even more unusual was the situation at Yorktown, where Hessian troops in the employ of Britain fought fellow Hessians serving in the Zweybrucken Regiment of the French. Baron von Closen of this regiment mentioned in his journal that the soldiers of his unit had "found many relatives in Philadelphia . . . which necessitated our redoubling our efforts to prevent desertion, for there are many of them who would prefer to seek their fortune in this country."[84]

By the end of the war, more than 30,000 German soldiers had been shipped to America. It has been estimated that at any given time the Germans "averaged a minimum of 34 percent" of the total British effective fighting forces.[85] Moreover, more than half of the Hessians (14,532) did not return to Europe. Of this number, roughly 7,554 died of natural causes or battle-related deaths. Thus almost a quarter of the German troops "made a conscious decision to not return to Europe."[86] Many of these men ended up in the Continental ranks at some time during the course of the war. Captain Wiederhold, a Hessian prisoner at Reading, Pennsylvania, observed Armand's Legion passing by his barracks in 1780 and noted that all four hundred of these men were former Hessians.[87]

Former Hessians roving about the town of York, Pennsylvania, may have been typical. Lewis Miller, a local wit and amateur artist (decades after the end of the war) took it upon himself to sketch 293 prominent residents of the city. Of this number, twenty-two men were casually labeled by Miller as Hessians or "about whom Miller made some comment regarding their service with the German armies."[88] York had a large and growing ethnic German community. A number of Hessians, "seeing how their German-speaking Landsleit were living in America, deserted and settled in towns and countrysides" that they culturally identified with. York's labor needs and strong ethnic ties proved irresistible to some Hessians. At least ten of these former enemy soldiers and their families can be identified in the York borough on the 1790 census.[89]

The records of the Brunswick (Hessian) Regiment support the hypothesis that many of the deserters ended up in the American service. Of the 5,723 Brunswick men sent to America during the course of the war, 3,015 did not return to Europe.[90] Many of these men were captured at Saratoga by American forces and eventually became part of the famous Convention army of war prisoners. Initially quartered at Winter Hill Barracks near Cambridge, Massachusetts, the Hessians were transferred as far south as Virginia. Thus, during their years of captivity, they had ample opportunity to desert or be recruited by American forces.

German archives recorded the disposition of 1,700 of the 3,015 Brunswickers who did not return to Germany. These men had deserted, joined the U.S. service, received discharges in North America, became prisoners in places known or unknown, or became disabled in service. Six hundred men (35.2 percent) were known to have deserted from their prisoner camps or while on the march with their units. At least eighty-three (5 percent) were identified as having served with American combat forces.[91] Thus nearly 41 percent of the positively identified Brunswickers who did not return to Germany were found to have assisted the American war effort in some fashion.

This trend was the same in other Hessian formations. In the Waldeck Regiment, more than 63 percent of its 758-man total complement did not return to Germany. In Johann Ewald's Jager company, 43 percent of its 83-man complement remained in America. More than 2,353 German soldiers came to America from Ansbach and Bayreuth. Of this number, nearly half (1,170) did not return to their homeland.[92]

The reasons for their defection had as much to do with their fear of an uncertain future as it did with American appeals to Republican virtue or offers of land. Some of the Hessians had neither seen nor heard from their officers or countrymen for more than five years. Because it was customary in the eighteenth century for the opposing forces to pay for the health and welfare of their own prisoners of war (something the British government refused to do for the Hessians), it was not unreasonable to assume that the prisoners took care of themselves the best way they could. In lieu of payment, the prisoners often (conveniently) joined the Continental army. The British offered the same "bargain" to American prisoners of war in order to fill up their provincial force ranks. Thus for many Hessians "it was only a small step from prisoner of war to American citizen."[93]

Despite tremendous efforts by officers such as Major Baurmeister to recover their prisoners of war, the end of the fighting increased rather than decreased defections. Baurmeister noted that 240 men from the Frederickstown (Maryland) prisoner barracks had deserted since the Hessians began their march to the embarkation ports of New York. Furthermore, one-sixth of Burgoyne's army had failed to show up from the other camps, and many of the prisoners had been "farmed out" to the countryside where it was nearly impossible to locate them.[94] Many former Hessian prisoners had long since abandoned the locales where they were supposedly being interned. Some, as we have seen, were wearing Continental army uniforms. Others had married or become an integral part of the local economic infrastructure. Moreover, to protect local farmers who had been supporting the Hessians, William Jackson, assistant secretary of war, informed Major Baurmeister at a meeting in July 1783 that "the War Council has no jurisdiction over the Hessian, Brunswick, and Hesse-Hanau soldiers who have been sold out of imprisonment to the inhabitants," and that "no German soldiers may return to the British army unless their [American] owners are reimbursed in cash for their outlay."[95] An analysis of the Von Lossberg Regiment confirmed Baurmeister's dilemma. The returns of the regiment revealed that only one soldier in five who was "farmed out" chose to return to his unit.[96] To overcome economic hardship or to survive, many Hessians joined the American army or served in a war-related industry in the countryside. These men, and others like them in similar situations, became citizens of the new republic.

The participation of ethnic Germans in the Revolutionary War was critical for the success of the American army. While Hessian desertion was certainly a legacy of the war, the formation of purely German military units represented congressional recognition of the necessity of keeping the German element on the colonial side. Service in the American army enabled redemptioners like Johann Buettner to survive in a world where survival was no easy matter. It offered Hessians who had little connection with their communities in Europe a new start in a new world and perhaps a better prospect for prosperity.[97] Motivated by economics or perhaps merely trying to stay alive in an English-dominated foreign land, Germans were willing to serve the United States—but only when such service was in their interest.

The exact level of German recruitment into the Continental army is nearly impossible to determine. Many, like Johann Leibheit, changed their names to Anglicized versions or simply disappeared into the Pennsylvania-German communities, like those Hessians whom Lewis Miller sketched in the early nineteenth century. A rough estimate can be made, however, by comparing the extant records of German enlistees with the total number of men Washington had available at a given time and place. Fifteen percent of all the Pennsylvania men who claimed to have had a foreign birthplace were from Germany. A larger number, around 25 percent of Pennsylvania's total force, were probably first generation German Americans. Because one-third of Pennsylvania's entire population was German, this number makes sense. Using 1778 as a benchmark, Washington's entire main army totaled approximately 7,600 effective rank and file. Of this number, perhaps one of every eight soldiers, or about 12 percent, was German or of German heritage.[98]

These German soldiers served in the Continental army but had the reputation of being a contentious lot. One of the first mutinies quelled by Washington (and there would be many) occurred in the predominately German Pennsylvania Rifle Battalion. As we shall see in chapters 6 and 7, Continental soldiers demanded a viable wage for their services. When their labor was stolen from them by Continental officials unable, or unwilling, to pay them their price, the soldiers demonstrated their dissatisfaction by insubordination, desertion, and mutiny.[99]

The high levels of German immigration resumed after the end of the war. No doubt influenced by the idealistic tales of returning war veterans, old stories similar to those told by "Neulanders" before the war surfaced again. Conveniently forgetting abuses by men like John Faesch, the former soldiers described a land where a "simple man enjoyed affluence seemingly unattainable by a farmer from Hesse or Ansbach." Most of the Hessian states went to great lengths to reaffirm prewar bans on emigration to America. "It was probably not accidental," stated historian Horst Dippel, "that in 1784–85 emigration to America made itself felt in exactly those states whose soldiers had returned shortly before."[100]

CHAPTER FOUR

Changing One Master for Another: Black Soldiers in the Continental Army

Tell them that if I am Black I am free born American & a revolutionary soldier & therefore ought not to be thrown intirely out of the scale of notice.[1]

Cash Africa, a free African American citizen of Litchfield, Connecticut, joined the Continental army along with thousands of other young men in the early months of the war. His decision to become a soldier was not hard to understand. After living nearly hand-to-mouth in a society where racial prejudice, bigotry, and poverty abounded, a few months' service in the army for good wages seemed like a very lucrative offer indeed. Remaining in the ranks until 23 November 1775, Africa was forcibly discharged due to a congressional policy change that had previously allowed African Americans the right to enlist in the Continental army as regular soldiers.[2] Yet there were hundreds like Cash Africa who eventually followed him into the ranks. The desperate need for military manpower overrode any concerns that the army command or Congress had for the propriety of using enslaved or free African Americans as combat soldiers. These soldiers worked for the wages offered, enlisted for longer periods of service than their white counterparts, and took the chance to become free.[3]

The American Revolution was a war that shook the foundations of the colonial concepts of armed struggle, private property, and slavery. Confronted with a conflict that presented opportunities to all racial and ethnic groups of the North American population, the colonial elite were forced to deal with a crisis of military labor in which they had to decide how to employ African Americans in an American army of liberation while maintaining and defending the institution of slavery.

Recent scholarship has revealed that the African American Revolutionary War experience was more complex than has been previously thought. Social pressures caused by the war created conditions that enabled African Americans to gain some leverage in their continuing negotiations with the dominant white culture. A number of important questions concerning race and the armies of the Revolution remain to be answered: How did slave resistance during the war affect the recruitment of African Americans into the Continental army? Did the participation of African Americans in the Revolution result in any appreciable social gains? How did the crisis of military labor affect the situation of African Americans during the war? In sum, the Revolutionary War needs to be seen as a multisided struggle in which slaves and free African Americans took initiatives against British and American elites to create the conditions for their own liberation or an improvement of their immediate situations.[4]

Prewar Resistance

During the period leading up to the American Revolution, historians have usually viewed the struggle between Britain and America as bipolar—that is, the colonies versus Britain. Since numerous colonial laws prohibited the arming of African Americans as militiamen, many failed to appreciate their role in the conflict. The New York colonial assembly, for instance, threatened—one hundred years before Lexington—to punish "grievously" any slave or servant who used "as Pretense of going to the wars against the Enemy to run away from his Master's service."[5] In Virginia, African Americans who appeared at militia musters were "fined one hundred pounds of tobacco." An early group of Carolina patentees feared African American retribution. They noted that military employment of slaves must be exercised with "great caution lest our slaves when armed might become our masters."[6] Provincial legislatures, "sensitive to the property rights of the master, were impressed by claims that tampering with his labor supply struck at the roots of colonial prosperity."[7]

The struggle was, in fact, a complex "triangular" or even multiangular process that involved peoples of many colors, including those from African American and Native American communities.[8] They seized upon the opportunity provided by the war to participate in the fervor of the times. Resistance by slaves and other repressed groups were part of a broader cycle of rebellion that existed throughout the eighteenth century. The

American Revolution was not only shaped by the British-versus-white colonial struggle but by the exigencies of racial and ethnic communities as well.[9]

The revolutionary participation of repressed groups residing in the colonial community was greater than has been assumed. Moreover, the fervor of the times was absorbed by these groups and transformed by them for their own purpose of gaining concessions from the dominant white culture. Following in the path of friends and relatives who participated in earlier revolutionary activity such as the 1747 Knowles Riot, the Boston Massacre, and the Stono Rebellion, African Americans participated in the Revolution in a number of ways, all of which helped them to reduce or control white dominance and oppression.

Between 1765 and 1776, North American slave resistance became a "major factor in the turmoil leading up to the Revolution." The 400,000 African Americans of North America were, by 1775, too large and active a group to be ignored. The social upheaval that led up to the Revolution found corresponding expression in increased slave unrest. In 1765, when Christopher Gadsden's Sons of Liberty demonstrated against the Stamp Act and chanted "Liberty, Liberty" throughout Charleston, African Americans soon began to do the same, causing the militia to be mobilized for at least a week.[10]

The slaves were far from passive observers of the impending struggle. Using an informal but effective network of communication, the American slaves, after 1772, passed around news of Lord Mansfield's decision in the Somerset case. With notions of freedom and liberty being bantered about by whites, there were reported instances of slaves attempting to run away to England "where they imagine they will be free." Archibald Bullock and John Houston, Georgian delegates to Congress, noted in correspondence to John Adams that slaves managed to carry information "several hundreds of miles in a week or fortnight."[11] Not surprisingly, the revolutionary ideas of the patriot movement made their way into this network in a rapid manner.[12]

At least four colonies reported escalating amounts of slave resistance in the 1770s, which followed an earlier period of revolt that occurred during the 1730s and 1740s and corresponded with similar tensions within the white community. In 1773 Abigail Adams mentioned a conspiracy of Boston's African Americans who volunteered their services to the royal governor in exchange for liberation "if he conquered."[13] Thomas Gage, military governor of Massachusetts, noted with interest the "grate Number of Blacks" who, after observing the intense political unrest evident within the white community, offered their services in exchange for freedom in the event of conflict. Likewise, in November 1774, James Madison wrote of a group of Virginia slaves who met secretly to select their own leader for the coming conflict between the British and Americans. Acting as an informal committee of correspondence, the slaves appropriated forms from the patriot movement but applied them to more revolutionary ends. The planters, not necessarily the British government, were their primary enemy. Their plans, however, were discovered and "proper precautions taken to prevent the Infection." White society, well aware of the slave's underground communication networks, purposely withheld news of growing African American unrest. After the November incident, Madison cautioned his correspondent, William Bradford, that "it is prudent such things should be concealed as well as suppressed."[14]

Turmoil caused by white revolutionary unrest corresponded with similar slave turbulence in the southern colonies. On 7 December 1774, a group of ten slaves in St. Andrew Parish killed their overseer and his wife, and "dangerously wounded a carpenter named Wright" and a boy who later died of his wounds. They then marched to the neighboring plantation of Angus McIntosh, wounding him as well. Proceeding further, they attacked the home of Roderick M'Leod, "wounded him very much," and killed his son. Finally captured by the militia, two slaves (one of whom belonged to McIntosh) thought to have been leaders of the revolt were burned alive: a method of death designed to inflict maximum pain and generate maximum terror.[15] Perhaps as a result of their experience with slave resistance, both Angus McIntosh and his brother Lachlan later became very active in revolutionary activities, the latter serving eventually as a general in the Continental army.

The excitement of the times was also evident in the slave populations of South and North Carolina. Anticipating imminent liberation by the British, slaves were thought to be conspiring against the white master class in two North Carolina counties.[16] In South Carolina, the Committee of Safety hanged and burned a free black river pilot named Thomas Jeremiah, who was suspected of offering to lead British ships over the harbor bar. This event occurred in St. Bartholomew's Parish, where the conspirators allegedly planned a general insurrection "to take the Country by killing the whites." Those prosecuted along with Jeremiah included several African American preachers, two of whom were women owned by prominent planters in the Cheraw region of South Carolina. With the exception of one absentee landowner, all the conspirators had owners who were active in the patriot cause. When the royal governor, William Campbell, attempted to defend Jeremiah, he was warned to "keep quiet unless he wanted the hanging to take place at the door of his mansion."[17] In a similar incident, Christopher Gadsden's Sons of Liberty had tarred and feathered two Irish Roman Catholic loyalists, James Dealy and Laughlin Martin, who reportedly favored arming Catholics, Indians, and slaves.[18]

Janet Schaw, an upper-class Scottish visitor, noted that the threat of black unrest seemed to pull the white community together despite their previous political differences. "Every man is in arms and the patroles going thro' all the town, and searching every Negro's house, to see that they are all home by nine at night." Schaw was escorted to her home by a patriot militia squad commanded by a local Tory. Other North Carolinians suspected that their deposed royal governor, Josiah Martin, was somehow involved in the unrest.[19]

Stephen Bull, a member of the South Carolina Committee of Safety, related to Henry Laurens in a rather incredible letter that more than two hundred slaves had deserted their plantations and were encamped on the Georgia sea island of Tybee, where they made contact with the British ships along the coast. Bull thought that it would be better for everyone if the runaway slaves were shot, for if they were captured by the British and sold, "it would enable an enemy to fight us with our own money and property. Therefore, all who cannot be taken, had better be shot by the Creek Indians, as it . . . may deter other negroes from deserting, and will establish a hatred or aversion between the Indians and negroes."[20] Bull and other planters saw obvious advantage in pitting African Americans against Indians in deadly conflict. Repressive measures against slaves were commonplace as the patriot elite responded to slave unrest.

The greatest panic among the white community was caused by Virginia's deposed royal governor, Lord Dunmore. In late 1775, Dunmore proclaimed, in no uncertain terms, liberty to all slaves who joined his standard. Virginia's slave-owning elite responded to Dunmore's less-than-veiled threat of social upheaval in sharp and predictable ways. Numerous broadsides were published in the *Virginia Gazette* urging white slaveowners to warn their slaves against joining the former governor. On November 23, 1775, the editors of the *Gazette* printed a stronger warning, recommending that owners remind potential runaways that their families would be held hostage: "The aged, the infirm, the women and children, are still to remain the property of their masters,—of masters who will be provoked to severity, should part of their slaves desert them." Finally, the editors addressed the slaves directly: "Whether we suffer or not, if you desert us, you most certainly will."[21] A Virginia surgeon described in his diary the type of treatment that Dunmore's black soldiers could expect. "Slaves who join or assist the [British]," remarked Robert Honyman, "are to be transported to the West Indies, or otherwise dealt with, as the Committee of Safety shall think fit, and the Masters of such are to receive the value of them."[22]

Disregarding the warnings of Virginia's slaveowners, slaves flocked in large numbers to Dunmore's ranks. It is difficult to estimate how many slaves actually escaped the plantations, but the former governor himself related in a letter to the British secretary of state that he was endeavoring to raise two regiments of troops, "one of white people, the other of black. The former goes on very slowly; but the latter very well, and would have been in great forwardness, had not a fever crept in amongst them, which carried off a great many fine fellows."[23] By the first of December 1775, Dunmore was able, nevertheless, to outfit more than three hundred slaves who, according to the *Maryland Gazette*, had emblazoned a "Liberty to Slaves" inscription across the breast of their uniform coats.[24] The governor dubbed them his "Ethiopian Regiment."

Dunmore's endeavors must have been moderately successful, as his implied threat of slave rebellion kept the Tidewater, Virginia, area in a state of upheaval for the better part of the war. Landon Carter complained in his diary that a number of his slaves escaped to Dunmore in a skiff:

> 26 Wednesday, June 1776. Last night after going to bed, Moses, my son's man, Joe, Billy, Postillion, John, Mullatto, Peter, Tom, Panticove, Manuel, and Lancaster Sam, ran away, to be sure to Lord Dunmore.[25]

Carter was especially upset by the defection of Moses, whom he felt he had treated rather benevolently "these past six or seven years."[26] Moses' desertion hinted at the precariousness of the entire patriarchal slave system.

Dunmore's threat was not confined only to Virginia. Within a fortnight of his pronouncement, African Americans in Philadelphia were aware of it as well. A few days later the *Pennsylvania Evening Post* reported an incident between a white woman and a black man who apparently refused to give way on a narrow sidewalk. When she demanded that he take to the street, the man shouted: "Stay you d[amne]d white bitch 'till Lord Dunmore and his black regiment come, and then we will see who is to take the wall." Peter Leacock, a Philadelphia silversmith, later published a play that lampooned Dunmore and his African American soldiers. The play was full of hatred for the governor and included "a very black scene between Lord Kidnapper (Lord Dunmore) and Major Cudjo (an escaped slave)."[27]

The American diplomat Silas Deane also recognized the efficacy of "tampering" with repressed peoples. In December 1776 he suggested that, in certain geographic areas at least, the British were as vulnerable to attack along racial lines as the southern colonies. In a letter to John Jay, Deane outlined a bold revolutionary policy by stating, "*Omnia tentanda* is my motto, therefore I hint the playing of their own game on them, by spiriting up the Caribs in St. Vincent's, and the Negroes in Jamaica to revolt."[28]

In fact, there was a slave insurrection scare in Jamaica in 1776. The conspiracy was centered in the Hanover parish and was precipitated ostensibly by the removal of a British army unit to North America. Other evidence, however, indicates that the leaders of the revolt were apparently informed of the progress of the American war and seemed to have been inspired by revolutionary events on the mainland. The Reverend John Lindsey, rector of the parish of St. Catharine and Spanish Town, wrote in a letter to Dr. William Robertson that "in our late constant disputes at our tables (where by the by every Person had his own waiting man behind him) we have I am afraid been too careless of Expressions, especially when the topic of American rebellion has been by the Disaffected amongst us, dwelt upon and brandished of with strains of Virtuous Heroism."[29] Lindsey concluded his letter by warning that "Dear Liberty rang in the heart of every House-bred Slave, . . . and as soon as we came to blows [meaning the commencement of American Revolution] we find them fast at our heels. Such has been the seeds sown in the minds of our Domestics by our Wise-Acre Patriots."[30] Two years later, another conspiracy was discovered at St. Kitts. According to the governor, William Mathew Burt, the slaves intended to "murder the Inhabitants, deliver the Island to the French, or any Person who would make them free."[31]

The cumulative effect of the slave unrest of the mid-1770s, and especially Lord Dunmore's proclamation, caused some white revolutionaries to see the African American population within their midst more as a liability than an asset. James Madison thought that Dunmore, by tampering with the slaves, had discovered the way to military success in Virginia. He lamented that "if we should be subdued, we shall fall like Achilles by the hand of one that knows that secret."[32] John Adams feared that "if a British commander landed one thousand regular troops in Georgia, and would proclaim freedom to all the negroes who would join his camp, twenty thousand [slaves] would join in a fortnight."[33] Planter William Henry Drayton noted with satisfaction that the First Provincial Congress, determined to smash the slaves' "high notions of liberty," appointed a special committee to investigate potential African American insurrections. They formed three regiments not only to guard against British amphibious invasions but to "keep those mistaken creatures [the slaves] in awe." Meanwhile the merchants of Charleston ordered three companies of militia to patrol the city's streets, one by day and two at night, "to guard against any hostile attempts that may be made by our domesticks."[34] "Mistaken creatures" or not, slaves used the turmoil of the times to their best advantage, and their resistance forced the colonial elite to consider their value as combatants for liberty.

Recruiting African Americans for War

Despite facing pervasive racial prejudice and white fears of insurrection, African American soldiers were heavily recruited for service in the Continental army at Cambridge, and later in other areas. At first, American recruiters resisted enlisting African Americans because it was thought that such a policy was "inconsistent with the principles that are to be supported." In July 1775 Horatio Gates reminded recruiters not to accept "any deserter from the Ministerial army, nor any stroller, negro, or vagabond." African Americans, however, still appeared in sizable numbers in nearly all Continental regiments.[35]

One of the reasons for this phenomenon was that African Americans often took the initiative to join the manpower-starved army, with or without their master's permission. Israel Ashley of Westfield, Massachusetts, was drafted by his town's militia for Continental service. Intending to furnish his slave Gilliam as a substitute, Ashley soon discovered, to his chagrin, that Gilliam had already enlisted without his consent. Ashley complained to Horatio Gates, requesting that Gilliam be sent back to

Westfield. Gates declined, insisting that Massachusetts had not defined its policy on such volunteers nor had it passed a law "on behalf of slaves who have or will assist us in securing our freedom at the risk of their own lives." A law was needed, continued Gates, because of the "great number of soldiers in that class in this department, and in your own [Massachusetts] troops."[36]

By the fall of 1776, the young United States faced a full-scale crisis in military manpower. Congress had ordered the formation of an eighty-eight battalion army, to which each state was required to contribute an assigned number of men on the basis of their prewar white male population. The states' responses to their assignment, however, were inadequate and remained so throughout the war. Not having the power to force the states to comply with their quotas, Congress enjoined them to use their militia "and to pursue every Means in their Power in order to forward the recruiting service."[37] Frederick MacKenzie, a British officer in occupied Rhode Island, observed that the Continental army was having difficulty obtaining (white) men. They were, however, doing a brisk business with African American recruits.[38]

How brisk a business depended on the location of the recruiter. In New England, several officers noted the presence of African American recruits in the ranks. William Heath, one of Washington's generals, noted the great diversity of units from the northeastern United States: "There are in the Massachusetts Regiments some Negroes. Such is also the case with the Regiments from the Other Colonies, Rhode Island has a number of negroes and Indians, Connecticut has fewer negroes and a number of Indians. The New Hampshire regiments have less of both."[39] A Hessian officer observed in 1777 "that the Negro can take the field instead of his master; and, therefore, no regiment is seen in which there are not negroes in abundance, and among them there are able-bodied, strong and brave fellows."[40]

Compared to their numbers in New England, African Americans joined the Continental army in significant numbers. The free black population of Massachusetts during the war years was only about forty-four hundred; of these some five hundred served in the Continental army.[41] In Connecticut, "close to three hundred African American soldiers can be unmistakably identified as serving in Connecticut's regiments of the Continental army."[42] These men were identified by the typical African American surnames of the period such as Cuffe, Jack, or classical names like Jupiter or Cato. Some African Americans, however, had adopted

European names, so there is no certainty that a larger number were not in Connecticut's ranks.

More than any other region, the New England states seemed to encourage African Americans to join the Continental army. With small free black and slave populations, they did not have the extreme fear of arming African Americans experienced by states farther to the south. Moreover, by 1778 the crisis in military labor in New England had escalated to such a level that even cash bounties of over one thousand dollars were failing to attract enough free whites to man the ranks. The patriots were thus forced to consider larger recruitment of slave and free black manpower.

From the beginning of the war, however, slaveowners had been discouraged from allowing their slaves to serve as soldiers. Laws were passed that defended the rights of property holders, and slaveowners were required to post one hundred pounds to "guarantee that their former chattels would not become public charges" in the event they became disabled through battle or disease. The exigencies of the war, however, caused the Assembly of Rhode Island to pass a new law quickly that "absolved masters of this responsibility and made the state liable for the support of such slaves as should come to want."[43] The state also resolved the problem of indemnification by purchasing the slaves at a price not exceeding four hundred dollars in Continental currency.[44] The way was finally cleared for full African American recruitment. In February 1778, the Rhode Island Assembly passed a law that allowed "every able-bodied Negro, Mulatto or Indian Man slave, in this State [to] enlist into either of the . . . two [Continental] Battalions" then being raised by the state in fulfillment of its congressional quota.[45]

Noting perhaps the success that the Continental army had in recruiting a battalion of ethnic Germans in 1776, General James Varnum recommended to George Washington that one be formed entirely of African Americans as well. Because both of Rhode Island's regiments were severely undermanned, Varnum wanted to consolidate them into one and recruit a new regiment composed primarily of African American soldiers. He assured Washington that "a battalion of Negroes could easily be raised [in Rhode Island]."[46] Varnum's proposal met opposition as six slaveholders petitioned the Rhode Island Assembly against it. They opposed the decision to purchase slaves to defend "the Rights and Liberties of the Country." More importantly, the petitioners felt that "great difficulty and uneasiness would arise in getting masters to sell their slaves." In fact, the petitioners believed that "some owners would not sell their slaves at any price, fearful of the effect it would have upon those [African Americans] still in bondage."[47]

On 25 February 1778, the first three African Americans enlisted under Rhode Island's new law. Cuff Greene, Dick Champlin, and Jack Champlin, all former slaves residing in South Kingstown, joined the Continental army. The state of Rhode Island reimbursed their former owners for the maximum value of 120 pounds (Jack was purchased for ten pounds less). The general treasurer's accounts from 25 February to 14 October 1778 revealed seventy-four enlistees. The largest number of these (63) occurred during the months of May, June, and July. Thirty-one of the enlistees came from the North and South Kingstown townships. This trend reflected the large concentration of African Americans in that part of the state.[48]

The unevenness of African American enlistment can be explained in two ways. First, to keep their slaves from running away and enlisting without their consent, slaveowners began to indenture their slaves to other whites, which greatly complicated matters. Slaves owned by an individual but worked for second parties as well were not authorized to enlist because of the complexity of reimbursement for their military service. Second, there was a concerted effort on the part of some disgruntled whites to derail the enlistment process by spreading disinformation among the slaves regarding Continental service. Captain Elijah Lewis, a recruiting officer present in Kingstown on 19 February 1778, reported to state officials that a Mr. Hazard Potter told the slaves gathered for enlistment that "they were [to be used] as Breastworks" and that, if taken prisoner, they "would be sent to the West Indies and sold as slaves."[49] Virginians had used the same argument against Dunmore's recruitment of slaves for his "Ethiopian Regiment" in 1775. Now, however, it was being used against the patriot's recruiting schemes.

White reaction to Rhode Island's new African American enlistment policy was so strong that the Assembly repealed the February enlistment law on 10 June 1778. Nevertheless, the state treasurer's records showed that at least forty-four more slaves managed to enlist between 12 June and 13 October 1778. The precise number of African Americans who actually served in the Rhode Island unit remains uncertain, the estimates ranging from 130 to 300. Taking into account all the incomplete muster rolls, treasurer's lists, payrolls, and casualty lists, the most probable number was between 225 and 250.[50]

Rhode Island's black regiment served for the duration of the war.

African Americans were highly valued as soldiers, not only for their fidelity but also because they drew "no other allowance than what is paid them by the continent." Other soldiers, wrote Governor William Greene, "received subsistence money, the amount of which has been more in one year than either of them [slaves or soldiers] were valued at." Significantly, Washington turned down Governor Greene's request for the return of the black regiment to Rhode Island, and he assigned the unit to duties with the main army.[51]

Following the lead of Rhode Island, other New England colonies also seriously considered the enlistment of African Americans as a way of alleviating their manpower dilemmas. In the spring of that year, the General Court of Massachusetts debated the issue. Thomas Kench, an artillery officer then at Castle Island, addressed the court:

> A re-enforcement can be quick raised of two or three hundred men. . . . And what I refer to is negroes. We have divers of them in our service, mixed with white men. But I think it would be more proper to raise a body by themselves, than to have them intermixed with the white men; and their ambition would entirely be to outdo the white men in every measure that the fortune of war calls a soldier to endure.[52]

Kench outlined for the court just how he intended to organize African American recruits and even hinted at using racial competition to get maximum efforts from the men. The unit would be commanded by whites, but the noncommissioned officers would be African American. They would serve for the duration of the war and "then be free men." African American enlistment "will be far better," continued Kench, "than to fill up our battalions with runaways and deserters from General Burgoyne's army, who, after receiving clothing and the bounty, in general make it their business to desert from us."[53] The court, however, was not persuaded; it voted to reject Kench's proposal. Instead, in order to appear less threatening to whites who feared African Americans with guns in their hands, Massachusetts recruiters enlisted African Americans as individuals rather than as whole units.

Besides Christopher Greene's Rhode Island regiment, there is fragmentary evidence that at least a few all-black units were formed during the war. Known as the "Bucks of America," such a unit was raised in Massachusetts. No service records remain except for a battle flag that had been presented to the unit by John Hancock. In 1781, Connecticut also formed a company of African American soldiers. The officers and noncommissioned officers were white, but the private soldiers were solidly African American. After the arrival of French forces in North America, the *Paris Gazette* noted that there were 2,979 "Europeans" and 545 "Colored: Volunteer Chausseurs, Mulattoes, and Negroes, newly raised at St. Domingo."[54]

While employment of African Americans as soldiers was a generally recognized policy in New England, such suggestions were met with resentment in the south. A 1779 congressional proposal to arm southern slaves was received "with horror by the planters, who figured to themselves terrible consequences."[55] Christopher Gadsden, radical member of the South Carolina patriot movement, agreed: "We are much disgusted here at Congress," he wrote to Samuel Adams, "recommending us to arm our Slaves, it was received with great resentment, as a very dangerous and impolitic Step."[56] The South Carolina Privy Council even went so far as to offer to the British General, Andre Prevost, that the colony would remain neutral for the rest of the war if the British would not invade it and liberate the slaves. Faced suddenly with invasion and the possibility of slave seizures by the British, the Privy Council was willing to risk the revolution and continental unity for the sake of maintaining racial and social dominance.

Eventually, the slaves themselves, with the help of the British during their abortive invasion of the southern colonies, provided the impetus for full recruitment into the Continental army. It was the threat of self-liberation, which might have been achieved with British help, that opened the way for the white ruling classes to use army enlistment as an alternative means of control. Even hardened slaveowners such as Henry Laurens changed their opinion about the employment of African Americans during the course of the war. Together with his soldier-son John, the elder Laurens led the movement for enlisting black soldiers in the South. Not only were American arms losing the war in the South, but the British had also made slave seizures an integral part of their southern strategy.

John Laurens, Washington's aide-de-camp, had long thought that arming African Americans was appropriate for the Continental army. To his practical mind, the obvious reason for British success in the southern theater was that the South Carolina and Georgia legislatures failed to make good use of their African American manpower. It appeared to both John and Henry Laurens that large portions of the militia were tied down garrisoning the frontier or tidewater, where they fearfully awaited slave or Indian insurrections.

Moreover, the younger Laurens was present when James Varnum discussed raising the African American Rhode Island battalion with George Washington. John Laurens implored his slaveowning father to "cede me a number of your able bodied men slaves," to begin training them as soldiers. This would, thought Laurens, put African Americans on the way to "perfect liberty" and at the same time "reinforce the defenders of liberty with a number of gallant soldiers."[57] Laurens informed his father that "even Washington was convinced that the numerous tribes of blacks in the southern parts of the continent offer a resource to us that should not be neglected."[58] Washington, however, did not offer any of his own slaves (he owned hundreds) for the defense of the south.

But just as had happened in Rhode Island, the rights of private property, indemnification to owners, and racial prejudice overrode cooperation, despite the fact that the British army was ransacking the countryside and attracting slaves by the thousands. The reasons for southern reluctance to arm African Americans were not hard to understand. There were many in South Carolina who would rather have lost the war than give up their dominant position in the social hierarchy of the colony. The legislatures of South Carolina and Georgia, dominated by the planter class, would be the least likely to agree to any plan that involved liberation of slaves.

Nevertheless, on 25 March 1779, a congressional committee, led by Henry Laurens, reported that because no troops could be spared from Washington's main army for the defense of the South and because it was necessary "for the great proportion of citizens . . . to remain at home to prevent insurrections among the negroes, and to prevent desertion of them to the enemy," at least three thousand slaves should be immediately recruited for the southern army, in exchange for freedom at the close of hostilities.[59] Significantly, the recruited African Americans did not receive a land bounty; instead they received fifty dollars and freedom if they survived the war.

Alexander Hamilton noted that Laurens's plan would "have to combat much opposition from prejudice and self-interest." Hamilton observed that a "thousand arguments" will be offered against recruiting African Americans. "It should be considered," he warned, "that if we do not make use of [them] in this way, the enemy probably will; and that the best way to counteract the temptations they will hold out will be to offer them ourselves." "An essential part of this plan," he continued, "is to give them their freedom with their muskets. This will secure their fidelity, animate their courage, and I believe will have a good influence upon those who remain, by opening a door to emancipation."[60]

Soon after Congress resolved to recommend raising African American battalions, Henry Clinton, commander of all British forces in America, struck back, declaring that because "the enemy have adopted a practice of enrolling Negroes among their troops," he would sell all captured African American Continental soldiers, "the money to be paid to the captors." Moreover, Clinton proclaimed a general emancipation of all slaves who escaped to his lines, with the interesting proviso that each runaway could choose "any occupation [with the British army] which he shall think proper."[61]

To counter Clinton's offer of emancipation, Congress agreed to appoint "an officer to levy a Corps of one thousand able bodied negroes in Georgia and South Carolina" under the authority of their respective governors; the same offers of pay and provisions were to be provided to them.[62] The new resolve was two thousand African American soldiers fewer than the original Laurens plan called for. There is, moreover, evidence that the legislatures of South Carolina and Georgia refused to arm the men, using them instead as labor and pioneer troops.[63]

Predictably, Laurens's plan received only twelve votes from the South Carolina legislature. The plan had been, as Henry Laurens stated, "blown up with contemptuous huzzas." In 1782 John Laurens tried once more to convince South Carolina to enlist the slaves before the British seized them. This time, however, he proposed that "one of the best ways to employ the profits from among the confiscated estates was to raise a corps of 2,500 troops from among the slaves on them." Laurens evidently offered this revision of his original plan to secure the loyalty and property of the planter class in the state legislature. His whole plan was now linked to the sequestration and confiscation of loyalist estates and would not force the planters themselves to make any sacrifices.[64] Despite what Governor Rutledge described as "a hard battle," Laurens's proposal was once again easily defeated.[65]

Immediately before his death in an obscure skirmish, Laurens wrote to Washington and suggested that the state of Georgia might be receptive to his new plan, because it admitted in 1780 that arming slaves was a necessary military step. Washington's reply, however, revealed a deep pessimism over the whole affair:

> I must confess that I am not at all astonished at the failure of your Plan. That spirit of Freedom which at the commencement of this contest would have gladly sacrificed every thing to the attainment of its object has long since subsided, and every selfish Passion has taken its place; it is not the public but private Interest which influences the generality of Mankind . . . under the circumstances it would have been rather surprizing if you had succeeded, nor will you I fear have better success in Georgia.[66]

Rather than recruit African Americans, the South Carolina legislature, in an "Act to Procure Recruits and Prevent Desertion," used the slaves of Tories as a bounty to encourage white enlistment.[67] The state of Virginia offered "a negroe worth 60 pounds specie at the end of the war" in addition to cash and land to stimulate enlistments during the southern invasion.[68] After Yorktown, however, the manpower emergency was over. The moment Cornwallis surrendered, Washington posted guards on the beaches to prevent blacks from escaping aboard British men-of-war.[69] With the bulk of the British forces now headed for prison camps, all plans for African American enlistment became essentially moot and no less agreeable to planters, who were not about to change their minds now that the British threat had diminished.

If the Continental forces did not always open their arms to blacks, the British certainly did. Slaves took advantage of the turmoil of war to liberate themselves by deserting their plantations for the British army. The colonial historian, David Ramsey, estimated that South Carolina lost "twenty-five thousand negroes." George Abbot Hall, a Charleston merchant, estimated that more than 20,000 slaves (about one-quarter of the entire slave population of South Carolina) ran away from their plantations when the opportunity presented itself. In Georgia, the loss was even proportionately greater, with estimates of "three-fourths to seven-eighths of all slaves freed by the British." Thomas Jefferson, as the wartime governor of Virginia, estimated that during 1778 alone, the British had enabled more than 30,000 Virginia slaves to flee from bondage. As late as 1786, a corps of runaway African Americans calling themselves the "King of England's soldiers" formed a North American "maroon" community in the swamplands of the Savannah River, harassing settlements well after the Treaty of Paris.[70]

Many African Americans must have hoped for the success of British arms. Henry Melchoir Muhlenberg, a Lutheran pastor, wrote in his journal of a conversation he had with two black servants of an English family leaving Philadelphia. "They secretly wished that the British army might win," stated Muhlenberg, "for then all Negro slaves will gain their freedom. It is said that this sentiment is almost universal among the Negroes in America."[71] During the British occupation of Philadelphia, a correspondent for the *Pennsylvania Packet* observed that "the defection of the Negroes [to the British], [even] of the most indulgent masters . . . shewed what little dependence ought to be placed on persons deprived of their natural liberty."[72]

Despite the "universal sentiment" that the British were liberators, their policy concerning the enlistment of African Americans was nearly as hesitant and disjointed as that of the colonists. With the exception of Dunmore's "Ethiopian Regiment" of 1775–76, most African Americans were not armed by the British as red-coated combat soldiers. Groups of former slaves, however, operated as guerrillas in the "neutral ground" near occupied New York, while mounted former slaves served the British near Savannah, rounding up deserters.[73] Three items in patriot newspapers of 1780 related the depredations of an African American guerrilla leader by the name of Ty, a veteran of Dunmore's Ethiopian Regiment of 1775. With a force of "twenty blacks and whites," in the vicinity of occupied New York, Ty was credited with "carrying off prisoners, Capt. Barns Smock and Gilbert Vanmater; at the same time spiked up the iron four pounder at Capt Smock's House. . . . The above mentioned Ty is a Negroe, who bears the title of Colonel, and commands a motley crew at Sandy Hook."[74] Thomas Peters was the slave of one William Campbell in Wilmington, North Carolina. He fought for the British and was twice wounded.[75] Thomas Bee, a South Carolina planter, complained to state authorities about "Black Dragoons who have been out four times within the last ten days plundering and robbing."[76] African American labor was fully utilized by the British against the colonists wherever possible.

British military personnel even engaged in slave trading: "During the occupation of Georgia, General Andre Prevost acquired 100 slaves and put them to work on his plantation on the Ogeechee River." Another general gave a fellow officer a "twenty-two year old black man as a present." Frequently, African American prisoners from the Continental forces were marketed to provide cash for sustaining the British army.[77] Many British officers regarded their black servants as their personal property. General Leslie warned that "every department and Every Officer, wishes to include his slaves in the Number to be brought off." Leslie proposed the appointment of officers to supervise the transportation of runaway slaves to places such as Jamaica, East Florida, St. Lucia, and other parts of the empire where slavery was still legal.[78]

British efforts at slave seizures, however, should not be confused with any sentiments of emancipation. John Cruden, a loyalist who had previously used slave-soldiers to guard the property of sequestered estates in the South, wrote Lord Dunmore and proposed that the British raise and arm 10,000 African Americans to regain the South "with its own force." Cruden revealed, however, some underlying reasons for his proposal. The recruitment of former slaves changed nothing in the social order. "'Tis only the changing one master for another," he stated, "and let it be clearly understood that they are to serve the King for ever, and that those slaves who are not taken for his Majesty's service are to remain on the plantation, and perform, as usual, the labor of the field." Cruden significantly added a side benefit to his plan in that by employing slaves as a military force, they were "disciplined and brought under command . . . [and were] prevented from raising cabals, tumults, and even rebellion, what I think might be expected soon after a peace."[79]

Despite resistance from southern slaveowners and the tendency for the slaves themselves to take their chances with the British, black soldiers were scattered liberally throughout the lines of all the states except for South Carolina and Georgia and appeared in greater numbers than has been previously supposed. In no other area of the United States, however, with the exception of New England, were African Americans incorporated into completely black units.

Historians have estimated that five thousand blacks probably served in the Continental army during the Revolution.[80] An examination of the muster rolls of the various regiments of the Continental army revealed that recruiters (with the exception of Rhode Island) took African American enlistees as they found them, in ones and twos, to fill chronically undermanned Continental battalions. Benjamin Quarles's five-thousand-man estimate represents approximately one African American soldier for every sixty white soldiers. Black soldiers, however, generally served four and a half years in the Continental army, three years longer than whites, who, however, saw substantially more militia service. The percentage of African Americans to whites in Continental service at any given time, therefore, was much higher than one in sixty.[81]

One way to determine a more exact percentage of African Americans in Continental service is to look at the rolls of blacks who were present for duty in the army as listed by Alexander Scammell, adjutant-general of the army, on 24 August 1778. This is the only known military document in existence that identified (in a general personnel return) the number of African Americans in each regiment. We can compare Scammell's total figure of black rank and file present for duty with the overall figure of the rank and file for each brigade on the army's monthly personnel return to come up with the percentage of African Americans present in each brigade. Parson's Brigade (Connecticut troops), for example, reported for the month of September 1778 a total of 1,065 rank and file (117 of whom were African American) present for duty,[82] or nearly 10 percent of this single unit.[83] Most of the other brigades listed fell within Connecticut's rate. The North Carolina Brigade showed 670 men present for duty, Scammell listing 42 African Americans, for a total of 6.2 percent of the unit. Muhlenberg's Virginia battalions were 13 percent African African.[84] When compared against the total number of white soldiers present for duty, African Americans appeared in larger numbers but were scattered throughout the whole army (see fig. 2). In February 1778, Washington's army was estimated to have only 7,600 rank and file fit for duty. The 755 African Americans within it thus comprised nearly 10 percent of the entire army.[85]

Several foreign officers commented on the racial diversity of the American army in the latter years of the war. The Marquis de Chastellux, a French officer, observed the Continental army in 1781 and commented that the large number of African Americans in the ranks "were strong, robust men, and those I saw made a very good appearance." Another French officer at White Plains, New York, commented that "three-quarters of the Rhode Island regiment were negroes, and that regiment is the most neatly dressed, the best under arms, and the most precise in its maneuver" of any unit he had ever seen.[86]

Despite the paucity of formal records, there is evidence that African Americans were rather common in the ranks. Contemporary art depicting scenes from the Revolution nearly always revealed the presence of black combatants. In both the Sully and Leutze paintings of Washington's Christmas Eve crossing of the Delaware River in 1776, an African American soldier was present. The soldier has since been identified as Prince Whipple, the bodyguard of a New Hampshire general.[87] Trumbull's famous painting of the Battle of Bunker Hill (painted in 1786) prominently featured an African American soldier, purported to be Peter Salem. A portrait of Lafayette by Jean-Baptiste Le Paon shows Lafayette's black assistant, James Armistead Lafayette, to be both armed and exquisitely turned out in perfect uniform. Particularly interesting is a watercolor drawing entitled "costumer de l'Armee Americaine en 1782," which portrayed the uniform and equipment of four American soldiers, one of whom was unmistakably black.[88] A portrait of the Battle of Cowpens by William Ranney (painted in 1845) revealed an unknown African American cavalryman saving the life of Lieutenant Colonel William Washington by firing a pistol into a British dragoon.[89] Most artists of the Revolutionary era routinely portrayed African Americans as combatants and not as auxiliaries in their paintings.

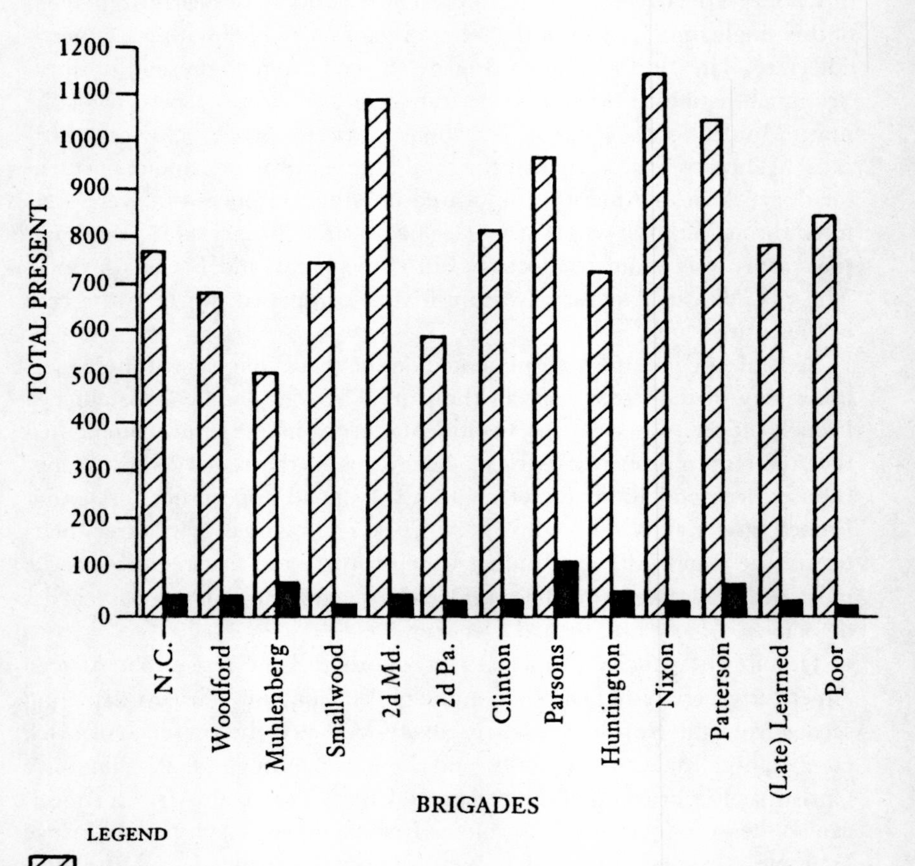

Figure 2. African-American Soldiers in the Ranks

While a remarkable number of blacks served as long-termed Continental soldiers, few served in the state militias. Steven Rosswurm's definitive study of the militia in the city of Philadelphia revealed only one African American enrollee on any of its muster rosters.[90] This disparity indicated that African Americans fulfilled the onerous continental manpower quotas for the states but were still discriminated against on the local level. Moreover, Continental service placed African American soldiers under strict military discipline and transported them to regions remote from their place of recruitment.[91] Militia duty, of course, would have kept them in the same locality. These conditions for African American service apparently satisfied the objections and fears of members of the white master class in every area except the Deep South, where arming slaves in any way remained anathema throughout the war.

Instead of being used as general military manpower, African Americans were used as a specific kind of manpower. Filling the arduous military roles of infantryman, pioneer and wagoner, their social characteristics were remarkably similar to the hordes of Irish and German immigrants who served the Continental army as well. Most African American enlisted men were in the lower socioeconomic strata of colonial society. A survey of fifty black soldiers' pension records showed that one-fifth had listed laborer or servant as their prewar occupation. Other occupations mentioned were the semi-skilled occupations of weaver or wagoner. One famous soldier, Cuff Tindy, called himself a farmer. He was a slave before the Revolution, received his freedom as a result of service and listed one horse, three sheep, three lambs, and one rake as his only assets upon applying for a pension in 1819. Cato Freedom, African by birth, won his freedom and last name by service and listed ownership of thirty-three acres of land, a plough, cow, ax, and other small household articles when he applied for a pension, whereas Devonshire Freeman merely listed an "old violin or fiddle" as the sum of his worldly assets.[92] In no case did any of the pensioners indicate that they achieved any sort of financial success during their lifetimes.

Conclusion

How had the war, army service (British and American), and the Revolution affected the overall situation of blacks in America? Gary Nash, in his study of African Americans in Revolutionary-era Philadelphia, recently offered evidence to show a subset of African Americans who were probably affected most by the war. Comparing a list of blacks who were evacuated with the British army with information on those slaves who did not seek refuge with the British, Nash found that of those still in the city by 1779, 72 percent had been under the age of sixteen when the British occupied Philadelphia in 1777. Of those who left with the British when they evacuated, two-thirds were single males between the ages of seventeen and thirty-five; the average age of the males was around twenty-seven. Taken together, the two sets of data "indicate that a large proportion of the slaves who were not immobilized (by family ties or age) risked their fortunes with the British."[93] What this meant was that if African Americans were mobile enough to take advantage of the turmoil of war, they usually did so without equivocation.

The enrollment of African Americans as soldiers and their subsequent manumission as the result of their wartime cooperation served to create a larger and more visible group of free African American citizens. A comparison of the compiled service records of Connecticut's African American soldiers with a 1790 census of "free black heads of families" revealed many of the same names. At least forty African Americans out of a total of 195 soldiers also matched names listed on the rolls of the 1790 census as free heads of households. During the Revolution, African American soldiers were frequently given classical names or the surname of their former masters. Often the muster rosters revealed many with the same first and last names. It was impossible to distinguish between these particular soldiers with any degree of accuracy. Yet more than 20 percent of Connecticut's African American soldier enlistment records matched a name on the 1790 heads-of-household census.[94]

Free African Americans became a permanent legacy of the Revolution. Maryland's free African American population, which was 1,817 in 1755, reached 8,000 by 1790.[95] By the end of the first decade of the nineteenth century, "there were over 100,000 free African Americans in the southern states and they composed almost five percent of the free population and nearly nine percent of the (total) [African American] population."[96] William Gaston, chief justice of the North Carolina Supreme Court, noted in 1835 "that previous to the Revolution, there were scarcely any Emancipated Slaves; and that the few free men of color that were here at that time, were chiefly Mulattoes, the children of white women."[97] Of course freedom for service was not the only causal factor in accounting for this substantial increase. Army enlistment, however, must be acknowledged as a viable and traditional avenue of emancipation.

Another way that African Americans emancipated themselves was through self-liberation. The war presented the large slave population of the southern colonies with a paradox. On the one hand, they could remain passive and hope that the war would somehow change their fortunes for the better. To do so would not be consonant with long-established Atlantic traditions of resistance. Slave flight, therefore, should be seen as a form of slave revolt. It is an active process whereby the slave makes the conscious decision to leave his or her present circumstances and risk sickness, reenslavement, or death in a variety of ways. It is ironic that the high level of slave flight caused by the individual actions of the slaves themselves or the nearby presence of the British army was perceived by the white master class to have been a principal causal factor in overall slave resistance; yet it also served to lessen the possibility that the rebellion would become an organized social revolution.[98]

The recognition of slavery as a national problem and the incentive given to a nascent abolition movement by the Revolution caused a number of states to ban slavery or revise their manumission policies by 1787. By 1790, "manumission was a slaveholder's prerogative throughout the South, except in North Carolina."[99] While this did not necessarily mean freedom for the slaves, it did lessen the obstacles for obtaining individual manumission, which represented the first cracks in the system.

Freedom for relatively few, however, did not mean racial toleration. In 1793 Virginia passed a law that required all free African Americans to be registered and numbered by their towns of residence. Georgia likewise demanded the annual registration of free African Americans. The most restrictive law was passed by North Carolina in 1785. Not only were free African Americans required to register, but they were also made to wear a cloth badge inscribed "FREE."[100] Throughout the two decades that followed the war, free African Americans were seized by southern county sheriffs to prevent "domestic insurrections." Advertising and describing their detainees in various newspapers from New York to Georgia, blacks were sold back into slavery for "passing as free and Supposed to have Been Mannumited by their former owners."[101] It is easy to imagine that former slaveowners who lost their slaves to British raiders might claim these slaves as their own without regard to their actual place of origin.

That the Revolution had loosened the social bonds of both African American and white communities is indisputable. However, the most significant changes occurred for the free African American communities and urban slaves—artisans, river pilots, sailors, or domestics—who wit-nessed the Revolution firsthand and were best able to take advantage of the social upheaval. They gained a working knowledge of the language of revolution and were able to express themselves in ways that broke down the old patterns of white authority "that traditionally had controlled slaves fairly well" before the war.[102]

Freedom was the most powerful motivator for African Americans in the Revolution. They seized upon the occasion to procure their freedom in at least four ways: (1) as escaped slaves working for and against the colonial forces, (2) as Continental soldiers who expected to be free at the end of the war, (3) as substitutes for their masters, and (4) as persons owned or hired to perform wartime services for government.[103]

Service, however, was not without its dangers. Any African American who joined either side took the chance "that when his regiment or ship moved away from the place of his [enlistment] or manumission, where witnesses to the event could be summoned, he might be spirited back into slavery."[104] Samuel Sutphen was a New Jersey slave who was hired as a substitute for his master, Caspar Berger. When the war ended, Sutphen was seized by his former owner and forced to remain a slave for twenty years, until he bought his own freedom with some money he had managed to save in the interim.[105] Ned Griffen, a "man of mixed blood," served in the North Carolina line as a substitute for his owner, William Kitchen, a deserter from Nathanael Greene's army. Kitchen had deserted after the Battle of Guilford Court House and would have been made to return to service if he had not forced Ned Griffen to serve in his stead. Although Kitchen promised him his freedom at the end of the war, he was seized by his former owner and sold to another owner in Edgecombe County, North Carolina. It took an act of the General Assembly for Griffen to win freedom from both masters.[106] Various underprivileged groups recognized the Revolution as an opportunity to escape oppression. For the slaves, "the Revolutionary War as a black declaration of independence took on a power of its own, fueled by residual revolutionary rhetoric and sustained by the memory of fallen heroes and the cloud of living black witnesses."[107] St. George Tucker, a Virginian, commented in 1800 on the slave conspiracy inspired by a man named Gabriel. Tucker observed that there was a "difference between the slaves who responded to Lord Dunmore's proclamation in 1775 and those who took part in Gabriel's plot in 1800. The slaves of 1775 fought for freedom as a good, whereas those of 1800 claimed freedom as a right."[108]

1. Guilford Court House, 15 March 1781, courtesy of the Center of Military History, Department of the Army. The illustration depicts the veteran First Maryland Regiment about to repulse a British attack with bayonets. 2. Trenton, 26 December 1776, courtesy of the Center of Military History, Department of the Army. The illustration depicts the surprise attack on the Hessians at Trenton on the day after Christmas, 1776. The ragged American continentals overwhelmed Colonel Johann Rall's defenses at a dead run and forced the Hessians to surrender. The American success at Trenton and a later victory at Princeton ensured the survival of the army and the Revolution.

3. *The Battle of Yorktown*, by Howard Pyle, courtesy of the Wilmington Society of Fine Arts, Delaware Art Center. The scene depicts the American continentals storming British redoubts at Yorktown.

4. *Battle of Bunker's Hill, 1775*, by John Trumbull, courtesy of Yale University Art Gallery. The illustration depicts the British final assault on Bunker's Hill. Note the African American soldier at the extreme right of the picture. 5. *On the Road to Valley Forge*, by William Trego, courtesy of the Valley Forge Historical Society. The illustration depicts the long-suffering and ragged continental soldiery on their way to winter quarters at Valley Forge in December 1776.

C H A P T E R   F I V E

Scalp Bounties and Truck Houses: The Struggle for Indian Allies in the Revolution

Nine days after the Boston Tea Party, a white family that had recently moved into newly acquired territory near the headwaters of the Ogeechee River in the colony of Georgia was massacred by Indians. The following month, the Coweta Creeks attacked a fort west of Wrightsborough and killed twenty more whites. Two weeks later, the Georgia militia were routed by Creek warriors. The Georgians refused to serve any further and went home "with this silly speech in their mouths," according to the *Georgia Gazette,* "that their families were dear to them, that they were in danger, and that they were wanted at home to protect them." Five weeks later, however, a group of peace-minded Creeks led by a man named Mad Turkey came to Augusta, Georgia, as guests of the local militia captain, William Goodgion. A blacksmith named Thomas Fee offered Mad Turkey a drink. When the Indian took the blacksmith up on his offer and raised his cup, Fee treacherously smashed Mad Turkey's skull with an iron bar. But rather than face trial for murder, Fee was hailed as a hero by the backcountry farmers. When the governor later confined Fee in the stockade at Ninety-Six, South Carolina, "a mob broke into the jail and set him free."[1] Fee's elevation as frontier hero rather than condemnation as cold-blooded murderer clearly illustrates the attitude held by the majority of backcountry Americans toward their Native American neighbors.

The complete history of Native American participation in the American Revolution has yet to be written; what the role of the Indian was during the war is usually relegated to the periphery of history. Older texts wrongly characterized eastern Native Americans as wandering nomads "having no towns or villages," no settled life, and hence no real effect on the outcome of the war.[2] However, a newer generation of historians has begun to recognize the complexity of the relationships among various tribes and their interactions with colonial backcountry settlements. Independent, active Native-American tribes helped to define the politics of this region for all peoples who lived there. The place and role of Native Americans in the conflict were much more complex than has been surmised.

Indians were employed as warriors both for and against colonial independence. Because most Native American tribes resisted induction into regular armies and viewed the regulations and European-style tactics as stifling and ridiculous, British and American commanders sought to use the fearsome image of the Indian in a psychological tug of war against each other. William Gordon, for instance, suggested to Horatio Gates that arriving Hessian forces should immediately be attacked by five hundred to a thousand "brave and daring" American soldiers dressed and painted as Indians. These men should be chosen, stated Gordon, from among those who could best imitate the Indian war hoop. He thought that "such dark painted enemies would go near to terrify" the Hessians.[3]

Few authentic Indians, however, saw actual service as Continental soldiers or red-coated British troops. The enlistment records of both sides say little about the induction of Indians into either army. However, the role played by the native tribes during the Seven Years' War convinced many whites of the value of Indians as allies and trading partners. The image and reputation of Indians as redoubtable guerrilla fighters remained firm in the memories of white European and colonial Americans. For whites, the Indian was both "noble savage" (an idealized innocent state similar to Adam and Eve before their fall) and "ignoble savage" (an individual utterly devoid of any redeeming qualities and undeserving of mercy, assistance, or quarter in battle).[4] During times of war, of course, portraying Indians as ignoble savages was much more convenient when it appeared that they would ally themselves with the other side.

If we examine the Native American problem from all points of view, not just those espoused by white colonial Americans, we see a new role played by the frontier tribes. Not only were most Native American tribes avidly pro-British in the conflict, but they also had good reason for being so.

The American policy of recruiting Native Americans for warfare evolved over time. John Adams admitted to Horatio Gates that he did not know much about Indians, but thought that having them as "Confederates in war" was "troublesome" and "expensive . . . besides the incivility and Inhumanity of employing such Savages with their cruel, bloody dispositions, against any Enemy whatever."[5] Adams hesitated, but in the end he did not "refuse the assistance of the Indians."[6]

Native American tribes held the decisive position on the American frontier. Native American/white commerce and trade with frontier settlements were part of everyday life in the backcountry. During the Seven Years' War, British and American officers remembered from experience that Native American tribes usually allied with the side that promised them the best chance of cultural and economic survival and continued access to western trade goods. When war began, British and American commissioners were mobilized to convince the tribes that it was in their interest to choose their particular side. Offers of weapons, powder, and shot—items not normally produced by Native Americans—were quickly made. The British, however, were better prepared to trade with the tribes than the patriots. They could give guarantees of reduced white encroachment on Indian land, whereas the Americans, because of land-hungry western settlers, refused to do so. Thus it was especially important for the patriots to get the Native Americans at least to remain neutral during the war.[7]

The groundwork for a treaty of neutrality between the Northern tribes and Americans had been built at the Fort Pitt Conference of 1775. A Seneca chief, Guyashusta, was given a great belt of wampum, a beaded symbol of peace that signified the importance and gravity of the relationship between the white colonials and the Iroquois. Moreover, the American commissioners urged Guyashusta to show the belt to other members of the Confederacy "so that they may know the sentiments of the United Colonies."[8] Sending a similar speech to the Lenni Lenape (Delaware) Indians, American commissioners urged them to "hold fast the great Belt of Peace & Friendship. . . . Consider us and you as One People. [Do] not hearken to any speech that the [British] Commandants of either Detroit or Niagara may send as they only mean to Deceive you. [Please] sit still & Enjoy Peace."[9]

Meanwhile, British emissaries sent similar messages to the Indians, causing great confusion in many tribal councils. Colonial officials even arrested a Dr. John Connolly who had organized a plan to enlist the Indians to attack American frontier settlements. Advocating an alliance of Indian and British soldiers, Connolly suggested that this force attack the Americans at Pittsburgh and drive east to the coast. Both Indians and British would benefit from such a campaign. The British would sever the American lines of communication and the Indians could partially recover much land already encroached upon by white settlers.[10] Thoroughly frightened at the prospects proposed by Connolly and other British emissaries on the frontier, Congress strongly wanted the Indians to maintain the terms of neutrality offered at the 1775 Fort Pitt conference. In fact, keeping the Indians neutral was especially important to the newly united colonies, because Native American nations represented a thousand-mile second front if they decided to attack the patriots in concert. The threat of Indian attack was even used to further the Patriot Party cause in South Carolina. British Indian Superintendent John Stuart reported to Henry Clinton:

> The newspapers were full of Publications calculated to excite the fears of the People. Massacres and Instigated Insurrections were words in the mouth of every Child—The pretended Discovery of an intention to Instigate Insurrections of the negroes and bring down the Indians was the pretence for tendering an Instrument of Association to every Person in the Province. It was assigned as the Reason for arming the militia and for raising Troops.[11]

George Washington was one, however, who thought that the Indians would be dragged into the conflict sooner or later. "In my opinion," he said, "it will be impossible to keep them in a state of neutrality; they must, and no doubt will, take an active part either for or against us. I submit to Congress whether it will not be better immediately to engage them on our side."[12]

Washington was correct in that the Indians were eventually dragged into the war despite American efforts to keep them out. The best way to describe this process is to divide up the colonies into two distinct geographic regions, north and south.

In the north, the largest, most powerful confederation of Native

Americans were the Iroquois or Five Nations. Commanding more than 10,000 warriors, the Iroquois had long been allies of the crown. In fact, elements of this great alliance touched upon the frontiers of every state from Virginia to New Hampshire, excluding Maryland, Delaware, and Rhode Island. Moreover, most of the triangular fighting between the British, Indians, and Americans occurred there.

The Iroquois were wooed by both belligerents, and this suited the Iroquois people well. Alliance was a goal commonly sought by them with "everyone in the universe." Alliances were dynamic and continuing sets of relationships with British, colonial, or other Native American tribes and stressed kinship and reciprocity.[13] Before the war, the British had cemented their alliance with the Iroquois Confederation and established a tributary relationship maintained by a steady supply of white man's goods upon which the Iroquois had become dependent by 1775. This was particularly true of firearms and ammunition which the Iroquois needed for hunting, self-defense, defense against white encroachment, and for the domination of neighboring tribal enemies. The Indians had become so dependent on this supply of goods that the Wyandot informed George Croghan, a colonial Indian agent in 1759, that "you . . . know very well that no Indian nation lives now without being supported either by the English or the French, we cannot live as our Ancestors did before you came into our Country."[14] Warfare between the British and Americans caused a dislocation of trade between the whites and the Iroquois. This interruption of trade caused the Iroquois to seek an accommodation with any belligerent group that could best fulfill their commercial needs.

By 1775 the British had fifty officers devoted to maintaining good relations (the covenant chain) with the confederation, while the hasty attempts of the Continental Congress to influence the Iroquois was plagued with factionalism and dissension.[15] In negotiations between the American Indian commissioners and elements of the fierce Mohawk tribe, Little Abraham, a Mohawk sachem, informed the commissioners that they considered the hostilities between the British and Americans as "a family affair" but still had two fundamental concerns: land and trade. The British blockade of trade and the colonial lack of a manufacturing base made Indian requests for trade goods, arms, and ammunition difficult for Americans to satisfy. White encroachment and patterns of settler aggression since 1763 also worried the Mohawks. Both issues clearly favored the British.[16]

Because Congress and American military leaders recognized that the British had the advantage in recruiting and that America could not compete economically with them, they tried a different approach. Ethan Allen reminded the Indians how easy it was to kill the British during the last war and assured them that they would receive "Money, Blankets, Tomahawks, Knives, and Paint" in return for their support. They would also receive all the war booty they wanted from the bodies of the dead British regulars, just as they had in the last war.[17]

The British, however, appealed to Native American cultural rituals instead. By inviting the Caughnawagas Indians to "feast on a Bostonian and drink his Blood," the British revealed that they were much more in tune with tribal customs than the Americans. Substituting an ox to represent the "Bostonian" and a pipe of wine "as blood," the British effectively used the symbology of an ancient Caughnawagas ritual against the colonists.[18]

John Butler, an Indian agent for the crown, went even further and ridiculed certain Indian sachems for declaring that they were determined to "receive no Ax from either [side]."[19] Butler stressed the relative poverty of the colonists in comparison with the wealth and power of the king:

> Your resolutions are very surprising; where is any one body of men to be compared to the King? As for Genl Schuyler (and other Commisrs) of whom you boast so much, what is he? . . . He has no men, guns, cannon and ammunition, or clothing, and should he survive the summer he must perish by the cold next winter for want of blankets. But the King wants [lacks] neither men nor numbers.[20]

The British were much more aggressive than the Americans in recruiting the northern tribes to their cause. Friendship with a tribe incurred a financial burden that the Americans were not willing to assume. The tribes, in turn, used the war to get what they needed from either the Americans or the British. Stephen Moylan wrote to the chairman of the Newburyport Committee of Public Safety that the Penobscot tribe in Maine demanded powder for their loyalty and stated bluntly that if the Americans did not supply their needs, "they would apply to the enemy who would be glad of the opportunity of making friends with them."[21]

The expense of providing for Indian allies caused the colonists to avoid assistance to Native Americans even when it was in their interest to do so. Philip Schuyler, the commanding officer of the Northern Department, noted that he was "daily tormented" by parties of Indians who applied to him for support and ammunition for their weapons. Schuyler discovered that he simply did not have the means to support his own forces as well as those of any potential Indian allies. He even suspected the Tories of urging the Indians to inundate colonial depots with requests for supplies. Finally, an exasperated Schuyler threatened to confine anyone caught encouraging Indians to ask for supplies from Continental authorities "with a Lodging in the Simsbury Mines."[22]

The key issue to success or failure with every tribe on the frontier centered on the issue of trade. The British even used the vast tributary network they had established prior to the war as a weapon. The Maine tribes noted that "we are in much want of Powder to Hunt with—the Old English people will not let us have any, Unless we will fight against our Brothers & Countrymen."[23] Trade was so important that nearly every commission formed to negotiate with the Indians included trading agents who were well known to the tribes before the war. For instance, George Morgan, a prominent partner in a Philadelphia trading firm familiar with the tribes west of Pittsburgh, was appointed by Congress as Superintendent of Indian Affairs for the Middle Department.[24] Such trade relationships had military value as well, "for if the Indians trade with us," observed Jonathan Elkins, "we need no Soldiers."[25]

The Massachusetts Provincial Council made repeated attempts to keep the eastern tribes in Maine provisioned. A Council report stated that "it was absolutely necessary that the Truck house at Machais should be supplied with Cloth, Corn, Rum, and every Kind of Stores Necessary for such a Department as the best means to secure the several Tribes of Indians from taking part with the Enemy."[26] By cementing the tribes to the patriot cause through trade, the Provincial Council hoped to avoid the expense of defending the backcountry.

The colonists also utilized religion as another method of retaining Native American loyalty. Samuel Kirkland, a colonial missionary, had been active among the Oneida tribe for years prior to the war and was partly responsible for the Oneidas' break with the Iroquois Confederation and siding with the Americans. The eastern tribes of the St. John's Indians and Micmacs had been converted to Catholicism during the years of French dominance. Using religion as a means of gaining the loyalty of the Maine tribes, Colonel John Allan, a militia officer responsible for maintaining friendly relations with the tribes in Maine and Lower Canada, sent Father De La Motte, a French chaplain, to the Passamaquody tribe, which had long been asking for a priest "that he may pray with us to God Almighty." Not only did they desire spiritual assistance but they also included a request for "Ammunition, Provisions, and Goods for us . . . and [we] give you fur and skin, and take our support from you in return."[27] Getting the Indians a priest was no small matter and one that Protestant Britain was loathe to provide. Henry Mowat noted that Pierre Tomo, an Indian chief, had accused the British of a breach of promise by not providing them a priest and regretted that "many of them are now with Mr. Allan on the faith of General Washington's having promised to furnish them with a Priest and everything else they require."[28] Religion, therefore, was also a powerful determinant in which side the tribes chose.

De La Motte's appointment had been long awaited. Reminding the Passamaquody of their former relationship with the king of France, who was their "common father," De La Motte told them that "our common father will not neglect to gratify all your wishes and to make you happy."[29] While the French offer to satisfy the commercial needs overcame the material poverty of the patriots, De La Motte's presence cloaked the possibility of renewed French interest in their former Canadian territories.

The Massachusetts Provincial Assembly did not wait for the French to enjoin the tribes to their cause, nor were they anxious for the introduction of any "popish" influence in their vicinity. Instead, they sought to enlist individual Indians into their ranks before the British made allies of them. General Gage complained about these Indians who assisted the Continental forces during the siege of Boston. "The Rebels," stated Gage, "have brought all the Savages they could against us here." Gage heard camp rumors that some of the British dead on Breed's Hill had been scalped. Because the issue of whether or not to enlist the Indians in their cause had been debated with British administration circles, Gage now thought that "we need not be tender of calling upon the Savages, as the Rebels have shewn us the example."[30]

In May 1776, Congress abruptly changed its policy of neutrality and authorized Washington "to engage up to 2,000 Indians for war against Canada." Moreover, Washington was allowed to offer "a reward of one hundred dollars for every commissioned officer, and thirty dollars for every private soldier, of the King's troops, that they should take prisoners in Indian country or on the frontier of these colonies."[31] While Congress refused to offer such terms to their Continental forces, they perceived the value of the tribes as allies and the disastrous consequences if the British were to enlist their aid. However, the enlistment of Indians would inevitably split the tribes of the Confederation into opposing factions.[32] In fact, there is evidence that Congress encouraged this policy. Washington approved the idea of Colonel David Brodhead to "inflame the rivalship which is said to subsist between the Wyandots and Mingoes, and I shall be glad it may be in your power to induce the former to aid you in some decisive stroke against the latter."[33] The Mingoes inhabited the Ohio country claimed by Virginia. Washington, Benjamin Franklin, and other senior American officials also had land interests in the region. Thus removal of the troublesome Mingoes by the Wyandots may have had other purposes as well. Moreover, the division of the Iroquois Confederation into smaller factions would make it easier for the Americans to conquer them later.

Congress also allowed whole tribes of Indians to enlist as Continental soldiers, although, as we shall see, few did. The American Indian superintendent for the Middle Department, George Morgan, was one, however, who disagreed with congressional plans to enlist Indians. Morgan protested that using the Indians was a violation of the Fort Pitt treaty. Months of work getting the Indians to remain neutral were jeopardized. While the Americans might gain some few hundred recruits, they were more than likely creating thousands of enemies. Most of the tribes were opposed to allowing armies to march through their territory in any case.[34] Unfortunately for the Indians, the only way for the rebels to attack the British in Canada was through their territory. Congress, however, was probably reacting as much to information they had received from Philip Schuyler as anything else. Schuyler had informed Congress that Guy Johnson, who opposed the "Belt of Peace" given to the Seneca, sent among the Indians "a large Black War belt with a Hatchet depictured on it." While the Indians accepted the belt, they "would neither eat nor drink nor sing the War Song."[35] Their actions signified, more than anything else, their desire to stay out of the fight.

While American commissioners concentrated on keeping the powerful Iroquois neutral, they allowed the Stockbridge tribe of Massachusetts to enlist en masse in the Continental army. The Stockbridge had acted as minutemen since 1775, and their presence at Boston had been noted by Thomas Gage. Father John Sargent, a missionary to the tribe, wrote to Congress in 1776 and observed that the tribe

> had made themselves acquainted with the merits of the controversy and have taken an active part in our favor, enlisting their young men in our

> army, while their counsellors and sachems have carefully sent presents of belts of wampum . . . to the Six Nations, to the Canadian Indians, and to the Shauwanunese on the Ohio, addressing in such terms as they judged would have the greatest tendency to attach them to the interests of the United States.[36]

Congress gave each Indian who enlisted a blanket and a yard of red ribbon,[37] whereas white soldiers received a cash bounty.

In October 1776 the Stockbridge, under their sachem Abraham Ninham, applied to Congress for permission to enlist members of their tribe into the Continental army. The Indians were directed to report to General Gates for duty, and Ninham and his enlistees were paid two hundred dollars "for the use of himself and his companions, and as an acknowledgment for their zeal in the cause of the United States."[38] Unfortunately for the Stockbridge, zeal was not enough. They were severely mauled in a battle with British troops near White Plains, New York, the following year. A British lieutenant noted that their forces had "put a period to the existence of thirty-seven Indians and a number of Rebels; there were ten prisoners taken, amongst them one Captain and two Indians of the Stockbridge tribe."[39]

After the destruction of the Stockbridge, the Indians employed by Congress for the northern frontier appeared to be connected to the army in a haphazard fashion. Congress authorized the recruitment of four hundred Indians from among the northern and southern tribes. Washington noted that the Oneidas had "manifested the strongest attachment to us. . . . Their Missionary, Mr. Kirkland, seemed to have an uncommon ascendancy over that tribe and I should be glad to see him accompany them."[40] Colonel Timothy Bedel's Abenaki (St. Francis) recruits shivered near Haverhill, New Hampshire, throughout most of the war. Never given any ammunition or clothing for his troops, Bedel was able to report he had only about "30 fighting Indians and double the number of Women & Children all Naked and daily coming in." "If they had clothes," stated Bedel, they "might be of service." By 1780 seventeen Abenakis were in Caughnawaga captain John Vincent's company. General Bayley sent George Washington a report of the Abenaki company, stating that "a much larger number has been here at times but are rambling in the woods[;] those inserted have been serviceable as scouts &c."[41]

The St. Francis Abenaki Indians had been heavily recruited for Continental service. During the Seven Years' War, these people had been viciously attacked by Robert Rogers and his rangers in 1759. The principal Abenaki village was burned to the ground, and many inhabitants were killed in the process. The Abenakis recovered from the attack, but forever afterward held the British in contempt. Rogers became known to them as "the White Devil."[42] Migrating into the Coos Country of Vermont and New Hampshire, the Abenakis had inhabited the upper Connecticut valley for hundreds of years. Few Americans had yet penetrated this inaccessible part of the country. Recruited too late to participate in the 1777 Saratoga campaign against Burgoyne, the Abenakis signaled their willingness to support the patriot cause. When another invasion of Canada was planned for in 1778, Horatio Gates sent orders to Colonel Timothy Bedel to raise five hundred of the "Best Woodsmen, Hunters, and Indians" in preparation for a campaign against St. Johns.[43] Unfortunately for Colonel Bedel, he was able to raise few woodsmen or Indians for any expedition.

Throughout the war, each side combined terror with propaganda to influence the Indians who lived in proximity to the colonists. Allegations about the use of Indian mercenaries, scalp bounties, and atrocities were commonplace. During the fighting at Vincennes, Colonel Henry Hamilton testified that fifteen or sixteen captured Indians were serially tomahawked to death by the Americans at the direct orders of their commanding officer, George Rogers Clark. Hamilton noted that the Americans killed them "as [the Indians] sang their death songs."[44] Prior to Vincennes, however, Hamilton reported that Shawnee Indians had captured seventy-three prisoners (including the famous Daniel Boone) and brought 129 scalps into Detroit.[45] Not to be outdone, the American commander of the Northern Department, Philip Schuyler, offered a terrorist bounty of "1000 dollars in specie," if a Caughnawaga Indian known as "Colonel Louis" successfully burned British ships on Lake Ontario or in the St. John's area.[46] Schuyler offered Colonel Louis this money at a time when the Continental treasury was nearly bankrupt.

The intense fear of the Indians was used as a means of control as well. A group of Hessian deserters was advised to "thank circumstance for saving their scalps; the savages who seized them, as well as the Yorkers, became lame. Henceforth, if a Jaeger deserts, a party of savages will be sent out with full permission to scalp the deserter immediately."[47] Colonel La Corne St. Luc, a French Canadian who allied himself with the British, was very blunt about employing the Indians. St. Luc stated that he "thought it was necessary to loose the savages against the miserable rebels in order to impose terror on the frontiers. . . . It is necessary to brutalize affairs."[48] The portrayal of Indians as instruments of terror was a common tactic used throughout all wars in colonial North America.

The Americans were just as bloody. As the war continued on the frontier, the Pennsylvania legislature sought to brutalize affairs in its own way and initiated a scalp bounty to counter the terrorism employed by St. Luc and others. During the autumn of 1777, a scouting party of Westmoreland County militia took the scalps of five Indians in an engagement near Kittanning. Colonel Lochery, the county lieutenant, reported to the Supreme Executive Council that "a reward for scalps would be of excellent use at this time and would give spirit and alacrity to our young men and make it their interest to be constantly on the scout."[49] Pennsylvania's chief executive, Joseph Reed, agreed with Lochery's assessment and offered awards of "THREE THOUSAND DOLLARS for every Indian prisoner or Tory acting in arms with them, and a reward of TWO THOUSAND FIVE HUNDRED DOLLARS for every Indian scalp."[50] Reed's offer was incredible even in such inflationary times, for it far exceeded the bounties and wages of the Continental soldiery or even the militia. Moreover, the bounties encouraged "private" warfare on the frontier.

Just as sailors recognized the economic rewards possible for service on a privateer, soldiers on the border gained similar rewards for butchering Indians. Scalp bounties always created conditions for offensive war. However, the grisly "trade" of hair buying was usually only temporary security for white settlers as each side engaged in ambushes that successively surpassed previous incidents in atrocity and brutality. Moreover, scalp bounties posed an even greater threat to friendly Indians, for they were "the easiest to scalp of all." In an obvious effort to prevent his own demise, a Tuscarora Indian (a tribe allied with the colonies) embarrassed everybody by turning himself in to the Pennsylvania militia before they got around to scalping him for the bounty.[51]

Warfare on the southern frontier was different from that waged in the north. The Cherokee and Creek tribes had been fighting colonial militia forces for a number of years. Lexington and Concord were exceedingly irrelevant to them. Moreover, the 14,000 warriors of the Cherokee and Creek nations were formidable potential antagonists. In 1774–75, Lord Dunmore had led a band of militia against the Cherokee in Virginia and Mingo tribes in the Ohio country. Embittered by increased encroachment of white settlers, the Cherokee had risen against the British and backcountry settlers, and sporadic outbreaks of violence between Indians and settlers continued into the Revolutionary War period. Throughout the twelve years between the Seven Years' War and the Revolution, pressure from land speculators and illegal squatters caused colonial assemblies and Indian agents to exact cessations of large quantities of Indian land. In prewar Georgia alone, "6,695,429 acres were acquired."[52] Thus even without encouragement by the British, the southern Indians were predisposed against the American backcountrymen. Moreover, both Cherokee and Creeks were beholden to white traders and were sometimes forced to cede huge territories of land to cancel their debts. Playing the Creeks off against the Cherokee, Sir James Wright, the Georgia royal governor, got them to cede about two million acres on the upper Savannah. More radical factions within the Creek council disputed the terms of the treaty and occasionally attacked "squatters" who were flooding into the "New Purchase."[53]

During the winter of 1775–76, the Cherokee debated renewing their attacks against "the Virginians" (as all southern squatters and frontiersmen were called by them). By April 1776 the Cherokee Council fires burned constantly. British agents Alexander Cameron and Henry Stuart arrived at the Cherokee town of Chota with fifteen hundred pounds of powder. Although the Cherokee Council was split over whether to go to war, the arrival of the powder made the position of the war faction stronger. Eventually the war faction prevailed, and the Cherokee struck at frontier settlements in the backcountry of Georgia and the Carolinas. The patriot forces saw the attack on the settlements and the corresponding attack by the British against Charleston as a conspiracy of heinous proportions and used it to recruit frontiersmen into militia companies and the Continental army.[54]

Militia forces from Virginia eventually regained their composure after the initial Cherokee attacks and led punitive expeditions into the mountains and valleys of southern Appalachia. The Cherokees melted into the forests, but the militia burned town after town in retribution. Eventually agreeing to a truce in May 1777, the Lower and Middle Town Cherokee representatives agreed to a peace—in conjunction, of course, with another huge land cessation. This was not the last of the land penalties that were ultimately inflicted on the Cherokee by the young United States.

The only southern tribe that was inclined toward the rebel side was the Catawba. According to the British Indian Superintendent John Stuart, the Catawba was "domiciliated and dispersed thro' the Settlements of north and South Carolina, it is no wonder that they should be practised upon and seduced by the Inhabitants with whom they live." No sooner had Stuart written his letter when he was forced to admit that "this ingratefull Little tribe" was already lost to the crown.[55] In ways strikingly similar to the Stockbridge Indians to the north, the Catawbas, already engulfed by the surging white population, saw it in their interest to side with the Americans. Immediately before the war, William Henry Drayton had warned the Catawba that if the British prevailed against the Americans "you will be obliged to buy your blankets, your match-coats, your shirts and your rum, a great deal dearer."[56] Drayton, on the other hand, promised the Catawbas pay for their services against the king. Despite their predisposition toward the patriot cause, the South Carolina Assembly thought it was necessary to warn the Catawba that "if you do not mind what we say, you will be sorry for it by and by."[57] Having recognized the patriot mailed fist as thinly covered with a velvet glove, the Catawba reluctantly took the South Carolina Assembly up on its offer.

A militia captain named Boykin wrote the Provincial Council and stated that he had been to Catawba town "and [they] were willing to come down anytime you think proper." Boykin paid them a ten-pound bounty for enlisting and used them to terrorize runaway slaves in the parishes of St. George, Dorchester, St. Paul, and St. Bartholomew. There was also evidence that this same force assisted the South Carolina militia in the destruction of a group of runaway blacks who had fled to Sullivan's Island in Charleston harbor.[58] The militia commanders liked to use the Indians as shock troops to terrorize blacks who contemplated insurrection as well.

Little is known about how long or in what capacity the Catawbas were used by the rebels. Fragmentary evidence indicates, however, that they were used as light forces to catch or terrorize runaway slaves or act as scouts. James Wright, the former royal governor of Georgia, wrote that an American raiding party composed of "about 25 Indians" tried to capture him near Cockspur Island. Managing to escape with the loss of only one royal marine, Wright noted that "the man who was killed was scalped."[59]

The pay records of South Carolina troops listed only one single voucher for Catawba Indians. They were commanded by a Captain Thomas Drennan and had forty-one men in their unit. Other Catawbas helped with logistics for the army. Driving cattle from their own stocks, Richard Winn noted "that several times [the Catawba] brought out their whole force" in support of the Americans. In another instance, Catawba warriors were noted to have developed a novel way to stop the charging British cavalry, something that white soldiers in the southern theater had never been able to do. Robert Wilson noted that they had "put a strange feature upon the ground by stretching cowhides between the trees."[60] In this way the British horsemen could not run down the retreating militiamen. One Catawba named Monday was so despondent over the declining fortunes of American arms that he committed suicide.[61] Like other Indians who fought in the Revolution, Monday was employed informally. Few official records were kept on the Indians' service. The only Catawba who received a pension for service was Robert Marsh, a Pamunky who had settled among the Catawba. In 1818 he received an annual pension of ninety-six dollars for his service in the Virginia line.[62]

The largest body of Indians on the Georgia and Carolina frontiers, however, were the Creeks. Past Creek friendship, as with most other Indian tribes affected by the war, was predicated on trade. One item, however, was absolutely necessary for their survival: ammunition for their rifles. Moreover, powder was not produced by any of the tribes. Whenever trade was discussed, these items were invariably raised as an issue of concern. Occupying a central geographic position between the white settlements, the Cherokees, and the Choctaw to the west, the Creeks were conscious of their strategic position and vulnerability to increasing colonial encroachment. To maintain their position of centrality, it was imperative that they secure a reliable source of ammunition.[63] The group that best provided this commodity quickly gained the affinity of the tribe for as long as the supply lasted.

Superintendent Stuart recognized the importance of gunpowder and provisions. Addressing the Cherokee in January 1776, he informed their headmen that "powder, ball, arms, and clothes are sent you annually from Britain. The Americans stand as much in need of such supplies as you do. . . . They cannot make clothes, powder & arms for themselves; how then can they supply you?" Stuart, however, went even further. "You know," he warned, "with what Eager wishes they [the Americans] look upon your hunting grounds."[64]

When news of the war between the British and Americans reached the Creeks, David Taitt, one of Superintendent Stuart's deputies, immediately sent to the British base at Mobile for powder and ball to get the Creeks to favor the crown. Soon afterward, American policy was made to offset the actions of the British: "In case any agent of the Ministry shall induce the Indians to commit actual hostilities against these colonies or to enter into an offensive alliance with the British troops, thereupon the colonists ought to avail themselves of an alliance with such Indian nations as will enter into the same."[65]

The Americans even sent their own agent, George Galphin, among the Creeks to obtain their neutrality. Galphin tried to pass himself off as the "successor to John Stuart" because it had been rumored that Stuart was in poor health. A Creek chief known as the Cussetah King did not believe Galphin's ploy, however, and remarked that only after he was assured of Stuart's death would he "look for new friends." From the Indian point of view, the British were still supplying them with ammunition. They were aware that Stuart had been ordered by Thomas Gage to "supply the Indians . . . and bind them more firmly to you."[66] Although promises had been made to the Creeks from both sides, it was the British who were ultimately better able to supply the southern Indians. From their bases in West Florida, the Creeks were furnished small amounts of ammunition, weapons, and tobacco. Stuart emphasized in all his dealings with the Indians that the crown was better able to supply their needs, whereas Galphin had promised supplies but failed to deliver.[67]

One other event also may have been a factor in turning the Creeks against the Americans. The Americans refused to punish those who murdered Indians on the frontier. During a conference with George Galphin, a Creek chief known as the Chevulkey Warrior demanded that some frontiersmen be punished for the murder of a member of his tribe. Galphin promised justice and suggested that two of the Indians remain behind to see the murderers executed. The Chevulkey Warrior's emissaries reported, however, that the Americans attempted to deceive them by hanging a man convicted of murdering his own wife and then stated that this man also killed their tribesman. Moreover, the infamous Thomas Fee, the blacksmith who had previously killed Mad Turkey, murdered another Coweta warrior on the Ogeechee River. Both events served to remind the Creeks that whites could not be trusted. From then on, the Coweta Creeks remained opposed to American interests on the frontier.[68]

As for the Cherokees, after being severely mauled by Virginia and Carolina militia in 1775–76, they entered into a peace agreement with the Americans. Peace treaties with Americans, however were long known to the Indians as "euphemisms for land cession." The Cherokees were forced to cede a huge amount of land on the western North and South Carolina borders leading up to the Cumberland Gap and extending all the way down to the Georgia state border.[69] Like a dagger pointed toward the heart of Shawnee territory farther to the west, white settlers, led by Daniel Boone and others, quickly went beyond the limits of the treaty and encroached on Indian land in the Kentucky area. Even lands guaranteed by the treaty itself did not keep the Cherokee free from further encroachment. The Raven of Echota, an Overhill Cherokee, complained to Governor Caswell of North Carolina that white settlers were extremely close to Overhill towns and were "marking trees all over the country," a common sign of settlers staking out land claims. From experience, the Indians knew this procedure well. The only response that they received was the assurance from the governor that he would warn the settlers not to damage the trees. Only after the governors of South Carolina and Virginia complained that the actions of the North Carolinians might spark another war was Caswell moved to do something. When he attempted to appoint another commission to negotiate a new treaty with the Indians, the commissioners declined to serve on the grounds that a new treaty was not needed. Rather, the old one needed to be enforced.[70]

In conclusion, the Revolutionary War and its outcome laid the foundation for the destruction of the Native American tribes east of the Mississippi. Moreover, the colonial pattern of violence and expropriation of Indian territory would continue into the twentieth century. The policy of the United States toward Indians in the Revolution varied over time but generally denied them their place as allies in the War for Independence. It is ironic that while the Americans were engaged in a struggle against the British Empire, they were also attempting to *build* an empire to the west at the expense of the Indian nations.

Indians scalped settlers and were scalped, in turn, by avenging whites. In fact, just being an Indian was enough to cause some backcountry whites potentially to commit murder against the nearest Native American they could find. During the summer of 1777, a group of pro-American Shawnee and Lenni Lenape Indians led by Chief Cornstalk of the Shawnees attempted to warn the colonists that other British-led Indians were coming to attack the frontier settlements. When Cornstalk's party arrived at a Kentucky fort, they were placed in the stockade. The next day, the body of a scalped soldier was carried into the fort. Immediately, angry soldiers broke into the stockade and slaughtered Cornstalk, his young son, and another man named Red Hawk. Indian Commissioner George Morgan eventually had to warn Native American ambassadors to stay away from Fort Pitt because of the possibility that they would be murdered.[71]

Immediately following the war, many states resumed their prewar preoccupation with the Indians on their respective frontiers and attempted to make separate treaties with the tribes. Despite the large number of high-sounding treaties enacted in the years following the war regarding Indian rights to land, the large expansiveness of the frontier served to circumvent the ability of the government to keep its own citizens from encroachment. On other occasions, smaller groups of Indians such as the group of Creeks at the Treaty of Shoulderbone, pretending to speak for the entire nation, ceded all Indian claims to all lands in Georgia east of the Oconee River.[72]

After the colonists had, by terror and devastation, largely driven the British-allied Indians into Canada, the Oneida and Tuscarora tribes, which had remained loyal to the United States and provided soldiers, still suffered greatly. Building huts near Schenectady, they lived on the handouts of a white government that had become disinterested in them as a result of a lessened frontier threat. Former soldiers such as Lieutenant John Sagaharase of the Oneida Wolf Clan died of smallpox in the Schenectady camp. Their native hunting culture irrevocably altered, the Oneida gave in to offers by the state of New York for all the rest of their remaining ancestral lands. Good Peter, an Oneida sachem, rejected their offer, however, recalling the shabby treatment of the Stockbridge Indians who now lived on the charity of the Oneida. Unfortunately, the Oneida did not listen to Good Peter's advice. Thus began a series of land sales that eventually dispossessed the few tribes that had supported the American cause. The once powerful Iroquois Confederation was broken forever. The remaining nations settled on land provided by the crown in Canada.[73]

Chief White Eyes of the Lenni Lenape was a longtime supporter of the patriot cause. White Eyes favored the creation of a "fourteenth Indian state" located in the Ohio territory. White Eyes envisioned a state capital at the Lenape town of Coshcoton and wanted his people to elect tribal members to take their seats in the United States Congress.[74] The thought of an Indian state was anathema to many who had postwar ideas for conquered Native American territory. Generals Lachlan McIntosh and Brodhead promised White Eyes statehood for the Lenni Lenape if he agreed to allow the Continental army to attack Fort Detroit. He was even given a colonel's commission. The mission to Detroit turned out to be a ruse to get White Eyes assassinated by McIntosh's soldiers. Claiming that he died of smallpox, a subsequent investigation revealed that White Eyes had been "treacherously put to death,"[75] a sad ending for a gallant ally.

The Native American tribes had been caught in the middle of a war they little understood. Striving to protect their cultural identity against devastation and encroachment, they were classic examples of a weaker power caught between the titanic struggles of two stronger ones. The struggle of the Indians, therefore, needs to be viewed from this new perspective.[76]

Looking upon the Indians as defeated allies of the British, the Americans thought they now had a rightful claim to all Indian lands within the recently won political boundaries of the young United States. The legislature of North Carolina summed up their view perfectly. By rights, they stated, we now own *all* the Cherokee lands, but the Cherokee may live upon it as tenants until otherwise directed to vacate the property in favor of white settlers. The Iroquois, on the other hand, were not given a tenant option. Forced to remove to Canada, their former tribal lands in northern and western New York were divided up as spoils of war for Continental army veterans and speculators. Chief Cornplanter, a surviving Iroquois sachem, told President George Washington in 1790 that his name in their language now meant "Town Destroyer, and to this day when that name is heard our women look behind them and turn pale, and our children cling close to the necks of their mothers."[77]

For most Native Americans, the entire patriot movement meant nation destroyer. By the end of the war, frontiersmen, emboldened by the weakened state of the Native American tribes as a result of the years of fighting and the devastating raids into their territory, began to engage in plundering expeditions. According to one frontier observer, Major William Croghan, "The country talks of nothing but killing Indians and taking possession of their lands." Plunder seized by raiding militiamen against Indian towns was later sold at Wheeling, Virginia, for nearly £20,000.[78] Intermittent warfare between white militia and Native American tribes continued in the Ohio country for the next thirty years, when the Northwestern tribes, led by Tecumseh and The Prophet, were nearly annihilated by William Henry Harrison, a future president of the United States, at the battles of the Thames and Tippecanoe. The legacy of the war set a pattern that was to be repeated again and again, culminating at Wounded Knee, South Dakota, in 1890. White land hunger always overrode any considerations of the Indians, an old story that was reinforced by the outcome of the fighting.

CHAPTER SIX

To Get as Much for My Skin as I Could: The Soldier as Wage Laborer

At Uncle Joe's I liv'd at ease;
Had cider and good bread and cheese;
But while I stayed at Uncle Sam's
I'd nought to eat but "faith and clams."[1]

Like "circuses come to town," Continental recruiting parties in 1776 fanned out across the thirteen colonies in hopes of enticing men to join the army. Joseph Plumb Martin was one of the many drawn to the commotion caused by the fifes and drums of musicians who entertained the gathering crowd with martial tunes. Martin lived with his grandparents in Connecticut and had already served a short enlistment earlier in the war. But an "elbow relation," with "a Lieutenant's commission in the standing army," continually harangued his grandparents whose consent was necessary for his reenlistment. The lieutenant had even sent a squad of soldiers around to harass Martin, "using [as] much persuasion" as possible; they gave him the impression that he had little choice in the matter. Martin thought, "As I must go, I might as well endeavor to get as much for my skin as I could." He agreed to sign the "terms of indenture" of a soldier at the next scheduled militia muster day.[2]

When muster day finally arrived, Martin stated that he "went to the parade, where all was liveliness, as it generally is upon such occasion; but I felt miserably; my execution day had come." He was hesitant to "put his name to enlisting indentures," but the lieutenant insisted, marching him toward the house where the recruiters were signing people up for "the duration of the war," and where he saw the same squad of soldiers who had previously "used much persuasion" on him. He then enlisted as a substitute for a militiaman. "The men gave me what they agreed to," wrote Martin. "I forget the sum. . . . They were now freed from any further trouble, at least for the present, and I had become the scapegoat for them."[3]

Now a private in the Continental army for "the duration of the war," Martin had entered into a complex agreement between himself and the state. His use of the terms "indenture" and "execution day" were in many ways apt. By agreeing to abide by the military code of justice known as the Articles of War, Martin had temporarily traded his civil liberty and possibly his life for more immediate wages, food, and clothing. His length of service was specified on the enlistment papers; rations of food and clothing were implied but usually stipulated by law.[4] Martin felt that his service was a sort of indentureship: "soldiering" was a form of unfree labor. Indentureship and servitude were commonplaces in early America. Masters who purchased such labor were required by custom to provide food, shelter, and clothing, but service was restricted to a specified number of years.[5] Martin, who enlisted "for the war," was committing himself to perpetual servitude with the state or until he himself died in the war. He, like most other soldiers, dreaded indefinite service and equated it to "contracts for perpetual servitude."[6]

Few historians have considered the contractual nature of "soldiering" in the eighteenth century. Most have become ensnared in the radical Whig ideological rhetoric of the times and assumed such motivation applied to everyone. The rough and tumble existence of soldiers in camp or on the march was nearly foreign to most Continental army officers. Concerns about how long they would serve, where their next meal was coming from, monthly pay, and the harshness of discipline were more pressing issues than taxation without representation, or Parliament's right to tax the colonies. Liberty and freedom were nice ideas, but most soldiers only had time to think about where their next meal was coming from. Martin remembered standing with a group of soldiers in a field during the campaign of 1776, cold and hungry. Spying an officer nearby, one of the soldiers decided to inform him that the men needed something to eat. The officer, "putting his hand into his coat pocket, took out a piece of an ear of Indian corn burnt black as coal." "Here," he said to the complaining man, "eat this and learn to be a soldier."[7]

Learning to be a soldier meant different things, especially to those who had to accept burned corn or go hungry. For officers, "learning to be a soldier" meant that enlisted men did not question authority, quietly endured privation, and persevered until "liberty" was won. The experience of Continental army enlisted men, however, gave them their own distinct ideas of "liberty," separate and apart from the definition used by officers and colonial elites. "Liberty" to soldiers meant that they were free to bargain for their time and labor, for as we have seen, their labor was about nearly the only thing they owned. Each soldier recognized *before* he enlisted that he was customarily due a wage, food, and shelter in exchange for agreeing to abide by limited terms of recruitment. When it appeared that these terms were being abrogated or being extended indefinitely, the soldier was apt to view himself as enslaved. Sarah Hodgkins wrote to her soldier-husband Joseph, who was in camp at Boston, that she was afraid he would stay in service until he had agreed to make himself a slave. Congressman Roger Sherman of Connecticut argued that "long enlistment is a state of slavery. There ought to be a rotation which is in favor of liberty."[8] When the time of enlistment ran out for Caleb Haskell, a soldier who participated in the 1776 invasion of Canada, he refused to go on outpost duty along with the rest of his company. These men perceived that their enlistments had expired. Haskell noted that "they had been "looking upon [themselves] as *freemen* since the first of January." Haskell's officers, however, refused to recognize his status. Haskell and his mates were placed under guard and rushed before drumhead courts-martial and soon informed that if they continued to refuse their officers they would "again be confined and receive 39 stripes." Choosing discretion as the better part of valor and being deep in Canadian territory in the heart of winter, Haskell and his squad mates found that "arbitrary rule [had] prevailed." They decided to do their assigned tasks "much against their will."[9]

The concerns of men like Martin and Haskell revealed two important dimensions of the soldiers' experience as a waged military laborer: (1) the wages and bounties given by various jurisdictions in exchange for service, and (2) resistance to demands by Congress and the army for an indefinite term of enlistment. The chapter will also trace the extensive though rarely appreciated amount of wage bargaining that took place between the soldiers and the government throughout the war. Refusal to reenlist, desertion, and resistance to authority were all part of this bargaining process, as was the soldier's ability to play local against national jurisdictions, using the understocked military labor market to advantage. Soldiers struggled to remain volunteers and violently resisted attempts by officers or the government to limit their mobility by forcing them to enlist for "the duration of the war." Effectively resisting involuntary military servitude, one prewar Virginia frontiersman explained that they were "soldiers [only] when they chose to be."[10]

Soldiers looked upon themselves as volunteers who were at liberty to fight or not to fight as they pleased. Theirs was a status that implied certain rights and deferments that officers often were not willing to grant. Colonel Otho Williams remarked that when a group of riflemen showed up in camp, the soldiers declared that "they are Volunteers and should be treated with distinction." Washington, however, refused volunteers sent to him by his home state of Virginia in 1777. Men of the "Volunteer kind," stated the General, "are impatient of Command, ungovernable; and, claiming to themselves a sort of superior merit, generally assume, not only the Privilege of thinking, but to do as they please."[11] When an unruly group of independent Pennsylvania riflemen arrived at camp in Boston, Washington was heard to remark that he sincerely "wished they had never come."[12]

With the war barely a year old, General William Heath reported mass disobedience in his regiment. He wrote to Washington that one of his battalions "had drawn up and were determined to march home." Heath stated that when he went over to find out why the soldiers were taking such action, he was informed that it was due to "the want of money and Blankets and the Severe Duty of the Camp." They were, after all, "volunteers." Threatened with the "severest punishment," many soldiers decided to desert anyway. The unrest soon spread to the "other Rifle Battalion of Pennsylvanians who are extremely uneasy and talk of going home in a Body."[13] As volunteers, soldiers considered themselves entitled to all contractual and implied rights of freemen who willingly offered their services to the state.

The enlistment contract shaped the ways in which soldiers joined or dodged, re-enlisted or deserted the Continental service. This concept of military contract had begun to take shape during the Seven Years' War. New England soldiers viewed service as a "contractual agreement" between an individual and the state. New Englanders "in every rank from general officer to private soldier, reflected an almost unfailing tendency to base arguments and actions upon contractual principles whenever they confronted what they regarded as the unwarranted pretension of superiors."[14] The soldier's diaries revealed numerous examples of contractual principles at work. Private Enoch Poor, for example, observed in 1760 that all the soldiers garrisoned on the New England frontier "was of One Mind [and] That was Not to work with thout Pay." A provincial Massachusetts unit kept in service beyond its allotted time delivered "a round robin [petition] to the Colonel desiring to get us sent home according to the enlistment."[15]

Many of the contractual attitudes of colonial soldiers found in units during the Seven Years' War were renewed and extended during the Revolution. In Connecticut, for instance, state contractual offers of pay, clothing, and rations in exchange for an amount of time served played a large role in recruiting forces for Continental units.[16] General Enoch Poor of New Hampshire complained to Mesech Weare, governor of the state, that he had problems punishing deserters. He reckoned that if the state expected their soldiers to do *their* duty, then the state had better live up to its side of the bargain too:

> If any of them desert how can I punish them when they plead in their justification that on your part the Contract is broken? That you promised and engaged to supply them with such things . . . this they say they had an undoubted right to expect. You promised they should be supplied with the common necessaries of life at a reasonable rate.[17]

But enlistment contracts were broken almost as soon as they were signed. Many soldiers saw this as an abrogation of their bargain with the state and chose to desert or not reenlist.

Not only were enlistment contracts neglected but they were not uniform either, causing an endless number of problems for the national and state governments. The need for Congress to provide military forces on demand caused the revolutionaries to emphasize economic incentive as their principal motivator for recruiting forces for the war. Each state, however, employed its own methodology for enlisting recruits. Some states were able to supply the contractual needs of their soldiers; others never did. As the Revolution progressed, old intracolonial conflicts became renewed over this issue. Colonies competed for scarce military recruits and were willing to offer nearly unlimited amounts of money to get them. These conditions, of course, favored the soldiers. John Adams feared such competitions among state governments. "I wish," he lamented, that

> there was a laudable Spirit to give Bounties in Money, and Land, to Men, who would enlist during the War. But there is not. Congress offers Ten

Dollars Bounty to inlist for three years when New Jersey, New York, Connecticut, Mass. Bay and New Hampshire are voting six, Eight, or Ten Pounds a Man to serve for Six Months. This Economy at the Spigot, and Profusion at the Bung will ruin us.[18]

Adams was hinting that enlistments "during the war" would negate the ability of soldiers to play local jurisdictions off against the national government. It also allowed soldiers simply to refuse to enlist until the government offered shorter terms of enlistment for higher wages.

The length of enlistment, the selling of one's labor for a military tour of duty, was the chief cause of tension between the army leadership and its laborers, the foot soldiers. Richard Smith noted in his diary that "the New England Men are adverse to inlisting for a longer Term than One year & not fond of serving under any but Officers of their own choosing." Connecticut Yankee Joseph Plumb Martin was one of the many who declined to enlist for more than a year. During his first enlistment he considered one year's service to be "too long for [him] at first trial," and "wished only to take a priming before [he] took . . . the whole coat of paint for a soldier."[19]

The British astutely grasped this tension and sought to exploit it by spreading an ingenious bit of disinformation against Congress. Publishing an article in the *Philadelphia Evening Post* that bore "all the marks of a genuine Act of Congress," the British attempted to get soldiers who had already enlisted for a specified period of time to believe that Congress had involuntarily extended their service for the duration of the war.[20] Washington quickly disavowed the authenticity of the article. But the conflicts between the state and its soldiers remained.

A biting satire later appeared in the rebel controlled *New Hampshire Gazette* that expressed some of the bitterness soldiers felt toward their lot in the Continental ranks. Dripping with irony and sarcasm, the author of the article wrote:

We are well informed that by far the greater part of the brave Americans, under General Washington, have re-enlisted during the war. . . . The men are highly pleased with their excellent clothing. . . . They are equally pleased with the plenty and quality of their provisions, and the attention that has been paid by the several States, as well as Congress, to their families. Many of these noble-spirited men, upon re-enlistment, have laughingly said, "The term is too short; the war, we know, can last but a little while; bring us an indenture for ninety-nine years.[21]

The soldiers, almost everywhere displeased with their clothing, provisions, and family arrangements, were, at the moment these words were written, bitterly contesting their "indentures," their terms of service.

A recruiting poster displaying a martial-looking soldier performing the manual of arms appeared in the streets of Philadelphia in 1776. The broadside boldly promised each soldier who enlisted a bounty of twelve dollars, an annual suit of clothing, large and ample rations, and sixty dollars a year in silver and gold for pay. "Who shall embrace the opportunity of spending a few happy years in viewing the different parts of this beautiful continent," enticed the advertisement, "after which . . . he should return home to his friends with his pockets FULL of money & his head covered with laurels." Finding that most men were not as gullible as they had supposed, Congress was forced to resort to other, more traditional ways of recruiting. Following the European practice of "beating up" for enlistees, a sergeant or junior officer (who sometimes received a portion of the bounty money that was offered) paraded through an area with a detachment of drummers to attract a crowd. Local taverns or inns were ideal locations, because the people were attracted not only to the commotion of the drums and circuslike atmosphere created by the recruiters but also to the generous supply of liquor freely dispensed to loosen the inhibitions of a skeptical citizenry.[22] John Claspy, a recruiting sergeant in Virginia, stated that his destination while on such duty "always was where there were the largest gathering of the people in their civil capacity and where whiskey was most likely to induce them to assume a military one."[23]

"Liquor listees" were not unusual, nor were other nefarious recruiting practices. In another method the recruiting agent hid the proffered bounty money on the person of a potential recruit, then would "find" the money in the recruit's pocket, and quickly haul the victim before a justice of the peace (who may have been in collusion with the recruiter), who would then hand down a sentence of a long term of service.[24] Such a trick was played on Joseph Doble. He was approached by recruiting officer, Second Lieutenant Thomas Jenny, at a tavern. Doble facetiously told Jenny that he "would take money from any body that would bestow it on [him], but not with any design for being a soldier." Upon hearing this, Jenny casually slipped ten shillings into Doble's pocket and announced to the gathering crowd that Doble "had enlisted." Realizing that he had been tricked, Doble tried to give the shillings back to Jenny, who refused them. In a panic, Doble threw the money down on the table and ran off.

Concerned that Jenny had advertised him as a deserter, Doble, in a counter-ad, recounted his side of this escapade to keep from being arrested.[25]

By 1777, these tried and once true methods of recruiting were no longer succeeding in getting enough men to join the regular army. The men actively resisted signing terms of enlistment that limited their ability to sell their labor to the highest bidder. Moreover, returning veterans brought with them horrid tales of mortality in camps that were swept by smallpox, and of battlefields littered with bloodied British and Hessian bayonets. Josiah Burr, a Connecticut private who had enlisted during the early period of enthusiasm for the war, simply grew weary of the harsh and poorly paid life of a soldier. Writing from camp in 1777, Burr proudly announced to his mother that he could "eat raw Pork & drink white fac'd Rum with the best of them." A year and a half later, however, he wrote his commanding officer of his inability to continue in the army: "It is really very surprizing to me that a person sick & infirm as . . . I am should be consider'd as an able bodied Man & as such drag'd by force & Arms & be obliged to join the Army dead or alive."[26]

Army recruiters responded to resistance by employing some shady reenlistment tactics that tricked soldiers into longer service. Four companies of the "German Regiment," few of whom understood English, petitioned Congress for release from active duty over what they felt was a misunderstanding over both their bounties and their intended term of service: "We Being First Inlisted for Three Years and Received Ten Dollars Bounty, at the Expiration of Three Months There Being Ten Dollars More Given to us, Being Persuaded that it was Only a Present [of the state of Pennsylvania], But Now we are tould by Our Officers that we are Inlisted During the War."[27] Persistent localism was also a factor in preventing men from enlisting in the Continental army. A group of Pennsylvania frontiersmen were enlisted in Westmoreland County under the proviso that they were to remain there in defense of the frontier (and their homes) which were subject to Indian attack. When ordered to join Washington because of the impending British invasion of Pennsylvania, the men marched eastward to the main army only after receiving assurances that they would return to Westmoreland after "the emergency" was over. Washington, however, felt that the emergency was never over and refused to let the men return home once they were in camp. He feared that other units raised on the frontier would demand the same. He noted that the Thirteenth Virginia "was raised on the West side of the Alleganies with assurances from its officers, that the Men would not be drawn from that quarter." Because they were taken from the frontier, Washington claimed that "it has been the cause of great desertions and a present source of uneasiness."[28]

In most cases, however, militias took advantage of their short enlistment times, an option denied to soldiers of the standing army. Washington noted with alarm that bounties offered by states for extended military service had a negative effect, from his standpoint, on recruiting. He thought that the bidding over troops would cause soldiers to "feel their importance" and the states, consequently, would have to pay their price. "Indeed as their aid is so essential, and not to be dispensed with," stated Washington, "it is wondered, they had not estimated it at a higher rate."[29] James Warren was keenly aware of the soldier's ability to wage bargain with the state. He feared that Massachusetts' "excessive" recruiting inducements "would stop any further inlistments till the Soldiers can Extort from their Townsmen 50 dollars a piece in Addition to the Bounty already promised."[30]

Competition for scarce military labor created soaring bounties and a measure of bargaining power for prospective and active soldiers. John Hancock, one of the wealthiest men in America, was "Pained . . . at this Want of Public Spirit and the Backwardness in the Soldiers" who refused to reenlist for the wages offered. Hancock's characterization of the soldiery, however, proved to be inaccurate, for it was not a matter of public spirit and backwardness. To determine why men refused to reenlist, the Congressional Committee of Conference researched the journals of Provincial units that were fielded by the colonies during the Seven Years' War. During the "Years 1758 & 1759 . . . [the soldiers] received fourteen pounds bounty & had thirty six Shillings per month pay, which as their Engagements were for Six months only, was much higher Terms than the present when no other Bounty is allowed than a Coat to each Man."[31] When soldiers were not being paid what they considered were adequate wages, comments like that of General Edward Hand appeared: "New Englanders do not enlist as was expected."[32] While the government sought to aggregate its military labor and limit the prerogatives of soldiers, the enlisted men resisted these attempts by their collective refusal to agree to the army's terms.

Near the end of the first year of the war, Washington noted that more than 19,000 men were due to be discharged. Few were inclined to reenlist. He reported to Hancock that "not more than 2540 men [had] reenlisted," and that only 966 had reenlisted prior to their eleventh-hour efforts to keep the army from walking away.[33] Samuel Ward noted from the letters he received from the army camp at Cambridge that Congress had "infinite Difficulty in reinlisting the army."[34] Fearing that the British would find out about their reenlistment woes, Congress empowered Washington to call out the New England militia, a function that had formerly been the sole prerogative of state governors. Hancock also hastily forwarded three months' back pay due the soldiers and a month's "extraordinary" pay for soldiers who reenlisted before the end of the year.[35] Still, the soldiers declined to reenlist. Washington observed that at the beginning of the war, "Men might have been got at Cambridge without a bounty for the War." But a half year later, the men "began to see that the Contest was not likely to end." He implied that they would not serve now without a significant offer of money and land.[36]

By the end of 1776, entire regiments of soldiers, frequently led by their commanding officers, marched for home as soon as their enlistments expired. General Horatio Gates pleaded with the New Jersey Brigade stationed in the Champlain Valley to remain in service for a few more weeks during the latter part of 1776. Nevertheless, the regiment of Colonel William Wind refused to stay past its allotted time. Gates had camp drums sounded "in derision of [those soldiers] who had the Baseness to quit their post in this Time of Danger." He later thanked the few soldiers who remained in service "for their Honour and publick Spirit they shewed in disdaining to follow the infamous Example of their Colonel and the deluded Soldiers who accompanied him."[37] Nearly the entire regiment, however, marched for home.

Edmund Phinney's Eighteenth Continental Regiment left Fort George en masse, and marched for home on New Year's Day, 1777. Officers had to scramble to collect local militiamen to replace them at nearly four times the cost of regular soldiers and for substantially less time in service. General Philip Schuyler found out that Phinney's officers soon followed their men, claiming that "they could get no Fire Wood, and the Men being come off they were obligated to follow their Example."[38] Following his retreat through New Jersey, Washington informed the president of Congress that "the term of the Jersey and Maryland Brigade's Service expired and neither of them would stay an hour longer."[39] Anthony Wayne reported that Charles Burrall's Connecticut Regiment refused to extend its service for two more weeks when it was expected it would be relieved by other troops. On 31 January 1777, with their time of service about to expire at midnight, the soldiers "went off in the Night." Wayne stated that "the chief part" of the Connecticut troops had "run away . . . taking along the publick Ammunition which they drew for the defense of this Post."[40] It was the dead of winter, and these men did not expect to see action. They probably reasoned that a two-week extension would have brought them more of the same garrison duty. They left because "their time" was up, and they felt no further obligation to serve.

Even Colonel John Glover's famous Marblehead regiment (a group of former sailors who were responsible for rescuing a portion of Washington's army from Brooklyn Heights and rowing him across the Delaware on Christmas Eve, 1776) decided eventually to take their chances on privateers rather than stay in the army. Washington laconically noted that much of Glover's regiment went to Philadelphia soon after the battle of Trenton "to offer their Services for the Continental Vessels [and] will not, by any endeavors of mine re-enlist."[41] Colonel Daniel Hitchcock wrote John Adams that "he was very sorry to hear" that Congress was only offering "Ten Dollars Bounty for those that will enlist for three Years; for it will not procure the Men, as that Sum is given by the New England States to the new Levies only for 5 or Six Months, and our Soldiers all know it."[42]

It was not always pleasant or safe, however, to depart from the army, even under these perfectly legal means. Those packing to leave were the targets of jeers and depredations by their officers. General Charles Lee even smashed the butt of a musket over the skull of one soldier who tried to persuade a comrade to come with him.[43] Therefore many soldiers did not wait for their time to expire, but used their feet to desert the army and the government (either temporarily or permanently).

Such actions by soldiers consistently surprised army officers and members of Congress during the early years of the war. They failed to recognize the "moral economy" that the soldiers were trying to establish when they demanded wages, rights, and traditional privileges in exchange for their service.[44] Moreover, viable wages were what set them apart from unfree forms of labor such as indentured servitude or even slavery. Longer enlistment terms coupled with low pay meant decreased recruitment. In November 1776 Congress was informed that it had gone too far in its efforts to establish an army whose enlistments extended for the duration of the war. James Sullivan wrote to John Adams and Elbridge Gerry and asked why he thought the army would never successfully recruit soldiers:

> There is not in my mind the shadow of a probability of [Congress] raising ten thousand men on the proposed Establishment. . . . [The soldiers] will not Engage for an indefinite Term of Time, and those who are Engaged in the Family way [married] are by no means willing to inlist for a Term the End whereof they are not able to see. Indeed few Americans would choose the Life of a Soldier and be willing to be bound during Life.[45]

Sullivan continued that "the Wages and bounty ordered by Congress Afford but Little Encouragement or when we consider that the persons who are to Engage for forty shillings per Month have near one half of them large Families to Support and the other half can have three pounds at home" working jobs in the civilian community. After considering the "depreciation of money" and inflation, Sullivan asked, "How is it possible that the Soldiery should live upon the proposed Wages" when "Goods of every kind are set at such sums that 40 [shillings] will not purchase near half so much at home as it would in April 1775 nor one third part so much (if reports are true) in the Camp?"[46]

Not only were the price of extra clothes and food high in camp but the soldiers were subjected to periods of reduced rations. Upon enlistment each soldier was promised a set daily ration of bread, beef, vegetables, milk, and spruce beer. To soldiers, the ration not only kept them alive but it was part of the contract for which they had enlisted. Congress estimated on 10 June 1777 that a soldier's ration was worth eleven cents. When the government failed to provide this pittance, soldiers were required to spend their monthly pay, if they got any at all, at sutler booths (food stands), where prices were not always controlled by Congress or the army command. Thus they felt not only cheated out of their due ration but doubly put upon by having to spend their hard-earned wages on items that were owed them by the government in the first place. Soldiers who had participated in the Canadian invasion during the winter of 1776 loudly complained of food, clothing, and supply shortages. Occasionally, soldiers were forced to spend their entire wages simply to avoid starvation. Years after the war, Joseph Plumb Martin still bitterly remembered his 1777 Thanksgiving repast of "a half a gill of rice and a tablespoon of vinegar." Thoroughly disgusted, he and his mess mates unsuccessfully attempted to "purloin" some beef from the commissary stores. His hopes for a meal "blasted" by an alert sentinel, Martin returned to camp and had his usual supper of "leg of nothing and no turnips."[47]

The sheer difficulty of staying alive as a soldier in camp also deterred enlistment. After an extraordinarily unsuccessful recruiting trip into

Pennsylvania and Maryland in 1776, Alexander Graydon stated that he was sorry that "the contest was not a religious one and [the] people been inflamed by a zeal on points of faith like the Crusaders or the army of Cromwell." Graydon wanted zealots, not rational, calculating, self-interested waged soldiers. He lamented that the soldiers "were to be taken as they were."[48]

Most soldiers did not intend to be "taken" at all. A 1776 Connecticut broadside urged men to "chearfully spring forward and offer themselves for the service of their country" and march to New York. In light of the military emergency, the Assembly offered each volunteer twenty shillings in addition to the money previously paid to earlier volunteers, and promised that the men would be under the command of the "most generous-spirited and humane" officers. Moreover, they were guaranteed that they would not be obliged to serve for more than two months and would be "much and generally sheltered in houses &c in the Jersies."[49] The Connecticut men who did enlist, however, declared that their term of service would not exceed three weeks "if it shall be necessary to serve so long." Further, they *demanded* the "same Wages and Incouragement" which the Assembly had offered to men who had enlisted for two months.[50] Because they were in demand, the soldiers—not the government—set the parameters of their terms of enlistment. The soldiers' ability to bargain for wages and set limits upon the terms of engagement were paramount goals. Moreover, as Nathanael Greene noted in a letter to Samuel Ward, men were not "obliged to resort to the Army for employment."[51] Short of impressment, the government simply had no leverage over them. In another example in which soldiers and not the government set the limits of service, Colonel William Ledyard reported that he was forced to recruit soldiers "hired by the day," as men refused to enlist for anything longer.[52] Shorter term limits allowed soldiers more effectively to bargain for wages with the government. It was imperative, from their point of view, to be able to negotiate the terms of service as often as possible.

Tired of negotiations with soldiers and anxious to create a European-style regular army, Washington, in 1777, hinted at another way men might be induced into "joining" the army. Writing to Governor Patrick Henry of Virginia, Washington stated that drafting men (outright impressment) might be the only way to obtain soldiers for the duration of the war. Ignoring the fact that grievance against impressment was a source of revolution for many in the first place, Washington stated that it was "fruitless" to attempt to enlist soldiers on the bounty offered by Congress, "as the Sums given for substitutes in the Militia, induces all those, who would otherwise have gone into Continental service, to prefer a line in which neither duty or discipline is severe; and which they have a chance of having the bounty repeated three or four times a year." Thus he favored impressing men into service rather than recruiting them with monetary enticements. If "experience has demonstrated, that little more can be done by voluntary inlistments," he stated, then "some other mode must be concerted, and no other presents itself, than that of filling the Regiments by drafts from the Militia."[53] In this way Washington could circumvent the soldier's ability to wage bargain by refusing to reenlist. Once enlisted, went Washington's thinking, the soldier became the military property of the state. As we have seen, the soldiers considered themselves "freemen" and violently resisted attempts to change that status. In worse cases, the men simply deserted or walked away from the army if they thought the state failed to live up to its agreement. Washington noted that long-term Continentals were "trying by every possible artifice to prove that their engagements were only temporary."[54]

Sometimes militiamen drafted for temporary duty with the regular army did more than just complain or desert. When men refused to answer an alarm or call-up, they were liable to be heavily fined for failing to appear at camp. Loyalist Benjamin Betts reported to Henry Clinton that the militia drafted to guard the Long Island shore "refused to serve—there were 1700 Writs served upon them for the Fines—upon which 400 of them arose and demanded General Sullivan but he was not to be found. They said . . . they would tear down or burn the Court house and Jails."[55] Burning the courts, of course, got rid of the records of those who failed to appear at muster when required. Like their counterparts in the standing army, these men were not wealthy enough to pay for substitutes and used the traditional soldier's threat of violence or desertion to circumvent rules they considered especially onerous or unfair.

Drafting drew a similar reaction in Massachusetts. When the Massachusetts General Court ordered the selectmen of Worcester to draft one-fourth of their militia to join the Continental army to help repel Burgoyne's 1777 invasion of northern New York, the citizens of the town informed the local justice of the peace that "many of their sons and servants had done a great Deal of service in the army" already and that the "rule of drafting was unjust," meaning that they thought there were other, more well placed members in the community who were not subject to the draft at all.[56] Moreover, the citizens demanded that others "who had not personally done a turn in the public service should be first drafted."[57] A Worcester militia captain named Ebenezer Lovel refused to turn out his men for the draft until the selectmen gave them a sum of money to cover their expenses while they did duty with the army. When the selectmen refused their request, "very few men turn'd out."[58] Of the forty-one men drafted from the town of Worcester, only eighteen actually marched to join the American forces at Bennington. The others "imagined they have discharged their duty and themselves too, by paying a fine of three pounds." "I fear," stated a citizen of the town, "we shall soon have more money than men."[59] While never quite abandoning the idea of drafting militiamen when not enough of the "lower sorts" joined the regular army, by 1777 the army had settled into a pattern of recruiting based on offers of a cash bounty that included the promise of some land if the soldier enlisted for the entire duration of the war. At the same time, Congress moved to reorganize the army and create an eighty-eight battalion army based on unlimited enlistment terms. But when it became clear that citizens would not enlist for the duration of the war and that the states could not fill their respective enlistment quotas, Congress allowed men to enlist for three years instead.[60]

By 1778, soldiers were actively resisting being forced to remain in service for an unlimited duration or to turn out for the low wages offered. Continental army officers countered this resistance by withholding the pay of their men to keep them from deserting, but this tactic, too, failed. Pay fraud and desertion were so rampant in the Eighth Pennsylvania that Washington convened a board of inquiry to determine why the men were abandoning the army. Washington hoped that "this may give us an Opportunity of doing justice, if the men's complaints are well founded, and may be productive of the most Salutary consequences . . . to the whole Army."[61]

Soldiers may have been cheated out of their pay, but, according to eighteenth-century custom, they were not completely reliant on a monetary wage. By custom and law, they were due for service, money, rations, clothing, and rum on certain occasions. When the Board of War recommended as a cost-saving measure that the army "call in the Old Clothes [worn by the soldiers] upon delivery of the new" and turn them over to the camp hospital, Washington was informed by his officers that the soldiers "looked upon it as an unjustifiable attempt to deprive them of what they had earned by their years in service."[62] Washington decided not to risk a general mutiny among the troops and let the matter drop. The soldiers kept their clothes.

When some of the barely literate soldiers in Captain Job Wright's company complained in a formal petition to him that they believed they did not receive the bread ration that was due them, he nearly had an open rebellion on his hands. The soldiers believed that commissary officers were siphoning off amounts of the soldiers' ration and selling it on the side for a profit. They requested that the amount skimmed was "a trifel, [but] Every Day it A Mounts [it] will Bee of Value to the Solgers Wich We think is our Just Right." They requested that Captain Wright require the baker to give the profit to them because he used their ration to get it.[63] Customarily due a set ration, the soldiers sharply reacted to schemes by officers to expropriate even a tiny portion of what they considered was rightly theirs.

Wages, however, were customarily low; nonetheless, the soldiers jealously guarded their right to be paid, even when it amounted to a small pittance of what was originally offered. But there was a tremendous difference of opinion as to what was an appropriate level of pay. Initially, Continental soldiers were paid a salary of six and two-thirds dollars per month. Southern members of Congress thought that soldiers were paid too much and the officers too little; they proposed that the pay of a private soldier be reduced to five dollars per month. John Adams admitted that he did not know how much pay was appropriate for the soldiers but he feared that "a Reduction of it would . . . give Such a Disgust [among the soldiers] as to endanger the Service."[64] Joseph Plumb Martin, Daniel Allen, Elisha Stevens, John Smith, and Ephriam Squier all noted in their diaries the significance of pay to soldiers. Both Smith and Squier mentioned that "some of the Company refused to goe [on campaigns] Unless they were Paid their wages which was due them Before they went out of town."[65] Smith's company had refused to board a ferry boat until they were paid. The men reasoned that once aboard, they would have little recourse against their officers. Smith insisted that he had been made a sentry on desolate Goat Island in Narragansett Bay "as punishment for the Sin of a Soldier Standing out for his wages."[66]

To keep soldiers, as a body, from "standing out for their wages" and perhaps to provide some incentive, on 27 May 1778 Congress established a differential pay scale that reflected a higher wage for more skilled subgroups of soldiers. The common infantryman still received only six and two-thirds dollars; corporals, drummers, and fifers got two-thirds more of a dollar than infantry privates; higher enlisted grades such as fife majors, drum majors, and sergeants all received nine dollars. Artillerymen, due to the higher level of skill required to man their weapons, received eight and one-third dollars; artillery corporals and bombardiers drew the same pay as infantry sergeants (nine dollars), while artillery sergeants drew ten dollars. Cavalry specialists such as farriers, trumpeters, and saddlers also received ten dollars a month. Engineers were paid at the same rate as artillerymen.[67] By 1778, however, most people recognized that such wages had become nearly valueless due to galloping inflation.

Potential recruits demonstrated their "disgust' at the low, noncompetitive wages by refusing to enlist at those rates. During the winter of 1777, Samuel Blanchley Webb was sent into Connecticut to recruit soldiers for his state's Continental quota. Finding that just two days prior to his arrival in the state the legislature authorized an additional thirty-three and one-third dollars more than the Continental bounty and had adjourned without provision for his recruits, Webb wrote Washington that "Men will not enlist for 20 dollars with Me when others will give them 53." Pennsylvania specifically targeted "inhabitants of the city of Philadelphia not possessed of real estates" and offered them a bounty of ten dollars for only a month's service in the militia. Compared to long-term Continentals who drew just six and two-thirds dollars per month and were obliged (for the most part) to serve more than three years, the official soldier's wage quickly became laughable.[68] Washington thought that this policy had "poisonous effects on the army."[69]

During the Revolution, a soldier's wage became superfluous in a short period of time. By the fall of 1777, the Congress had issued nearly $250 million and the states another $210 million in bills that had little or no financial backing. The results were hyperinflation and financial chaos. By 1778, the rapid depreciation of currency had negated the soldier's ability to live on the wages provided him by Congress or his home state. Moreover, Congress increased the emission of paper money by another $63.4 million. By 1779, the amount of Continental paper required to buy one dollar in gold or silver began to climb sharply.[70] When advised that paying part of a bounty in silver dollars might aid the recruiting business, Washington warned strongly against it. He was afraid that the soldiers would "have ocular proof" that would "open the eyes of the whole and setting them to reasoning upon the difference between specie and paper."[71] By 1780 some regiments of soldiers—with their officers—refused to accept pay in paper money and instead demanded specie. A Continental dollar was worth one cent in hard money.[72] In fact, some soldiers received no pay at all. In 1781 Virginia's troops had not received pay for nearly two years. At the same time, Nathanael Greene complained that "he had not been furnished with a shilling in specie since he assumed command." Not knowing where else to turn after this governmental breakdown, Greene illegally drew on the account of Robert Morris to pay his troops. Even these creative efforts were not enough. In May 1782 Greene's troops threatened to mutiny and turn him over to the British. His own personal servant was part of the scheme.[73]

From the common soldier's perspective, the problem was a matter of equitable pay for the time engaged. Military pay was not comparable to civilian wages, which made prompt payment of wages all the more important to the soldiers. In 1776, well before currency depreciation took effect, civilian artisans (tailors, coopers, and carpenters) in Rhode Island earned one hundred shillings a month, while common laborers were paid sixty shillings. A private in the Continental army earned forty shillings. Maryland militiamen earned thirty-seven shillings, and New York provincial soldiers received fifty-three shillings for the same amount of served time.[74] Moreover, military pay was subject to deductions over which the soldier had little control. Deductions for costs to replace uniforms, arms, and equipment lost or destroyed on the march or battlefield reduced monthly wages as well. Paymasters simply introduced what was called a "stoppage" in a soldier's pay. A private who was owed seventy-two dollars yearly often received only about twelve dollars per year after deductions for arms, clothes, family support, and fines.[75] Some soldiers ended up with little to show for even a few months' service. Private Elijah Fisher complained that officers, through various deductions and subterfuges, sought to cheat soldiers out of nearly all of their meager pay. "If I had anone [*sic*] of [pay deductions] before I had Engaged I never would have gone [enlisted] the six months. But jest so they use the sholgers. They will promise them so and so and after they have got them to Enlist they are Cheated out of one-half they ought to have by one or another of the offisers."[76]

To prevent wholesale desertion over the issue of pay, Congress offered depreciation certificates to the soldiers. Congress even maintained an official table of exchange based on depreciation, but it rarely reflected what was actually happening in the marketplace. In September 1777 Continental paper currency held at face value. Four months later, a hundred dollar "Continental" bill was actually worth sixty-eight dollars. By 1779 the same bill had the purchasing power of only thirteen dollars, and by February 1780 it had dropped to a mere fifty cents in hard money. Charles Thomson, secretary to Congress, reported that the official rate of exchange differed sharply from the actual rate of the town of Philadelphia. While the official rate was 40 to 1, the black market rate exceeded 100 to 1. The governor of New Jersey bemoaned the fact that his salary of 8,000 pounds was worth no more than 150 pounds sterling. By December 1781 Continental currency stopped circulating, because no one would accept it as legal tender. Inflation affected state currencies even more drastically.[77] By 1780, soldiers were serving virtually without pay. Hundreds of men clamored to be released from their enlistments and officers feared massive revolts from within the army.[78]

What was worse for Washington and Congress was the tug of war that developed between the civilian sector and the army for scarce labor resources. One angry Connecticut citizen noted that the troops were "employed daily in a matter very inconsistent with the very end for which they were raised." Rather than sit idly in camp, many soldiers would spend a few hours in the morning attending to some camp drill and would then "let themselves out at the husbandry business, for eighteen pence per day."[79] Farmers, worried that their seasonal labor force would be depleted by each recruiting drive, were not adverse to "dissuading men from enlisting."[80] Joseph Plumb Martin and his mess mates volunteered to pull up turnips for one farmer in return for the tops of the vegetables, which they brought back to camp to eat.[81] Like Martin, soldiers who let themselves out to civilian employers while in camp were usually paid by the farmers in kind or in hard currency on a daily or weekly basis. The food or money sustained them when the army failed to pay on time.

Private Elijah Fisher made an agreement with a farmer to clear some land for him in exchange for one hundred dollars in paper currency. However, "if Headquarters moved before [Fisher] had finished [the farmer] was to pay [him] for what he had Dun according to the agreement."[82] Fisher must have been one of the most enterprising soldiers in the army, for he enlisted on four separate occasions, and probably got four different bounties. He also hired himself out to civilians as a laborer regularly to supplement his low or nonexisting pay.

Thus soldiers sought to develop on their own various ways to offset wage depreciation or the designs of officers to expropriate portions of their pay. Martin remembered how important basic wage supplements were with the soldiery. During the campaign of 1777, Joseph Plumb Martin mentioned that his unit had a thirty-two-pound cannon but no ammunition. The opposing British had the same type of cannon and lobbed shot at Martin and his squad mates at irregular intervals. "The artillery officers," according to Martin, "offered a gill a rum for [the retrieval] of each shot fired from [the British cannon]."[83] He noted that he had "seen from twenty to fifty men standing on the parade waiting with impatience the coming of the shot, which would often be seized before its motion had fully ceased. . . . When the lucky fellow who had caught it swallowed his rum, he would return to wait for another, exulting that he had been more lucky or more dexterous than his fellows."[84] Sergeant Samuel Bixby noted in his diary that after a general awarded a party of soldiers with two gallons of rum for the retrieval of a British cannonball, "soldiers chased down balls . . . as if they were gold."[85] In a more chilling example of the wage plight of the soldiers, Lieutenant Jeremiah Greenman noted that some of the men were reduced to "begging money from the Inhabitants of the City." One soldier was later acquitted of this crime due to a "lack of evidence."[86]

Many of the soldiers became convinced by midwar that the civilian stay-at-home population and Congress neither understood nor appreciated their sacrifice. Moreover, many of their letters expressed this resentment. Albegience Waldo, the Connecticut surgeon, stated that "People who live at home in Luxury and Ease . . . have but a very faint Idea of the unpleasing sensations, and continual Anxiety the Man endures who is in Camp. . . . These same People are willing we should suffer everything for their Benefit & advantage, and yet are the first to Condemn us for not doing more!"[87] Thomas Cartwright, a recruiting officer for Massachusetts, noted that Henry Jackson's regiment would only be filled by drafts but that "some men said they would join if paper money would pass" and also that "they were ready to fight when men of Fortune & monopolizers did."[88] Private Joseph Plumb Martin bitterly remembered the Continental army chaplain who, in a sermon to soldiers gathered for Sunday services, paraphrased John the Baptist's advice to soldiers to "be content with your wages."[89] Icabod Ward, a barely literate private from Connecticut, wished that critics of the Continental army were required to "undergo half so much as one of us have this Winter . . . that those grumbling at Soldiers New what they undergo."[90] "What expence we are at for Everything," moaned Ward. A pound of butter cost one-sixth of an entire month's wage and a small bread pie nearly half. "It is trublsum times for us all," he continued, "but wors for the Soldiers."[91]

In conclusion, the growing number of confrontations between the army hierarchy and its soldiers as the war wore on reflected the disparity felt by the men between what they were paid and the sacrifices they felt they had rendered in personal hardship and time. The serious American supply problems and monetary shortages are an old story but can be understood because of the difficulties of waging a full-fledged rebellion against one of the most powerful countries on earth. Yet the insubordination, desertion, and mutinies should not be viewed as some crass reaction of a pauper army but rather as indicators of a growing consciousness among the soldiers that their military labor could be bartered for something worthwhile.

By midwar, Washington became convinced that the intracolonial effort to recruit the army based on wages and bounties achieved "little purpose" and flatly stated that "nothing short of drafting will have the desired effect."[92] Yet it did not occur to Washington and others of his class that impressment was one of the issues that had started the Revolution in the first place. Furthermore, Washington reminded Congress that the impressment of soldiers was an important goal, because "voluntary inlistments seem to be totally out of the question; all the allurements of the most exorbitant bounties and every other inducement that could be thought of have been tried in vain and seem to have had little other effect than to increase the rapacity and raise the demands of those to whom they were held out."[93] He noted for the committeemen that he thought "the country had been already pretty well drained of that class of men [whose] attachments and circumstances disposed them [to enlist] permanently, or for a length of time into the army."[94] Yet neither Congress nor the states ever took the final step of officially drafting people into the army. As we have seen, the depreciation of currency was a two-way street. While it served to degrade the pay and tempers of those already in uniform, it also enabled others outside the army to easily come up with the cash to buy a substitute or pay the fine for refusing to appear at muster.[95] Those who traditionally possessed little to no tangible capital and whose only asset was the use of their strong hands and feet seemed to end up serving as Continental soldiers instead.

In an extraordinary letter, Washington admitted that wages in exchange for military labor had become a serious issue as the war wore on. Soldiers, in his opinion, had become conscious of their ability to demand

and receive higher wages for the sacrifices they perceived they w
making.

> It is vain to expect, that any (or more than a trifling) part of this Army will again engage in the Service on the encouragement offered by Congress. When Men find that their Townsmen and Companions are receiving 20, 30, and more Dollars, for a few Months Service, (which is truly the case) it cannot be expected; without compulsion; and to force them into the Service would answer no valuable purpose. When Men are irritated, and the Passions inflamed, they fly hastily and cheerfully to Arms; but after the first emotions are over, to expect, among such People, as compose the bulk of an Army, that they are influenced by any other principles than those of interest, is to look for what never did, and I fear never will happen.[96]

Washington's proposal to impress men into service as a solution to his problem of disinterested citizenry was his tacit admission that an army formed by men who were keenly aware of the moral economy that had traditionally existed between the recruit and the state had demands and requirements very different from his class or even the "middling sorts" who populated the state militias. The length of enlistment, the interstate competition for scarce military labor, the growing exorbitant bounties, and a general inability of the central bureaucracy to satisfy the basic demands of their wage laborers had created a very revolutionary army. It was an army, however, that the Whigs had long feared might demand, by collective action, a reckoning of accounts with rifles and bayonets against themselves instead of the British.

CHAPTER SEVEN

Through the Line Like Wildfire: Resistance, Punishment, Desertion, and Mutiny in the Continental Army

Cannons boomed out a warning and signal rockets lit up the New Jersey sky. Suddenly, cheering soldiers poured forth from their huts with their muskets. The men of the Pennsylvania line had mutinied. With pent-up fury and indignation, the soldiers seized several artillery pieces, loaded them with grapeshot, and rushed toward the parade ground. Officers who attempted to quell the mutiny were shot, bayoneted, or roughed up by their own soldiers.[1] Lieutenant Enos Reeves watched as General Anthony Wayne and Colonel Richard Butler pleaded with their men to disperse and return to their huts; their pleas "had no effect." The soldiers answered that "they had been wronged and were determined to see themselves righted."[2]

Led by a group of sergeants who jointly exercised command, the men filled the road and slowly marched toward Philadelphia and Congress. Their downcast officers followed ignominiously in the rear of their procession. The leaders of the mutiny took the title "generals colonel." This signaled to their deposed officers that they now outranked even Washington. Henry Marble, a New Englander who heard about the mutiny, stated that he would not "be surprised had the same disorder took place in every Line in the Army."[3]

Why did Marble believe that all the enlisted men of the Continental army were ripe for mutiny? Why were the soldiers willing to undertake an act punishable by death? Why undertake an act considered so heinous that special forms of punishment were reserved to deter it? Soldiers deserted, cursed their officers, and plundered civilians in practically all eighteenth-century armies. Yet mutiny was quite dramatically something else. This chapter will assess the frequency, causes, and meaning of mutiny as waged by Continental soldiers between 1776 and 1783. Resistance to officers, punishment, and official repression were all part of the process that led to the mutinous conduct prevalent throughout the army toward the end of the war.

In discussing questions of discipline and resistance within the ranks, many historians have missed the crucial underlying issues.[4] Resistance to discipline, however, may be rooted in a soldier's class experience. As we have seen in previous chapters, many of the soldiers of the Continental army were only a few steps beyond indentured servitude or slavery.

To some, it may have been perhaps comforting to describe eighteenth-century revolts as reactionary events triggered by "rebellions of the belly." Even contemporary observers downplayed the significance of mutinies. Washington, for one, informed his French counterpart Rochambeau that the revolt of the Pennsylvanians was caused by "foreigners and even some British deserters." Joseph Reed, president of the state of Pennsylvania, referred to Sergeant Williams, one of the leaders of the mutiny, as "a poor creature and very fond of liquor."[5] These accounts of resistance to spasmodic episodes struggled to deny the legitimacy of rebellions waged by soldiers. Had food and clothing been provided, went the conventional wisdom, the soldiers would never have had an occasion to revolt.

Soldier rebellions, however, were more than what was described by Washington and Reed. They were "highly complex forms of direct popular action." In every eighteenth-century crowd action, the participants "were informed by the belief that they were defending traditional rights or customs; and in general, that they were supported by the wider consensus of the community."[6] Indeed, the very words "mob" or "rabble"—used often by officers to describe Continental soldiers—suggest that the "crowd" possessed no honorable impulses of its own. This was comforting to officers who lost control over their men. Lacking definable motivation other than material need, the crowd was presented as the "passive" instrument of outside agitators, as Washington stated in a letter to French General Rochambeau following one particular mutiny.[7]

The men in the Continental army recognized that a "moral economy" existed between the soldier and the state. We know from earlier chapters that the average soldier in the Continental army was not a "yeoman farmer" nor was he always the "rabble" or "sweepings" of the street. Rather, citizens found themselves *temporarily* shouldering a musket for a great variety of reasons. They may have been willing to part with their civil liberties for a period of time, but not for too long. Such men hated officers who wielded the lash freely. They wanted to be paid for their services and were well aware of what a soldier was customarily due. As John Shy has suggested, many Americans—and historians—have chosen to forget the desertions, the whippings for minor infractions, the plundering, and the mutinies that were crucial parts of the Continental soldier's experience.[8]

Patterns of protest and defiance expressed by Continental soldiers were exceptionally complex.[9] In nearly every eighteenth-century war, soldiers were subject to prolonged periods of privation. Low pay or no pay, few if any clothes, and brutal conditions might have exacerbated dissatisfaction, but these matters do not, in themselves, explain why soldiers did not simply give up or disperse on their own accord, for they had many opportunities to do so.[10] A man also received customary dues or traditional privileges when recruited as a soldier, and these rights held some value for him. Moreover, these rights were easily known and understood by even the most illiterate recruit. As customary rights, these matters were not often listed in a soldier's contract, but the soldiers knew what they were, and they made sure their officers knew as well.

When a soldier enlisted, he understood that his temporary loss of civil rights required the state to pay, feed, shelter, and clothe him for the duration of his term. In August 1775 each soldier was allowed three-quarters of a pound of pork, one pound of fresh beef, or one pound of salt fish per day; one pound of bread or flour per day; and three pints of peas or beans per week, or vegetables. Added to this ample ration was one-half pint of rice, or one pint of Indian meal per week; one quart of spruce beer per man per day, or nine gallons of molasses per company of one hundred men.[11] In October 1776 Congress voted to give each man who enlisted for the war a suit of clothing, to consist of two linen shirts, two pairs of overalls, a leather or woolen waistcoat, one pair of breeches, a hat or leather cap, two pairs of hose, and two pairs of shoes.[12] To men who could barely afford one pair of pants, hose, and shoes, these items, customarily provided to all soldiers in the eighteenth century, had tangible value and were especially important to them.

Failure to regard the customary rights of soldiers could be deadly for both officers and enlisted men. The Pennsylvania mutineers warned Anthony Wayne "to be Punctual" in answering their demands "as we reasonably think," stated the sergeant, "it [was their] due." A year earlier, Private James Coleman, a deserter from the Pennsylvania line, called out from his execution scaffold in nearly the same language, warning his officers to "be punctual in their engagements [promises] to their men and give them no cause to desert."[13]

Soldiers prized their customary "due" above all things because this was what set them apart from unfree labor. Soldiers such as Caleb Haskell declared themselves "freemen" when they thought the terms of their enlistment had expired. Joseph Plumb Martin called his admission into the ranks not an enlistment but simply a matter of "indenture."[14] In 1776 William Heath, one of Washington's generals, was informed of mass disaffection in his unit. The soldiers told their officers that they were "volunteers," and as such, would "go home in a Body" if not paid and given their traditional clothing allotment. Threatened with the "severest Punishment," many soldiers deserted anyway.[15]

When the government tried to get New England soldiers to reenlist "for the war" in November 1776, the soldiers refused, stating that "such an engagement [was] a contract for perpetual servitude."[16] And when the soldiers perceived that the state was taking undue advantage of their sacrifice, they grew rebellious. Their reaction to violations of their personal rights within the Continental army thus paralleled their officers' quest for political freedom from the British. Anthony Wayne cocked his pistols when a sergeant informed him that his time of enlistment had expired a month earlier and "that [the men] looked upon themselves as at Liberty to go home." The sergeant relented only after Wayne threatened to kill him on the spot.[17] Many soldiers must have seen their officers as more immediate oppressors than the British ever were. Thus as the war ground on and soldiers were denied the basics of their enlistment contracts, they rebelled against those in immediate authority.[18]

In fact, conflicting interpretations of enlistment contracts seemed to be the principal cause of tension between the army command and its soldiers. Washington chose to think that "all the common soldiery of any country can expect is food and clothing."[19] The soldiers, on the other hand, sought to maximize their ability to sell their labor by limiting, in different ways, the terms of their enlistment, the authority of their officers over them, or to establish some sort of social wage to supplement the meager or nonexistent wage paid in money. When Congress increased the terms of enlistment in 1776 and imposed simultaneously a harsher set of Articles of War (to which each man was required to subscribe when he enlisted), many soldiers reacted by walking away from the army.[20] Washington admitted that

> the Mode in which the present Army has been collected, has occasioned some Difficulty in processing the Subscription of both Officers and Soldiers to the Continental Articles of War. Their principal objection has been that it might subject them to a longer Service than that for which they had engaged under their several [previous] Provincial establishments.[21]

Yet the Continental army continued throughout the war as a viable entity. The men who risked their lives to serve expected something for their service.

Washington's model for an effective standing army was essentially British. A newer, harsher set of Articles of War approved by Congress in the fall of 1776 was aimed at creating what Washington termed was "a Respectable Army."[22] His choice of words was significant, for not only was Washington attempting to impose a foreign set of regulations upon the soldiers, but he also aimed to curtail the ability of the soldiers to use their feet to desert or not reenlist, as they had after the first campaign. Washington and others strongly desired an army based on long-termed enlistees kept in line by an ironclad code of discipline. The soldiers of '76, however, observed the new code with jaundiced eyes. They began to repeat a new saying around camp: "New lords, new laws." It was clear to the soldiers that the new laws were directed at them and that the government's officers—the new lords—would enforce them.[23]

It was obvious to Washington and other officers that the original 1775 congressional Articles of War, which allowed only a maximum of thirty-nine lashes, was not harsh enough to keep soldiers from demanding concessions or defending their customary rights. Thus Washington deemed that a revised code was necessary to instill discipline in the ranks. John Adams even went so far as to recommend that the British Articles be copied verbatim. Enacted during the fall of 1776 and corresponding, not coincidentally, with an exploding rate of desertion, Congress increased dramatically the number of capital offenses. Besides changing the maximum number of allowable lashes from thirty-nine to one hundred, the revised section covering desertion stated explicitly that "all officers and soldiers, who having received pay . . . in the service of the United

States, and convicted of having deserted, shall suffer *death*, or such other punishment as by a courts-martial shall be inflicted." Moreover, for those enterprising soldiers who enlisted in two or more units (bounty-jumping), the offender was considered guilty of desertion from his first unit and thus liable for the death penalty even though he was still under American arms in some form.[24]

Why had the government enacted a newer, harsher set of regulations after only one year of war? The answer to this critical question can be found in the abundant source material collected in courts-martial records. The data reveal that the behavior of soldiers, frequently referred to as "criminal activity" by their officers, consisted predominantly of acts of protest and defiance. The majority of crimes listed in various orderly books surveyed were those of desertion, acts of defiance against officers, or plundering civilians. Of the 3,315 courts-martial entries culled from 168 sets of orderly books, more than 80 percent involved desertion or mutiny.[25]

Soldiers reacted to the harsher disciplinary code and reduction of customary provisions in three general ways: they committed "crime," they deserted, or they mutinied. The most threatening or dramatic statement was mutiny. There were, however, smaller, less dangerous steps that soldiers could take to protect their customary rights. Soldiers had plentiful opportunities to engage in situational crimes, whether on the march or in camp. They stole from civilians, officers, and each other.[26]

Soldiers did not necessarily look upon confiscation of goods as theft or robbery. Private Daniel Barber noted that "home and plenty are very different from the close quarters and deprivations to which a soldier is liable. The devil would now and then tell us, it was no harm to pull a few potatoes and cabbages, and pluck, once in a while, an ear of corn, when we stood in need." Private Daniel McCurtin, a soldier from Maryland, wrote in his diary with a touch of sarcasm that the upstanding citizens of Roxbury had "left their houses and given them to the Soldiers for to make Barracks of them for to protect their Rights and Libertys."[27] Thus to soldiers like Barber and McCurtin, theft was more a matter of survival than criminal proclivity.

Soldiers who plundered seemed to suffer little shame, and men who lived by their wits were objects of soldierly admiration. Joseph Plumb Martin, a former laborer from Connecticut, proudly recollected how he looted a citizen's cellar when the army was in New York. General Putnam's threat to hang him for this act did not deter Martin from other pilfering later in his career.[28] Soldiers who stole a farmer's goose joked about how they had captured a "Hissian." Others, such as Private John Smith, noted that "his Brother Soldiers" took what they could. Sergeant William Young observed that soldiers "cannot let anything Lay that comes in their way."[29] A Continental sergeant remarked that enlisted men and even some officers robbed homes around New York so frequently that it became commonplace. When an ensign named McCumber was ordered to desist from plundering, he replied that "he had a Right to take anything out side [Continental] lines." Soldiers, embittered over what they saw as shoddy treatment from officers and others in authority, saw nothing wrong in eating ill-gotten geese or "teaking [*sic*] what Came . . . to their hand. . . . by the whole Division of free Booters."[30] As "Free Booters" they tried to take advantage of any opportunity to supplement themselves "as every good soldier should."[31]

What did the soldiers' "crime" mean? Were they mere opportunists, awaiting their chance to walk away with their bounty money, to steal food and supplies for personal gain? Or were they expressing something else? The kinds and degrees of resistance practiced by the soldiers were connected to the kinds and degrees of repression and violence they suffered at the hands of their officers.

One of the most time-honored ways to avoid officer repression or to express dissatisfaction was for soldiers to desert at the earliest opportunity. The orderly books surveyed listed only nineteen desertion courts-martial convictions in 1775. By 1776, however, and coinciding with the imposition of the new Articles of War, desertion convictions had increased more than 700 percent (142 cases). Despite the harsher repression, the 1777 rate dropped only 40 percent below that of 1776 but still remained 400 percent higher than the 1775 court levels. But by 1779 the desertion courts-martial rate (109 cases) had once again reached the 1776 rate. By 1781, the number of courts-martial for desertion reached its highest point (157 cases). The rate was 9 percent higher than the rate of 1776 and more than 800 percent higher than the number of cases brought to trial in 1775.[32] Despite the increase in desertion convictions, the men still used their feet to express their disapproval of army life.

Not only was desertion a popular form of protest or escape for soldiers, but it was also sometimes condoned by the general populace as well. The British and loyalists were obviously interested in causing the rebel army to desert. But there were others, especially relatives or employers of deserting soldiers, who sheltered them. In "many instances," observed

Washington, "Deserters which have been apprehended by Officers, have been rescued by the People."[33] States offered rewards for the arrest of deserters or information leading to their incarceration. Civilians were threatened with flogging if they provided deserters protection or hid them from searching officers. None of these measures proved effective. Washington admitted that the country was "spread over with Soldiers, notwithstanding the pointed orders which have been issued."[34]

Desertion had always been the bane of eighteenth-century armies. It was one of the few recourses available to soldiers who felt oppressed by their situation. Even eight members of Washington's own "Life Guard," a group of hand-picked native-born soldiers, deserted during the course of the war.[35] Moreover, desertion was a contested term for many American soldiers. Around the camp at Cambridge in 1775, men strolled about the marshes and outlying villages looking for food to supplement their meager rations. At Charleston, both officers and men assumed that they had the right to leave the camp at will. Charles Lee noted that soldiers who were camped outside Williamsburg, Virginia, went in and out of town "without the least ceremony." After repeated attempts to curtail the soldiers' ability to move about freely, Washington still found stragglers far from camp "on a variety of frivolous pretenses and without passes." He called such practices "subversive of all discipline."[36] The soldiers called it survival. Their concept of what actually constituted desertion was much narrower than that of the generals.

Not only was the soldiers' definition of desertion much narrower, but some men deserted only to reappear in some other unit under a new name. Some men made it a lucrative practice to bounty jump (enlisting several times in different units and collecting the bounty). Washington once referred to this system as "a kind of business" among the soldiers. The soldier merely had to enlist under an assumed name, collect his bounty, desert, and reenlist in a different unit under a different name. The trick, of course, was to avoid being recognized by the officers as a bounty-jumper. John Welch of the New Jersey line enlisted in April 1777, deserted the following month, reenlisted in August, and deserted again the following year. In January 1779 he enlisted for his final time and was never caught by the authorities. One soldier, executed in 1778, was convicted of having enlisted seven separate times.[37]

Desertion took up much of Washington's and other officers' time. The exact level of desertion, however, is difficult to ascertain, because muster rolls were grossly inaccurate and brigade adjutants rarely reported all those who had walked away from the army.[38] Using three essential sources of data—the official muster returns of the army, the state muster rolls, and the muster reports of a selected group of units picked at random—it has been estimated that the rate of overall desertion in the Continental army was around 20 percent, though it varied greatly from unit to unit.[39] A Tory estimated that between 27 September 1777 and 26 March 1778, 1,134 men deserted the Continental army for British-occupied Philadelphia. He noted that the largest group of the deserters were former British soldiers who had temporarily fought for the Americans.[40]

Specifically, 50 percent of all runaways from the New York, Maryland, and North Carolina lines occurred within the first six months of enlistment. The desertion rates of the New Jersey line fell off sharply after men who were most apt to desert had left the army. In 1777 the New Jersey troops had a 42 percent rate of desertion. In 1778, the rate fell to 21 percent. After 1778, the line averaged about a 10 percent desertion rate.[41] New York's muster rolls indicated that one-third of all privates deserted. In one regiment, more than a fourth of the officers and nearly one-half of the privates deserted.[42] Twenty (47 percent) of Captain Alexander Johnston's company in the Fifth Pennsylvania Regiment deserted within the first four months of enlistment.[43] The harshness of army life, coupled with the soldiers' desire to use their bounty money, probably accounted for much of this early desertion.

Not only was desertion a frequent resort, but the expansive colonial frontier provided an ideal sanctuary for deserting soldiers to avoid the army. Washington noted that "the Grants," the mountainous area between New Hampshire and Vermont, had become "an asylum to all deserters; [and] to every person who wishes to avoid taxation"; moreover, the population growth of the Grants corresponded with the increased desertion rate of the Continental army. Writing at the end of the war, Washington described the situation in the Grants as a territory "populated by hundreds of Deserters from this Army; who . . . would be desperate in the defense of it, well knowing they are fighting with Halters about their NECKS."[44] Washington decided against recovering deserters, because he thought his own soldiers were unwilling "to imbue their hands in the blood of their Brethren."[45] After considering the consequences of forcing soldiers to subdue other soldiers, Washington rethought his impulse to attack the men living in the Grants.

Jails near the North Carolina frontier overflowed with apprehended deserters. Joseph Reed wrote Washington that Pennsylvania would not have had a severe desertion problem "if the Land-Office in Virginia had not afforded both an asylum and a temptation for desertion." Reed also noted that in Kentucky and other surrounding hinterlands, many deserters lived without fear of military service or taxation, enjoying "a sort of savage freedom." Pennsylvania officers argued against a bill that sold western lands to raise money for the war, not only because that land had been promised to them after the conflict, but because "a new Settlement invariably proves to be a Secure assylum [*sic*] for Deserters from every Quarter."[46]

One soldier named Joseph Parker ended up in New Hampshire after he served in both British and American armies. Parker was one of many American soldiers who opted for service in the British army rather than hazard a prisoner camp renowned for its lethality. As soon as the British outfitted him with a new suit of clothes and a weapon, he and a few "old countrymen" (meaning those born in the British Isles) decided to desert. Caught between two competing systems of military justice, Parker decided that New Hampshire was the best place to avoid a hanging by either side.[47] Continental deserters gravitated toward any frontier where governmental control was weak or nonexistent. David Cobb was informed by a loyal member of his regiment that "numbers of deserters" had gone into the Coos Country, the northern New England backcountry, "to settle some wild lands" and could not be induced to return by any means.[48]

Some soldiers may have chosen desertion over remaining with the army because of the intrinsic brutality of army camp life. Soldiers in the eighteenth century certainly experienced terror and cruelty daily. The lashings, canings, and summary beatings by officers were common occurrences. Officers strove to coerce their men into submission by violence and used the implied threat of a beating to keep soldiers from resisting their will, often without recourse to a formal courts-martial. Punishment was so frequently administered in the Continental army that even European volunteers noticed this practice. In the belief that such demonstrations deterred others from committing offenses, soldiers were required by their officers to witness punishments being meted out to their comrades and observe that one hundred lashes could turn a man's back into "jelly." "Kissing the Adjutant's Daughter" was a sentence sardonically given by officers to soldiers and held no prospect of campfire romance for the enlisted men. Usually the soldier was tied to a triangle frame specially designed for punishments and was lashed by the company drummer, who was, in turn, supervised by the unit drum major, who ensured that the lashes were "well laid on."[49]

Punishment or the threat of punishment was used by Washington and his officers as a means to keep soldiers within the confines of camp and thereby lessen their ability to desert or forage for food from the local inhabitants. He stated that any soldier caught straggling beyond the chain of camp sentinels after retreat (the end of the military day) would receive "100 lashes on the spot," which meant punishment without benefit of trial by court-martial. Any soldiers caught in the act of "perpetrating robberies" would receive "from 100 to 500 lashes at the discretion of the officer."[50] One hundred lashes were the maximum number authorized by the Articles of War, yet that did not seem to stop Washington from giving his officers authority to exceed that limit. Like sailors forced to serve a tyrannical captain, soldiers serving in the army were liable to be lashed, maimed, or beaten on the slightest pretext and had little protection against the capriciousness of the Continental army's military justice system.

The notoriously harsh punishments meted out in Continental army camps also deterred further enlistment. General David Cobb noted that men refused to enlist because of the stories told by returning veterans and deserters of the severity of Continental officers. "This is a prejudice that must be combatted with all force of art and Intrigue," cautioned Cobb, "for I conceive that this will have the most fatal tendency to the opposition of this Country, of anything that has happened during the contest."[51]

The soldiers, however, always seemed to find ways to lessen the ability of officers to inflict punishment. Sometimes soldiers were sentenced to "run the gauntlet with a bayonet at their breast," which meant that a soldier would have to walk through a double line of his comrades who were required to beat the man with sticks or fists. The "bayonet at his breast" made progress through the line more difficult. It also allowed officers to notice which soldiers chose not to inflict punishment upon their own comrades. The soldiers, however, sometimes faked the delivery of hard blows upon their comrades. Drummers usually performed the additional duty of wielding the lash during punishments. If a drummer became too enthusiastic about these duties, other soldiers might corner him "in a bye place" and force him to rethink the way he delivered lashes. Other soldiers literally "bit the bullet," placing a leaden cartridge between their teeth and biting it while the punishment was administered.

After one hanging in Pennsylvania, rioting soldiers severely beat the executioner and heroically hailed a soldier who had refused the task.[52]

Soldiers found yet other ways to contest the authority of officers. From the earliest days of the war, hats had served as a way to express one's patriotism. The "liberty cap" and the cockade were signs of loyalty to the United States and enmity for the British. Officers, however, tried to make hats into markers of discipline. Anthony Wayne ordered his officers to "compel the men to wear their Hatts in one way; in the most soldier like position."[53] To the officers, requiring soldiers to dress and act in accordance with their wishes not only reinforced a sense of discipline but also reminded the enlisted men of their lack of control over even such insignificant things as how a hat was worn or hair was cut. The privates, however, resisted and instead wore their hats without bindings and with the brims down. In 1779 hats even caused a mutiny among the sergeants in the Second Rhode Island Regiment. Rather than wear their hats as dictated by their officers, they ripped the bindings from them and delivered a "mutinous paper" to their commanding officer, Colonel Israel Angell.[54] Officers were never entirely successful at getting their men to wear their headgear in a standardized way.

Another way soldiers asserted their independence was to make their officers the butt of a practical joke. Joseph Plumb Martin, for one, always enjoyed a joke at the expense of his officers. During the month of January 1779, the officers ordered soldiers to cease firing their muskets while in camp. This made good military sense but did nothing to relieve the tedium of soldiers who were generally confined to their huts. Martin noted that "nothing could raise the officers' lofty ideas sooner, or more, than to fire [their muskets] in camp." So, "to make void [this particular] law," and to demonstrate their resistance to it, Martin and some of his friends decided to set up a loaded musket in an empty tent and attach a rope to its trigger. Pulling on the rope made the musket discharge and caused no small amount of pandemonium on the part of the officers who tore around the camp swearing and vowing vengeance on the perpetrators of the prank. Martin and his brother soldiers repeated their prank for much of the night, setting up the musket in different places within the camp. "But at length," he lamented, "the officers [got tired] of trying to catch Mr. Nobody." After this small prank with a larger message, Martin noted that "we fared a little better for a few days after this memento to the officers."[55] Small acts of defiance occasionally masked larger feelings of resentment.

Sometimes the men resorted to rougher forms of defiance. One soldier who observed the passage of a quartermaster (an officer responsible for supplying the army) through a row of soldiers' huts tied straw to the tail of the officer's horse and set it on fire. Another soldier, Private Dennis Kennedy, "threatened to desert as soon as he got shoes"; he was busy "cursing Congress" at the same time. Joseph Plumb Martin remembered a "gunpowder plot" devised by some of the men of his company. The leader of the "plot" informed Martin that they intended "to have some fun with the old man," their company commander. Loading a wooden canteen with three and a half pounds of gunpowder, they told Martin that they thought the blast would give their less than favorite officer "a hoist." Martin thought that the blast would probably kill the captain and quickly talked the men out of it. Not to be entirely thwarted, the men tried to scare the officer with a booby-trapped musket. Martin believed he had saved the man's life but added that "the men hated [their commander] and did not much care what happened to him."[56]

When officers were thwarted by the soldiers, they quickly used disciplinary repression to reassert their authority. Nathanael Greene, for instance, thought that hanging a soldier now and then served to terrorize the men into submission. He also thought that doing so without giving the condemned man the benefit of a court-martial was even more effective. He related to Washington that when officers tried to question some soldiers about a self-authorized foraging expedition, the men "threatened the officers if they offered to interfere."[57] The soldiers recognized that by collectively threatening their officers, they stood a greater chance of getting away with their foraging without being punished. It also served as a warning to the officers of the limits of their authority.

Court-martial records revealed how officers intensified discipline as the war progressed. The average sentence for desertion in 1775 was thirty-nine lashes, well below what most eighteenth-century armies meted out. British soldiers sometimes got five hundred or even a thousand lashes for similar offenses.[58] Of nineteen Continental army desertions recorded in 1775 orderly book data, the thirty-nine-lash penalty was given 53 percent of the time (10 of 19 cases). No one was sentenced to death for this offense. Even soldiers convicted of mutiny were accorded relatively mild treatment. One soldier who encouraged his comrades to desert and "spoke badly of America" received thirty-nine lashes and was forced out of camp with a placard labeled with the word "Tory" tied around his neck. Another convicted of "abusing his officers" was forced to wear a five-pound log around his neck for two days. Fines were not infrequent and were levied in conjunction with the lash.[59]

After the passage of the harsher 1776 Articles of War, the lash, firing squads, and gibbet were used with greater frequency. Fifteen soldiers had been fined for offenses in 1775. But by 1776 this method of punishment had all but disappeared. More than three times as many cases were heard in 1776, but there were less than half as many monetary penalties. The standard 1776 penalty for desertion was one hundred lashes unless the individual had actually gone over to the British, in which case the sentence was usually death.[60]

During 1776 the records listed nineteen men who were condemned to die. Sixteen of these (84 percent) were charged with desertion, the others with mutiny, plundering, and robbery. Two soldiers were offered pardons in exchange for enlistment for the duration of the war.[61] More than a few men received "gallows pardons" moments before they were to be hanged, to take maximum advantage of the terror such sentences evoked. In *Morale of the American Revolutionary Army*, Allen Bowman found 225 sentences of death, 40 of which were actually carried out. Suspensions of sentences were common. Those forced to continue to serve under a sentence of death lived in terror of the day when the camp guard would burst into their hut and haul them off to the gallows. If they deserted and were caught while under a sentence of death, the chances of a second reprieve were minuscule. Sergeant John Porterfield of the Third Pennsylvania Regiment was convicted of desertion and sentenced to be shot. Washington approved his sentence but granted him a reprieve of one week. Afterwards, his sentence was put off twice more until he was released back to his unit, still under the sentence of death.[62]

In 1780 Dr. James Thacher observed the theatrical drama of eleven men sentenced to die. General Orders had recently announced that "Criminals now under the sentence of death are to be executed tomorrow morning."[63] The camp color men (soldiers assigned to keep the camp in sanitary condition) were instructed to begin digging the graves of the condemned immediately. Ten of the eleven men had been convicted of desertion. On the following day, 26 May 1780, the eleven were brought to the place of execution in carts. Eight of the eleven were to be hanged, the other three shot, but not before they had observed the deaths of the first eight. Those to be hanged were placed on ladders with halters around their necks. A Continental army chaplain, noted Thacher, addressed the condemned "in a very pathetic manner," but loudly so that all those assembled could hear. "At this awful moment," recorded the doctor, "while their fervent prayers [were] ascending to Heaven, an officer comes forward and reads a reprieve for seven of them, by the Commander in Chief" as well as for the other three waiting to be shot by already-selected firing squads. Washington purposely refused to reprieve one soldier as an added twist of terror in this macabre theater.[64]

The staged scene was very emotional. Thacher noted that after they received their pardons, "the trembling criminals . . . were scarcely able to remove from the scaffold without assistance. The chaplain reminded them of the gratitude they owed the Commander in Chief . . . and that the only return in their power to make, was a life devoted to the faithful discharge of their duty."[65] It is impossible to tell if the individual soldiers remained grateful in the aftermath of such an experience. But it is clear that such "mercies" did not deter desertion, for more people were court-martialed for this offense in 1780–81 than in any other year.

Inconsistent punishments added to the terror of a court-martial. Two soldiers of the Fifth Pennsylvania Regiment, James Hammell and Samuel Crawford, were sentenced to death for suspected robbery. Crawford was pardoned, but Hammell was executed. Two other artillerymen were convicted of theft. One of the two, Jesse Peck, received fifteen lashes, but his comrade Rubin Parker got one hundred lashes for the same crime.[66] Like players in a deadly game of roulette, soldiers found themselves at the mercy of capricious justice. In one bizarre instance, three captured deserters were sentenced to death and forced to draw lots to see which one was to be executed. After hanging, the head of the condemned was severed from his body and placed on a pole in camp for all to see.[67] Mutilation of the body had always been reserved for the most feared colonial crimes: slave insurrections, mutinies, and piracy. The list was peremptorily expanded by Henry Lee to include army desertion as well.[68]

The number of soldiers condemned to die increased steadily as the war progressed. By 1778 the rate of capital punishment had risen 17 percent (23 cases listed) over the 1776 rate. Again, desertion was the principal offense (21 of 23 courts) that generated the death penalty. In 1779 the number of overall capital cases rose to twenty-nine (33 percent over the 1776 rate). Six soldiers (20 percent of the total) were sentenced to be executed due to the crime of mutiny. The overall capital punishment figures for 1780 were down slightly (25 cases), although the number of cases in which soldiers had been charged with mutiny or attacks on their officers or Sergeants had risen from six to fifteen. The year 1781 was the most lethal for soldiers convicted of desertion. Thirty-six men were sentenced to die (48 percent above the 1776 rate), though some of these men had their sentences commuted if they enlisted for the duration of the war. Again, the majority of the 1781 cases (83 percent) were related to desertion. By 1782, capital convictions tapered off (22 cases) but remained above the 1776 rate.[69]

These figures, important as they are, understate the number of executions, for not all soldiers sentenced to die received the benefit of a trial by court-martial. Colonel Israel Angell of Rhode Island noted the case of a Pennsylvania soldier caught in the act of plundering who "was hanged by orders of his Commanding Officer without a trial." Anthony Wayne, Nathanael Greene, and Henry Lee were apt to execute soldiers without the benefit of trial and usually as a terroristic example to others who might contemplate insubordination or mutiny. Not only did the use of the death penalty increase as the war progressed, but the use of the lash increased as well. One man was given fifty lashes for merely cutting up his blanket. Another, convicted of desertion, was sentenced to receive one hundred lashes and to serve on a "Continental Man of War." More than 81 of the 117 men (69 percent) convicted of desertion in 1782 were given sentences of one hundred lashes or more.[70] Soldiers sometimes got more than one hundred lashes if convicted of multiple offenses, such as desertion and insubordination, continual desertion, or mutiny and striking an officer. Washington admitted that because there were "no gradations of intermediate punishment" between one hundred lashes and death, courts-martial felt "bound in duty to decree the greater penalty . . . death." He suggested that he be "officially" allowed to impose five hundred lashes on soldiers rather than sentence them directly to suffer the death penalty. In this way he avoided the ire of soldiers who were forced to witness their comrades being gunned down by firing squads and appeared, ostensibly, more lenient. But as most soldiers were quite aware, five hundred lashes could be just as fatal as six bullets to the body, and a great deal slower and more painful in the end. Washington chose to allow a board of General Officers to consider the problem of punishments. They unanimously decided that severe, hard labor be recommended to Congress as an appropriate intermediate penalty. Toward the end of the war at least a dozen soldiers had their death sentences commuted by agreeing to serve aboard a Continental frigate or enlist for the duration of the war.[71]

Rather than desert or commit insubordinate acts and possibly become an impressed sailor aboard a Continental frigate for the duration of the war, some soldiers chose to protest collectively or mutiny over grievances. Organized mutinies within the Continental army had occurred before, the first in a company of William Thompson's Pennsylvania riflemen who mutinied at Cambridge in late 1775. Washington and Nathanael Greene merely had the headquarters guard surround the mutineers to compel their submission. "The Rifflers," noted Greene, "seems very sulky . . . but little is feared from them as the Regiment are all ready at a moments warning to turn out, and the Guards very Strong."[72] Officers who were not concerned about an aroused soldiery, as we shall see, quickly changed their opinions as the war deepened and mutinies grew more ominous.

By midwar, mutiny, actual or merely threatened, quickly became commonplace in the Continental army. Counting the mutinies of Thompson's riflemen and John Smith's company that were already mentioned, there were at least three recorded mutinies involving substantial numbers of men during the first campaign of the war (1775–76). When Benedict Arnold tried to forbid Ethan Allen's Green Mountain Boys from plundering the British after the capture of Fort Ticonderoga, he reported that he was insulted by Allen and "Often Threatened with my Life & twice Shot at by his Men with their Fuses." When Arnold informed Allen that he intended to take command over his men, the troops paraded and "declared they would go right home, for they would not be commanded by Arnold." Only after they were assured that Allen would remain their commander "were the men pacified."[73] The men continued to divide up the spoils, which "was most rigidly perform'd as to liquors, provisions, &c whether belonging to his majesty or private property."[74]

With the exception of the sergeant who confronted Anthony Wayne in 1777, there were no significant, large-scale mutinies during the campaigns of 1777–78. There were, however, at least twelve individual cases of mutiny or acts of defiance against officers. By 1779 soldiers began to "combine" their feelings of resentment over repression and to express their discontent collectively. Counting the aforementioned "hat mutiny" of the Rhode Island line, four major mutinies took place that year. Private Joseph Plumb Martin mentioned in his journal an uprising in the Connecticut line, in which the soldiers decided to "try once more to raise some provisions, if not, at least to raise a little dust." "After we had organized ourselves and regulated the plan for our future operations," stated Martin, an officer got wind of the mutiny as the men milled about and nipped the rebellion before it got underway.[75] That same year (1779), Sergeant Samuel Glover was executed for leading a mutiny in the North Carolina line in which he, on behalf of "His Brother soldiers"—unpaid for fifteen months—"demanded their pay and refused to obey the Command of his superior Officer, and would not march till they had justice done them."[76] Officers regained control as Glover suffered the death penalty for his actions in the affair.

One of the most ominous uprisings occurred in October 1779, when a group of militiamen marched into Philadelphia. The soldiers quickly surrounded the home of James Wilson, an inveterate opponent of price controls and an enemy among enlisted men and associators who depended on fixed wages for a living. Fighting broke out after someone fired a shot from the house and the militia responded, producing, in the words of Henry Laurens, "a very bloody scene in the streets" of Philadelphia. Only after the arrival of the "silk stocking brigade," a group of upper-class Philadelphians, was order restored.[77] Two days after the "riot," Benedict Arnold was accosted by a "mob of Lawless Ruffians" who "Attack'd [him] in the Streets and threatened [his] life," eventually driving him into his home in a replay of what had occurred two days earlier at James Wilson's residence. Arnold had recently submitted an expense account for nine months which many in Congress and in the city considered extravagant. Arnold's popular antagonists may have played a role in his decision later to betray the American cause. It may not be coincidental that American soldiers resented him well before he decided to change sides.[78]

In 1780 three more major revolts broke out in the lines of Massachusetts, Connecticut, and New York.[79] These mutinies terrified the officers, not only because they were better organized than those that came before, but also because they involved ever larger numbers of disaffected troops.

Mutinies were growing larger and more organized, and soldiers now expressed a willingness to seize by force those things traditionally due them or deemed necessary for survival. On New Years Day 1780, one hundred Massachusetts soldiers decided that their three-year enlistments had expired, and, in a collective body, they marched off for home. The mutineers, however, were recaptured; their leaders were punished and the rest pardoned. On 20 May 1780, thirty-one members of the New York line, whose soldiers had not been paid for nine months and "were destitute of Shoes, Stockings, and Shirts," deserted en masse from their regiment. When other soldiers who remained with the regiment refused to pursue the deserters, Lieutenant Colonel Van Dyck employed a party of Oneida Indians to go in search of them. The Indians trapped a small group of fifteen deserters as they tried to cross a stream. A firefight ensued in which thirteen of the fifteen were killed—a highly lethal engagement for the eighteenth century. The surviving soldiers got the point. Five days later, two Connecticut regiments decided to march in a body in search of something to eat. The ubiquitous soldier, Joseph Plumb Martin, was part of the group. After "growling like sore headed dogs," Martin stated, the men intended to march for home and wanted to "tear their Commissary [the officer responsible for providing the unit's food rations] to atoms." He related that, if necessary, the men were willing to "plunder for their sustenance on their way." Appeals by officers and a show of force by loyal Pennsylvania troops quelled the mutiny before it got fully underway but not before the commanding officer, Colonel Return Meigs, was severely injured in a scuffle with the men. Martin recorded that Colonel Meigs was run through the side with a bayonet "which cooled his courage at the time. He always considered himself the soldier's friend and thought the soldiers regarded him as such, but now had reason to conclude he might be mistaken." According to Martin, the "loyal" Pennsylvania troops were not informed that they were surrounding mutineers. After an inquiry about the commotion in the Connecticut camp, he noted that the Pennsylvanians wanted "to join them." Their officers quickly ordered them back to their own camp before they did. Nathanael Greene later wrote that he was fearful that the unrest demonstrated by the Connecticut troops "will run through the whole line like wild fire."[80]

By 1781, revolts around New Year's Day had become so commonplace in the Continental army that Anthony Wayne remarked, in a literary reference to Shakespeare's *Julius Caesar*, that he "sincerely wished the Ides of January was come & past."[81] Wayne's sense of foreboding was correct. Early January was always a tense time because most soldiers had been recruited to serve for a number of calendar years, usually ending on the last day of December. New Year's Day of 1781 proved no different: the enlistments of most of the Pennsylvania and New Jersey lines were due that day, at least according to the soldiers' accounts. In the famous mutiny of the Pennsylvania line on the evening of 1 January 1781, as many as fifteen hundred men (two entire brigades) participated actively in the revolt, with another five hundred playing a lesser role or being merely swept along by events. This mutiny was the largest and best-organized of the war. Sergeants chosen by acclamation of the men kept the soldiers cheering and firing their weapons into the air to frighten officers away from the camp. These leaders signed all correspondence "in conjunction" with each other to keep from being singled out and isolated by officers. Two regiments (the Ninth and Fifth) initially attempted to stay neutral, but the sergeants threatened them with artillery pieces "if they did not move off."[82] The mutineers literally filled the road to Philadelphia. The sergeants wanted to induce as many soldiers of the line as possible to participate in the mutiny so that officers could not divide the men against themselves.[83] Maintaining discipline on their march, the sergeants made it clear that they no longer acknowledged the authority of their officers. Those officers who had been especially obnoxious to the men had been chased away from camp by musket fire.[84]

Colonel Israel Shreve, the commander of the New Jersey Brigade, was ordered to intercept the Pennsylvanians. Shreve, however, could do little. Informed by one of his officers that "the cause of the Pennsylvanians is . . . too much considered the common cause" and that "some men in [his own] first regiment have been trying to foment an insurrection," Shreve concluded that he "could not have formed a Captain's guard" to march against the Pennsylvanians. He wrote Washington that the Jersey troops were "mortified and disgusted" about their own situation and could not be compelled to attack the Pennsylvanians.[85]

The Pennsylvanians demanded to be discharged and be "paid without fraud." Further, they wanted "no aspersions cast against them for participating in the mutiny" after their demands were met.[86] One group of sergeants mentioned to Wayne that "it was hurtful to the feelings of the soldiers to be prevented from disposing of their depreciation certificates as they please without consulting any person on the occasion."[87] The officers did not want the soldiers to get their back pay for a variety of reasons. Knowing the restlessness of the troops over their situation in the army, the officers feared that soldiers with money might find ways to buy their way out of service.

The crux of the mutineers' complaint was their enlistment contracts. The records indicated that they had enlisted earlier in the conflict "for three years or during the war." In turn, they had been given the standard Continental bounty of twenty dollars. The enlisted men took the phrase to mean that they would serve three years or less if the war ended sooner. Washington took the opposite view and interpreted the words to mean that three years was the minimum served and that they should continue in service if the war went on beyond that time. To compound their complaint, older soldiers saw new enlistees getting upward of two hundred dollars or more for enlisting on exactly the same terms that they did in 1776 when they received only a twenty-dollar bounty.[88] The soldiers appeared to have a point since it made little sense to specify a time limit for enlistment if they were to serve until the war ended.

Fortunately for the mutineers, Washington's army was thinned out, spread from Philadelphia to West Point, and the few remaining loyal regiments were situated well to the north of Morristown. Further, the sergeants had the foresight to move their camp to Princeton, a place equidistant between Congress at Philadelphia and British outposts in northern New Jersey. Fears that mutineers would defect to the other side quickly dissipated when the sergeants turned over two emissaries from the British to Anthony Wayne as a token of their true intentions. The Pennsylvania militia failed to turn out against the army, and merchants refused to comply with an order to supply the mutineers with their "Engagements"—that is, what the soldiers thought was due them in food and clothing. Joseph Reed, president of Pennsylvania, rode out to their camp and negotiated a settlement. He concluded that the entire affair was "a sore trial. . . . The men certainly had not those attachments which the officers supposed." Whereas he noted that "the mutineers are in all cases to be condemned," Reed admitted that "there are sometimes, in armies, just causes of discontent. The people of this State [Pennsylvania] are in universal sentiment with the men."[89] Remembering perhaps the sentiment of the city of Philadelphia during the "Fort Wilson" riot, when the militia, once again, had refused to turn out, Reed and others concluded that the people of the state identified with the plight of the soldiers.

The soldiers who claimed to have enlisted "for three years or the duration of the war" were allowed to testify before a commission. Reed observed that "many soldiers had [previously] been attested [enlisted] by their officers and others with so little formality, as to open a door to innumerable complaints both on that score, and the payment of the bounty."[90] As a result, most of the line claimed a right to a discharge. When officers attempted to present enlistment records to the commission, they were "forcibly prevented from producing them" by the soldiers, who feared that officers offended or injured during the mutiny would present fraudulent enlistment certificates. Many soldiers in Colonel Thomas Craig's regiment were deemed by the commission to have enlisted specifically "for the war," and therefore were not entitled to discharges. Soldiers began spontaneously to riot, swarming down to the Trenton wharf, where they had originally agreed to store their arms, breaking into the ship, reclaiming their firelocks, and threatening the life of Colonel Craig and any other officer who tried to halt their progress. Anthony Wayne later wrote Washington that he "wished the commissioners had given time for the officers to produce the Attestations before they made [the admission of a soldier's] oath so common," by which he meant that he wished the officers had time to counteract the commission's intention to take the soldiers at their word. Wayne noted that the papers signed by the soldiers were "for the War—but the birds [have] flown," meaning the soldiers had already been discharged.[91]

More than thirteen hundred privates were dismissed from further service, but Wayne hoped to reenlist two-thirds of them after a short furlough, noting that "the Soldiery are as Impatient of liberty as they were of Service."[92] Wayne meant that the soldiers were having difficulty finding jobs in the civilian sector. The mutiny thus ended with the virtual disbanding of a significant portion of the Pennsylvania line. Many of these soldiers ended up in Philadelphia, where they besieged the Board of War "in a hostile manner, and could not be satisfied, 'till they were assured that their Officers were in no better situation with respect to pay than themselves."[93] The soldiers had won but Washington vowed never to let it happen again.[94]

The Pennsylvania mutiny, the largest and most unusual internal upheaval in the history of American arms, was in large part recognized as such in its day, and subsequently by later historians. Jonathan Sullivan noted to George Washington that "the whole progress of this affair except the first Tumult has been conducted on their part [meaning the mutineers] with a consistency, firmness, and a degree of Policy mixed with candor that must astonish every theorist on the nature of the American Soldiery."[95] Not often noted by historians, however, were the numerous "post-mutinies" that occurred following the discharge of the Pennsylvanians. Like the aftershocks of a cataclysmic earthquake, unrest rippled through the Continental ranks until the very end of the war. More than a few of the "old mutineers" appeared as leaders of these "post-mutinies."

The unrest was not confined only to Washington's troops. Philip Schuyler informed Alexander Hamilton on 25 January 1781 that two regiments of the northern army threatened to "march to Headquarters unless some money is paid them, the certificates expedited, and in future better supplied with provisions." Five days before the revolt of the northern regiments, the New Jersey line had risen in mutiny as well, in apparent expectation of receiving the same bargain as had their brother soldiers from Pennsylvania. One New Jersey officer noted that "the Pennsylvanians previous to their Revolt had kept up a correspondence with our Line." Several sergeants shouted for the Jersey soldiers "to turn out and fight for your Rights. Let us follow the glorious example of the Pennsylvanians! Let us go to Congress who have money and rum enough but won't give it to us."[96] The Jerseymen had a real grievance. At the height of the Pennsylvania mutiny, General Arthur St. Clair observed that some of the Jersey troops had been kept from joining the revolt only after their commanding officer, Lieutenant Colonel Francis Barber, informed them that they would get whatever terms were offered the Pennsylvanians.[97]

Realizing that their officers were determined not to grant them discharges immediately, and placated by a promise that a state commission would judge their claim to release from service, the Jersey mutineers gave "three unanimous cheers." Thinking they had won, most of the soldiers returned to their huts and, with the exception of some troops at Pompton, accepted a general pardon offered by their commanding officer, Colonel Elias Dayton. The incident would have ended then and there except that Washington was determined to make a show of force and execute some soldiers despite the pardon. Washington saw the Jersey mutiny as "an opportunity" to reestablish his control over the soldiery.[98] The soldiers at Pompton were his targets.

Washington formed a force of five hundred New England troops under the command of Major General Robert Howe, whom he commanded to obtain an "unconditional submission" from the Jersey mutineers and "instantly [to] execute a few of the most active and incendiary leaders."[99] Howe carried out his instructions with a zeal seldom seen in the Continental army. Surrounding their camp in a predawn surprise attack, Howe's troops forced the groggy Jersey troops to point out the ringleaders of the revolt. In a step of "calculated brutality," Howe swiftly ordered the execution of two sergeants, the order carried out at the hands of their own men. He later wrote Washington that he thought that the executions "completely subdued" the spirit of mutiny and had "given place to a genuine repentance."[100]

Howe may have exaggerated; it was doubtful that the Jerseymen were contrite. Dr. James Thacher, a surgeon with the New England troops, noticed that the first six men detailed to execute one of the ringleaders missed their intended target, though he was kneeling in the snow only a few paces away. A second squad had to be used to kill both men. Lieutenant Colonel Barber reported to Howe that although he thought the spirit of mutiny had been destroyed, he was still "apprehensive of bad consequences should [the British] make any Progress in the State." A month after the end of the mutiny, a New England unit composed of the same troops who had assisted Howe in crushing the revolt at Pompton passed through Princeton and was promptly attacked by disgruntled New Jersey soldiers who remembered the unit's role in the suppression.[101]

The aftershocks of the January mutinies continued. In the spring of 1781, Anthony Wayne was ordered to march the Pennsylvania line south to join Lafayette in Virginia. Wayne experienced problems, however, in assembling his troops. The Pennsylvania legislature had not paid off the soldiers as they had promised to do back in January, and some did not think the men would march until they were given their clothing and pay.[102] Finally, after much cajoling by Joseph Reed and the Pennsylvania Convention, Wayne was able to get about one thousand men to march. But he got only as far as York, Pennsylvania, before trouble broke out once again. Wayne immediately attempted to impose harsh discipline upon the men, perhaps in memory of his recent humiliation at the hands of the mutineers during the January mutiny. Wayne arrested a soldier named John Fortesque for "mutinous behavior" and sentenced him to death. The soldiers saw through Wayne's terroristic ploy and, in a show of solidarity, began to defy their officers. One officer ordered the arrest of a soldier who cried, "God damn the officers, the buggers."[103] Wayne stepped up the arrests of soldiers for the slightest infractions.

One of the men Wayne had arrested was named "Macaroney Jack," who, according to witnesses, had been very active in the January mutiny. The officers, not surprisingly, wanted to make an example of him. They ordered him whipped "for a trivial offense" to reduce his stature with the men. Jack, however, did not accept his fate: "When he was tied up he looked around and addressed the soldiers, exclaiming at the same time: Dear brother soldiers, won't you help me!" The officers screamed "Take him down, take him down," for they saw an opportunity to charge him with the more deadly crime of mutiny. Macaroney Jack was handcuffed and ordered back to the guardhouse and confined with others whom the officers had locked up for "mutinous conduct."[104]

Without informing the men who had been detailed to act as executioners, Anthony Wayne had the Pennsylvania troops drawn up to witness the deaths of Macaroney Jack and several others convicted of mutiny.

"Whispered among the soldiers," however, was a plan to rescue their comrades, but it was not, apparently, put in place in time to prevent the executions. Macaroney Jack was the first to fall, followed by a soldier named Smith who had his head hideously blasted to bits by a volley of musket fire; the firing squads stood less than ten feet from their victims, so close that the handkerchiefs covering the mutineers' eyes caught fire. The fence and a field of rye that stood behind the place of execution were "covered over with blood and brains." Just prior to his execution, Macaroney Jack's wife attempted to run into the line to embrace her husband for the last time but an officer viciously "felled her to the ground with his sword, he having struck her with the side of it."[105]

Fifer Samuel Dewees remembered that soon after the executions, whenever he chanced to meet an officer, he would "avoid coming in contact with him . . . lest they might construe my conduct in some way or other into an offense. All disposition of mutiny was entirely put down by these steps of cruelty."[106] Soldiers talking to one another could be accused of "murmuring" by their officers. Others who did not move fast enough when ordered could be charged with exhibiting "mutinous conduct." Officers thus held absolute dominion over their soldiers, who in turn had few options for self-defense. Wayne later wrote Washington that "a liberal dose of niter" had purged the line of their "distemper."[107]

Mutiny within the Pennsylvania line did not end with Wayne's successful repressions. By the spring of 1782, the lines of Pennsylvania and Maryland had been sent south to reinforce Nathanael Greene's southern army. Greene wrote Robert Morris, superintendent of finance, that he thought members of the Pennsylvania line were "spreading Contagion"; "the seeds of discontent and mutiny" were "deep rooted among the Pennsylvania troops [and beginning] to spread through the whole army."[108] Greene added that "the natural consequence of [such] discontent [was] great desertions which we have experienced for a few days past." Moreover, Greene observed that soldiers had begun to put up placards around camp that asked, "Can soldiers do their duty if clad in rags and fed on rice?"[109] Greene wrote that it was "talked freely among the men that if pay and clothing did not arrive by such a day, they would march their officers to Dorchester, and allow them only a few days more, before they would deliver them to the enemy, unless their grievances were redressed."[110] He admitted that "the symptoms of mutiny appeared almost daily. It was difficult to fix it upon an individual." Using a now familiar tactic, Greene chose a Pennsylvania Sergeant named Gornell who had been "remarkably active in the former mutiny at Morristown" to be executed as an example to others. One of the accused was Greene's own servant, a soldier named Peters. Peters and three other soldiers were taken under guard and employed "in the service of the Laboratory," a place where munitions were produced and long renowned as an army hell-hole. "This," noted Greene, "had a better effect upon the army than their execution—The discontent has disappeared altho the sufferings continue."[111]

The executions of Macaroney Jack and other former mutineers at York and Sergeant Gornell by the order of Nathanael Greene suggests their successes as organizers of the January mutinies produced a desire for vengeance by the Continental army officer corps. The swiftness of their convictions and deaths testified to the power of Continental officers over their men. If an officer wanted to get rid of an individual considered to be subversive, it was not hard to find a charge that garnered the death penalty.

Other units, however, adopted the methods of the January mutineers, for they realized safety could be found in collective action. In early May 1782, the Connecticut line conspired to go to Hartford, where the state assembly had convened. The protest was to take the form of a march, supported by artillery pieces after the manner of the Pennsylvanians of 1781. On the eve of the revolt, a loyal soldier (or a disloyal one depending on the point of view) revealed the plot to the officers. Colonel Heman Swift quickly arrested the ringleaders and nipped the mutiny before it actually got underway. A week later, Private Lud Gaylord of the First Connecticut was convicted and sentenced to death for "endeavoring to incite a mutiny."[112] Washington refused to grant a reprieve.

The last large-scale mutiny of the war occurred immediately prior to the army's disbandment. Again, discontentment centered in the Pennsylvania line. For months the soldiers had been waiting to see what sort of settlement the government was going to award them when the army disbanded. When Congress attempted to furlough them without paying them "their due," the soldiers revolted as they had done in 1781.

The crux of their complaint was the army's intention to furlough them before pay certificates were issued. The soldiers reasoned that if they were disbanded prior to being paid, they would have little power as individuals to demand it later. Most men had not been paid since December 1782, a few even longer. General Benjamin Lincoln ordered Arthur St. Clair to begin preparations to pay off and furlough the Pennsylvania line. They were to be paid in "Morris Notes" (pay guaranteed to be redeemed later by the superintendent for finance, Robert Morris) for "the months of February, March, and April." He forgot the month of January, but the soldiers had not. Sergeants of the Pennsylvania line drew up a petition demanding that Congress pay them for January as well as for the other months. Before their petition reached Congress, however, the army discovered the pay error and ordered the appropriate restitution. Colonel Richard Humpton, commanding the troops at the Philadelphia barracks, reported that this "induced the Soldiery to believe they had been issued [their January pay] in consequence of their petition, and they appeared to exult in what they had done." Yet, when a paymaster from the artillery reported that he had been ordered only to pay for January unless the troops accepted their furlough, the soldiers organized a march to "the President's house."[113]

Trouble soon spread to troops quartered at the Lancaster barracks who also clamored for back pay. About eighty soldiers formed under the command of their sergeant, Christian Nagle, a German immigrant, and marched to Philadelphia. The discontented soldiers in and about Philadelphia, now numbering about three hundred, were a revolutionary mix of recently returned veterans of southern campaigns, new recruits, and old mutineers of 1781. Appointing two junior officers as their representatives, a group of insurgents surrounded the Pennsylvania State House on 21 June 1783. Giving President John Dickinson a mere twenty minutes to respond, the soldiers made it clear that if they did not get a satisfactory answer "they would turn . . . an enraged Soldiery on the Council, who would do themselves Justice, and the Council must abide the consequences."[114]

The soldiers were interested mostly in threatening the Pennsylvania Council (who had it in its power to pay the soldiers), but they inevitably threatened Congress too, who shared the building. When only thirteen militiamen showed up to quell the mutiny, Elias Boudinot, president of Congress, asked Washington to send loyal Continental troops. To make matters worse, when Boudinot attempted to enter the State House he was jostled by a group of soldiers. "To my mortification," noted Boudinot, "not a citizen came to our assistance." He issued a proclamation that he and other congressional members "had been grossly insulted" by the threats of the soldiery. He ordered Congress to flee Philadelphia (as they had been forced to do twice before by the British) and to reconvene at Princeton.[115]

It was clear that this time severe reprisals were not in order. The

Continental army was little more than a shell by this date, and all Washington wanted was to get the men to disperse peacefully. Earlier, Richard Peters noted that "the Difficulty which heretofore oppress'd us was how to raise an Army."[116] Now, however, the difficulty lay in getting the soldiers to accept a settlement and return home, an unlikely prospect unless some way were found to pay them their contractual due. Ironically, Lieutenant Benjamin Gilbert noted that rather than wait around for a dubious settlement from Congress, "a very great number of Soldiers" proceeded to New York and "offered themselves up for employment on the very ships that were evacuating the British and Tories"—a sad end indeed.[117]

In conclusion, patterns of protest and defiance found within the enlisted ranks revealed an army distinctly different from the one portrayed by traditional historians of the Revolution. "Crime," desertion, mutiny, and resistance to arbitrary rule need to be seen in a different light. Continental soldiers committed an abundance of offenses against their officers. Their behavior has been ascribed either to dissatisfaction at their loss of the personal freedom Americans were said habitually to enjoy or to plain licentiousness on the part of men with guns in their hands. And in some instances, this may have been the case. Most defiance, however, was more than that. When soldiers spoke of "teaking what came to hand," or getting what they considered "their due," they were attempting to remind their officers of their traditional customary rights or "moral economy" that existed between the officers and the men. The moral economy established by the soldiers had tangible value to them and was rooted in a centuries-old tradition of payment to freemen who surrendered their civil liberties, temporarily, in exchange for the wages and customary rights of a long-termed war fighter.

The irreconcilable conflict between the need for the colonies to field a long-term standing army and the moral economy established by the enlisted men placed the soldiers on a collision course with the imperatives of the state. While James Warren described Washington's troops as "the most undisciplined, profligate Crew that was ever collected" to fight a war, the enlisted men referred to themselves as "Brother Soldiers."[118] No clearer example can be given of the differences between those who did the fighting and those who were benefiting from it. Driven together by harsh Articles of War, the capricious justice of officers, and a commonality of experience, the soldiers demonstrated greater collective behavior as the war ground on.

While the war culminated in several large-scale mutinies, the evidence revealed that mutiny was commonly used by soldiers to express their dissatisfaction or defend their precarious moral economies throughout the war. There were at least ten major mutinies that occurred *before* the famous Pennsylvania line mutiny of 1781. Moreover, the successful 1781 mutiny was strongly connected, through common personnel and leadership, to four "post-mutinies." The reaction of the officers to all this was increased repression and extreme violence against the soldiers they deemed capable of fomenting further insurrections. The executions of Macaroney Jack and Sergeant Gornell and the banishment of Sergeant Peters to the laboratory served to remind the soldiers of the precariousness of their relationship with officers who had the power of life and death over them while they served in the ranks. When they mutinied, however, they visibly demonstrated their intention to achieve their "rights" and "due" with their own hands. The soldiers' collectivism was their only defense against reprisal by their officers.[119]

All else having failed, the soldiers could always desert, and many did. The threat of desertion was one way the soldiers could control their workplace, the army camp. The soldiers knew, as did their officers, that if things got too far out of hand, they could use their feet and slip away some dark evening or dodge into the woods on a march. They had little to fear from the general populace, who frequently offered protection against capture. The two years that required army reorganization—1776 and 1781—were also the years of greatest desertion. Desertion served to disaggregate the labor of the soldiers at the very moment that officers sought to force them to serve continuously for the duration of the war. Fleeing to the New Hampshire Grants or escaping to the frontier, soldiers sought to evade enlistments that amounted to perpetual servitude. It was also a check on the ability of the state to impress the services of those who desired to limit their time in the army.

In the end, the soldiers struggled to find some meaning to their long years of sacrifice. They felt that if Congress could be convinced that they were owed something for their efforts, then their service retained some tangible value. Joseph Plumb Martin sadly observed that "the country was rigorous in exacting my compliance to my engagements to a punctilio, but equally careless in performing her contracts with me. . . . Such things ought not to be." "The laborer," noted Martin, "is worthy of his meat."[120]

Conclusion

Toward the end of the Revolution, Joseph Plumb Martin chanced upon the army as it passed a crossroads. He stated that he had never before had such an opportunity to see the entire army as it marched. What he saw was "truly amazing." "There was Tag, Rag, and Bobtail; some in rags and some in jags, but none in velvet gowns." The army's soldiery, Martin insisted, "beggared all description." He marveled at the great array of dialects and languages spoken by the equally great variety of soldiers as they marched by. "There was the Irish and Scotch brogue, murdered English, flat insipid Dutch [German] and some lingoes which would puzzle a philosopher to tell whether they belonged to this world or some undiscovered country."[1]

This book has focused on the "undiscovered country" that was the Continental army itself, emphasizing the importance of the social origins and cultural diversity of the men who composed it. The historiography of the army in the Revolutionary era has itself suffered from a lack of attention to social and cultural questions. Fortunately, a newer generation of historians has risen to challenge the older, frequently mythic history of 1776 and finally to set things straight.[2]

The American fight for independence needs to be seen in a broader, more international perspective. After all, one rebellion "does not a revolution make." The men and women who joined or were associated with the Continental army were part of a larger group of free (and unfree) waged (and unwaged) labórers who found themselves in service for a variety of reasons. As contemporary observers of this group freely pointed out, "enthusiasm" for the cause usually had little to do with their participation in the rebellion. By looking at the longer history of the struggles and resistance of these working-class people, we can begin to see how the American Revolution "was part of a broader cycle of rebellion in the eighteenth-century world." By considering the Revolution as just one more rebellion in a series of upheavals in the eighteenth century, the participation of various racial and ethnic elements is now seen as much more crucial to the outcome of the event than has been previously supposed.[3]

Army recruiter appeals to the Irish or German elements of American society were attempts by the patriot movement to find common ground with other repressed groups and engender an international sense of solidarity. Thomas Paine, John Adams, and Benjamin Franklin all realized that by aligning the American cause with other rebellions or discontents outside the North American theater, the patriot movement was given greater legitimacy. It served to isolate the interests of the crown and cast it as the singular abuser of liberty against the freedom-loving peoples the world over.

But getting from a rebellion of small property holders to a revolt with international implications can be a long and winding road. The first task of any serious history on the Continental army must be to deconstruct the myths of Lexington and Concord. This myth long held that the British aggressively attacked America's peace-loving colonists who in turn had little choice but to abandon the plows in their fields and defend themselves, their families, and their national honor. All freedom-loving Americans willingly and self-sacrificingly abandoned their civil pursuits until the glorious fight was won.[4]

What we have seen was that the typical Continental soldier was not the "yeoman" farmer of legendary yore. In reality, it was those least-strongly connected to communities who were usually chosen as long-termed soldiers for distant campaigns. African Americans, ethnic minorities, and "free white men on the move" eventually formed the bulk of the Continental army. The state militias, on the other hand, usually retained those connected to the community by property and economic exigency.[5]

By appealing to racial and ethnic groups and luring the "lower sorts" into long-termed service, the army experience of the soldiers served to submerge former racial and ethnic identities and forged a new class consciousness from among those who had had little stake in the society that recruited them for war. The wartime experiences of these groups created a sense of commonality among them. Moreover, their army service undermined local loyalties and created a class of highly mobile, cosmopolitan-oriented laborers. As we saw with soldiers recruited in Virginia, few remained in the same locales that recruited them after the war had ended. Graveyards and cemeteries in states such as Tennessee, Kentucky, Ohio, Illinois, Indiana, and Michigan are heavily dotted with the tombstones of Revolutionary War veterans who left their family homesteads after the war and took their chances in the untamed lands west of the Appalachians.

Four overarching themes emerge and help to explain the origins of the Continental army. All four of these themes were interconnected with each other and served to create, in the end, a different sort of soldier than that envisioned by Congress when it first created its army. First and foremost is the issue of race and population. Fear of slave uprisings and a desperate need for military manpower proved to be a nearly impossible conundrum for American officials to solve. While the British could and did offer emancipation to slaves who fled their rebel masters, the patriots could not do the same. Thus what emerged was a disjointed policy that offered some African Americans freedom for service but denied others the right to enlist at the same time. Despite the restrictions, many blacks liberated themselves and served or avoided both warring parties to become free. Creating a newer, larger class of free men as a result of their wartime service, or just taking advantage of the turmoil of the times, free African Americans became a permanent legacy of the war and gave hope to others still enslaved. Moreover, the war needs to be viewed not only from the white colonial perspective but must also include the exigencies of the various races and ethnicities who participated. Thus much of the fighting was "triangular" and sometimes "quadrangular," with a number of races—black, white, and red—vying for survival or dominance. Never for a moment did the revolutionaries forget that they held in bondage thousands of African American men and women against their will. Resistance by slaves was far more pervasive than has been previously supposed. Indeed, if running away can be defined as a form of resistance, then slave revolts became pandemic during the Revolution. Although resistance by slaves did not achieve its revolutionary goals, "it did exert deep pressure on the slave system." The Revolutionary War became in many respects for slaves "a black Declaration of Independence" from the white master class. Fighting in the ranks of both armies, blacks sought to take advantage of any opportunity that would increase their chances for freedom.[6]

While the war for many African Americans must have appeared to have been a fortuitous event, it was a series of calamities for the Indians. Caught in a "baron's revolt," the Indians sought to maintain their cultural identity in the face of overwhelming odds. Having much in common with Irish peasants who resisted the English for similar reasons, they defensively fought against encroachment. Because the English offered them the best opportunity, most of the tribes fought on the losing side. The few who sided with the Americans (the Stockbridge and Catawba) had already been culturally engulfed by the surging colonial tide. Having little choice in the matter if they wanted to keep their crucial supply of western goods coming, they chose the patriot side. Because they were outsiders in the first place, white racism did not allow them to share in the final victory.[7] In the end, the war on the frontier devolved into a terroristic world of brutality, with each side (white vs. red) killing and butchering the other until the less populous Indians were finally driven off or exterminated. Even the egalitarian Thomas Jefferson had little regard for the Indians and had larger plans for their land after the war. Writing to John Page soon after the Cherokee began to attack encroaching settlers, he stated that "nothing will reduce those wretches so soon as pushing the war into the heart of their country. But I would not stop there. I would never cease pursuing them while one of them remained on this side of the Mississippi." A clairvoyant Jefferson remarked that "we [shall] never cease pursuing them with war until one remained on the face of the earth."[8] They never did.

The second theme revolves around ethnicity. Clouds of immigrants had arrived on America's shores in the years immediately before the war. Most of them, as we have seen, were responding to larger social and economic forces that were shaking much of their eighteenth-century world and were occurring throughout the entire Atlantic community. "Racked-rents" or the ravages of the Sun-King all served to drive throngs of emigrants into the waiting arms of America, but often only after a temporary detour into the world of unfree labor. These people "were redeployed" to create a swelling majority that depended on wages for their livelihood. Tramping about in search of cheap land or work, they represented a "seething" and extraordinarily mobile labor force. Indeed, the enlistment rosters of the Pennsylvania, New Jersey, and Maryland troops bear this hypothesis out. Large majorities of their troops claimed other colonies as their birthplace. Moreover, the presence of those who claimed foreign birthplaces seemed to predominate in the middle colonies.[9] Service in the army gave many immigrants (if they survived), who had had slight time before the war to earn their fortune, the opportunity to get some land, perhaps a wife (as did the Hessian prisoners who married American women), and gain a broader perspective on the rich possibilities of life in America when compared to what they had left in Europe. This experience created a medium for the eventual development of nationalism that occurred in the decades following the war. Former Irish and German ethnic soldiers were in the forefront of this movement.

The third theme is closely related to a developing class consciousness among the men who served as long-termed soldiers. The Continental army recruits were conscious that they were "freemen" and "volunteers" and went to great lengths to let their officers know that they were such. Many were only a few steps away from the experience of unfree labor; others had been only recently liberated from slavery or an indentureship; some had liberated themselves by joining the army, legally or illegally. These military workers—free and unfree, mobile, and of many nations and ethnicities—were all part of the prewar working class whose laborers were the most readily available to recruiters once the Revolutionary War got under way. When the initial enthusiasm for the war faded, opportunities for working-class men like Joseph Plumb Martin to maximize their ability to sell their labor became apparent. Martin, like many others, "endeavored to get as much for their skin[s] as they could." This was no small feat, because the government aimed to aggregate its military labor supply for the longest time possible and was loath to offer short enlistment terms. The soldiers, nonetheless, saw themselves as volunteers; as such they felt that the state owed them a traditional social wage in addition to what had been agreed upon at enlistment.[10]

Slowly, over time, the enlisted men became conscious of their status as soldiers. Soldiers recognized and defended their customary dues with a tenacity that grew as the war deepened. The idea of a social wage or "customary due" is critical to understanding the consciousness of the common soldiers, especially after inflation and depreciation robbed them of much of the true value of their wages. Recent scholarship has shown that rebellion by working-class men and women during the eighteenth century usually was due to the crowd being informed by a belief that they were defending "customary rights and traditions" and that these rights were recognized generally by the population at large. The Continental soldiers struggled to establish their own "moral economy" with their officers. In doing so, they created a common occupational consciousness that entailed the defense of their traditional dues and rejection of anything that limited their ability to remain free men. Soldiers who cried "No Meat—No Soldier" at Valley Forge were expressing more than their dissatisfaction at not being fed. They were defending their right to *be* fed and intimated that they would do no work until they were.[11]

The fourth theme emphasized was patterns of protest and defiance after the government reneged on its side of the social bargain between the soldiers and the state. As we have seen, the patterns of rebellion within the Continental ranks are exceptionally complex. Most historians have found it comforting to ascribe the mutiny and discontent in the ranks as "rebellions of the belly." A lack of food and support, we find, was only part of the protest-and-defiance equation. Rebellions within the ranks were not spasmodic episodes, nor was their rowdy behavior related to their being "a most desperate, profligate crew," as one member of Congress characterized the army. Rather, rebellion against authority was a long-established tradition of eighteenth-century groups such as immigrants and slaves. The actions of pre-Revolutionary crowds have been well documented. The "mob" that attacked the British soldiers at the "Boston massacre" was called "a motley rabble of saucy boys, negroes and mulattoes, Irish teagues, and out landish Jack Tarrs." Sailors, servants, immigrants, and blacks, not surprisingly, made up a large portion of such eighteenth-century crowds. Connected by lower-class social and cultural ties, these mobs were exceptionally militant in defense of their customary rights and prerogatives. The 1747 Knowles Riot, for instance, found gangs of "armed seamen, servants, and Negroes rioting against a press gang sent ashore in Boston." Sailors, servants, and waged workers were among the most radical groups pressing for independence in the years leading up to the war.[12] It is not surprising that they carried their revolutionary tendencies with them into the ranks.

Desertion, defiance, plundering, and mutinies were expressions of soldiers defending what was due them in return for their service. When they mutinied, they visibly demonstrated to their officers that a line had been crossed and they were determined to set things right. An analysis of the great mutinies of the Pennsylvania and New Jersey lines is crucial toward understanding this process. Moreover, there was a strong connection between these mutinies and number of "post-mutinies" that wracked the army up until it was disbanded in 1783. In fact, there were at least fifteen major mutinies of large numbers of soldiers during the course of the war. Their collectivism was an old and *learned* defensive mechanism taught in the streets of Boston, Philadelphia, and Charleston. It was a good defense against reprisals by officers as well.

Desertion, on the other hand, can be deemed an individual expression of mutiny. Most Continental army units averaged 20 to 25 percent of their entire complements as deserters during the course of the war. Desertion served to "disaggregate the labor" of soldiers as their officers sought ways to keep them in the ranks against their will. Desertion ebbed and flowed with the amount of repression used by officers to suppress it. It was no coincidence that the two greatest years of desertion (1776 and 1781) also occurred when the army underwent major reorganization. The evidence shows that the use of the lash, firing squad, and gibbet increased as soldiers sought ways to avoid continued service or as they were reacting to becoming "unfree labor" due to the failure of the state to pay them their wages.[13]

In the final analysis, one is struck by the "interconnections" of the participants in the American Revolution and the cosmopolitan nature of the Revolutionary struggle. The wartime experience of the soldiers served to create a shared or class experience for many who shouldered a musket in the cause of liberty. Individual men who joined the army in 1776 for the twenty-dollar bounty referred to each other as "brother soldiers" by the 1781 January mutinies. Banding together for self-defense against capricious injustice was the theme of the 1747 Knowles Riot as well as the 1781 mutiny of the Pennsylvania Line.[14]

The soldiers who revolted over their wages or chafed at being kept in service beyond their enlistment terms did not suddenly reach an epiphany over their situation in the army. Resistance to unjust authority had its foundation in the cycles of rebellion of the eighteenth century. These connections informed the soldiers of their customary rights and what was or was not worth risking by resisting authority. Thus class consciousness, race, ethnicity, and commonality of experience served to carry on the anti-authoritarian heritage of the English Revolution of the 1640s. The wartime experience of the soldiers reinforced this tradition and was later expressed in similar ways by former soldiers who participated in Shay's Rebellion and the Whiskey Rebellion years after the war.[15]

Notes

Notes to the Preface

1. John Adams quoted in John Ferling, "Oh That I Was a Soldier: John Adams and the Anguish of War," *American Quarterly* (Summer 1984): 258–75.

2. Charles Lee to James Bowdoin, 30 November 1776, Strictures on a Pamphlet (Philadelphia, 1774), in "Charles Lee Papers," *New York Historical Society Collection* (New York, 1878), 5, 323–24.

3. Lawrence Delbert Cress, *Citizens in Arms: The Army and the Militia in American Society to the War of 1812* (Chapel Hill: University of North Carolina Press, 1982), 7; James Kirby Martin, *In the Course of Human Events: An Interpretive Exploration of the American Revolution* (Arlington Heights, Ill.: Harlan Davidson, 1979), 132–34; and James Kirby Martin and Mark E. Lender, *A Respectable Army: The Military Origins of the Republic* (Arlington Heights, Ill.: Harlan Davidson, 1982), 3–6.

4. John Ferling, "Oh That I Was a Soldier," 258. An example of modern commentators erroneously skewing the true composition of the army is found in Merrill Jensen's statement that "most of the soldiers were free men: farmers and their sons and the independent mechanics and artisans of the towns." See Merrill Jensen, *The New Nation: A History of the United States during the Confederation, 1781–1789* (New York: Knopf, 1950), 32–33. Charles Royster, in *A Revolutionary People at War: The Continental Army and American Character, 1775–1783* (Chapel Hill: University of North Carolina Press, 1979), even used biblical terms—"the Army of Israel"—to characterize the Continental army as one with an elevated sense of motivation and composition. For an excellent criticism of Revolutionary War historians perpetuating the myth of the "yeoman farmer"-turned-soldier, see Mark Lender, "The Enlisted Line" (Ph.D. diss., Rutgers University, 1975), Introduction; Martin and Lender, *A Respectable Army*, 1–29.

5. John Shy, "A New Look at Colonial Militia," in *The Military in America: From the Colonial Era to the Present*, ed. Peter Karsten (New York: Free Press, 1986), 32.

6. John Shy, *A People Numerous and Armed: Reflections on the Military Struggle for American Independence* (Ann Arbor: University of Michigan Press, 1990), 23.

7. Martin and Lender, *A Respectable Army*, 6–8.

8. Alexander Hamilton to John Jay, 14 March 1779, *The Papers of Alexander Hamilton*, ed. Harold C. Syrett (New York: Columbia University Press, 1961–66), 2:1719; William G. Simms, ed., *The Army Correspondence of John Laurens* (New York: Bradford Club, 1867), 108–9, 114–18; *Journals of the Continental Congress*, hereafter *JCC*, vol. 2, 28 July 1775; vol. 5, 17 June 1776; Archives of Maryland, *Muster Rolls and Other Records of the Service of Maryland Troops in the American Revolution*, vol. 18 (Annapolis: Maryland Hall of Records), 563–65; *Staatesbote*, 1 August 1775, pamphlet collections of the Pennsylvania-German Society, Philadelphia, 34; George Washington to the President of Congress, 19 April 1776, in *Papers of the Continental Congress*, hereafter *PCC*, reel 186, item 169, 1:291–96; *Rhode Island Archives: Records of the State of Rhode Island, December 1777–October 1779*, 10:41; and "Journal of the Second Council of Safety," *Collections of the South Carolina Historical Society*, 3:253.

Notes to the Prologue

1. Voltaire, *Candide*, ed. John Butt (New York: Penguin Books, translated from the original French edition, 1758; reprint, 1947), 22–24 (page references are to the reprint edition). Voltaire chose as the setting for his satirical classic the German principality of Westphalia.

2. Ibid., 22–24; Dave R. Palmer, *The Way of the Fox: American Strategy in the War for America, 1775–1783* (Westport, Conn.: Greenwood Press, 1975), 18. After partially completing his punishment for desertion, every nerve and muscle in Candide's back had been laid bare. Rather than complete the punishment, he begged to be beheaded instead. Although Voltaire exaggerated the penalty given Candide, he nonetheless demonstrated for his reading public the capriciousness of military justice and the brutality of eighteenth-century army life.

3. Alexander Hamilton to John Jay, 14 March 1779, in *Papers of Alexander Hamilton*, ed. Howard Syrett (New York: Columbia University Press, 1961), 2:17–18.

4. Christopher Donnelly, *Red Banner: The Soviet Military System in Peace and War* (Alexandria, Va.: Jane's Publishing, 1988), 41. For a discussion of the contractual nature of soldiering in America, see Fred Anderson, *A People's Army: Massachusetts Soldiers and Society in the Seven Years War* (Chapel Hill: University of North Carolina Press), 1984.

5. Arthur J. Alexander, "How Maryland Tried to Raise Her Continental Quotas," *Maryland Historical Magazine* (1947): 185–86; [Council to Delegates at Congress], 22 May 1778, *Archives of Maryland*, 21:107–8; and Archer Jones, *The Art of War in the Western World* (New York: Oxford University Press, 1987), 200–201. For examples of congressional attempts to extend indefinitely the term of service for its soldiers, see John C. Fitzpatrick, ed., *The Writings of Washington* (Washington, D.C.: Government Printing Office, 1931–44), 6:152–56, 186–90, 200–201; and *JCC*, 5:854–56.

6. Johann David Schoeph, *Travels in the Confederation, 1783–1784*, I, trans. and ed. Alfred J. Morrison (Philadelphia, 1911), 30; Advertisement, *Pennsylvania Journal*, 17 April 1776.

7. Thomas Paine, *Common Sense* (originally published 1776; reprint, New York: Anchor Books, 1973), 29; and John Adams, *Works*, 5:491–96. An excellent treatment on the ethnic diversity of colonial America is found in Winthrop Jordan's *White Over Black* (Chapel Hill: University of North Carolina Press, 1968), 336–39.

8. For a more detailed explanation of the larger cycles of rebellion going on in the Atlantic community during the eighteenth century, see Marcus Rediker, "The American Revolution and the Cycles of Rebellion in the Eighteenth-Century Atlantic," paper delivered at the United States Capitol Historical Society meeting, 15–16 March 1989; and "The

Transforming Hand of Revolution: Reconsidering the American Revolution as a Social Movement," 1–2.

9. Bernard Bailyn, *Voyagers to the West: A Passage in the Peopling of America on the Eve of the Revolution* (New York: Vintage Books, 1986), 4–5, chap. 5; T. H. Breen, "Creative Adaptations: Peoples and Cultures," in *Colonial British America: Essays of the New History of the Early Modern Era*, ed. Jack P. Greene and J. R. Pole (Baltimore: Johns Hopkins University Press, 1984), 195–232; and Thomas J. Archdeacon, *Becoming American: An Ethnic History* (New York: Free Press, 1983), 1–26.

10. Hans Delbruck, *History of the Art of War within the Framework of Political History*, trans. Walter J. Renfroe, Jr. (Westport, Conn.: Greenwood Press, 1985), 4:43; Geoffrey Parker, *The Army of Flanders and the Spanish Road, 1567–1659: The Logistics of Spanish Victory and Defeat in the Low Countries' Wars* (Cambridge: Cambridge University Press, 1972), 173; and Archer Jones, *The Art of War in the Western World*, 200–201.

11. Joseph Galloway, deposition, in *Facsimiles of Manuscripts in European Archives Relating to America*, ed. Benjamin F. Stevens, 25 vols. (1889–98), no. 2094; *JCC* 4:392; Robert K. Wright, *The Continental Army* (Washington, D.C.: U.S. Army Center of Military History, 1986), 81–82; George F. Scheer and Hugh Rankin, eds., *Rebels and Redcoats: The American Revolution through the Eyes of Those Who Fought and Lived It* (New York: Da Capo Press, 1957), 88.

12. John Shy, "A New Look at Colonial Militia," *William and Mary Quarterly* (April 1963): 182. Fred Anderson argues that eighteenth-century soldiers viewed military service as a free and voluntary act, a contract between equal parties, in which each side had obligations to fulfill. Resistance by soldiers to low pay or no pay, inadequate rations, or nonfulfillment of contractual enlistment obligations had its basis in this belief, not, as some have supposed, in a reaction to European-style army discipline by freedom-loving Americans. See Fred Anderson, "Why Did Colonial New Englanders Make Bad Soldiers?" in *Military in America*, ed. Karsten, 36–52. E. P. Thompson argued in "The Moral Economy of the Crowd in the Eighteenth Century," *Past and Present* 50 (1971): 76–136, that popular discontent was not always simply "rebellions of the belly." Thompson thought that participants of riots and crowd actions were often informed by the belief that they were defending traditional rights or customs that were supported by a wide consensus of the community. The same might be said of the resistance of Continental soldiers to authority.

13. Marcus Cunliffe, *Soldiers and Civilians: The Martial Spirit in America, 1775–1865*, 2d ed. (Boston: Little, Brown and Co., 1968), 147–49; and Martin and Lender, *A Respectable Army*, 45.

14. Martin and Lender, *A Respectable Army*, 163–64. Soldiers were customarily due a set ration, a suit of clothes, and their enlistments had a predetermined beginning and end. Congress on a number of occasions failed to provide all three. Moreover, the civilian community seemed to recognize these customary rights as well. When the Pennsylvanians revolted for the final time in 1783 and swarmed about Independence Hall, few militiamen responded to the call to quell the revolt. See J. J. Boudinot, ed., *The Life, Public Services, Addresses, and Letters of Elias Boudinot* (New York: Houghton, Mifflin, and Co., 1896), 334–37; and *PCC*, reel 45, items 38, 49, 73.

15. Joseph Plumb Martin, *Private Yankee Doodle: Being a Narrative of Some of the Adventures, Dangers, and Sufferings of a Revolutionary Soldier*, ed. George F. Scheer (Boston: Little, Brown and Co., 1962), 186.

CHAPTER ONE *Few Had the Appearance of Soldiers*

1. Alexander Graydon, *Memoirs of "His Own Time" with Reminiscences of the Men and Events of the Revolution* (Philadelphia, 1846), 135.

2. Ibid., 135–36.

3. Ibid., 134; and Louis Duportail, undated letter quoted in Ernst Kipping, *The Hessian View of America, 1763–1783*, trans. B. A. Uhlendorf (Monmouth Beach, N.J.: Philip Freneau Press, 1971), 34–35.

4. Fred Anderson, "A People's Army: Provincial Military Service in Massachusetts during the Seven Years War," *William and Mary Quarterly*, 3d ser. (1983): 499; Allen Bowman, *The Morale of the American Revolutionary Army* (Washington, D.C.: American Council on Public Affairs, 1943), 14; Noah Brooks, *Henry Knox, A Soldier of the Revolution* (1900), 70; and Charles J. Stille, *Major-General Anthony Wayne and the Pennsylvania Line in the Continental Army* (1893), 44. Tench Tilghman, aide-de-camp to George Washington, lamented that the soldiers from New York City were "mostly old disbanded Regulars and low lived foreigners." See Samuel A. Harrison, ed., *Memoir of Lieutenant Colonel Tench Tilghman* (1876), 97; and Benedict Arnold quoted in John William Kruger, "Troop Life at the Champlain Valley Forest during the American Revolution" (Ph.D. diss., State University of New York at Albany, 1981), 172.

5. Carlos E. Godfrey, *The Commander-in-Chief's Guard: The Revolutionary War* (Baltimore: Genealogical Publishing Co., 1972), 42; Joseph Galloway, deposition, in *Facsimiles of Manuscripts in European Archives Relating to America*, ed. Benjamin F. Stevens, 25 vols. (1889–98), no. 2094; Carl Berger, *Broadsides and Bayonets: The Propaganda War of the Revolution* (Philadelphia: University of Pennsylvania Press, 1961), 123; *The Papers of George Washington*, ed. W. W. Abbot (Charlottesville: University Press of Virginia, 1985–94), 1:71; *Writings of Washington*, ed. Fitzpatrick, 8:56, 78, 264, 21:401. The more comprehensive *Papers* are only complete to August 1776. Therefore, the Washington letters edited by John C. Fitzpatrick were used for all dates preceding the most recently published volume of the Washington papers. See also *Journals of the Continental Congress* (hereafter *JCC*) (Washington, D.C.: Government Printing Office), 10:203, n. 1; *Archives of Maryland*, 47:196; William L. Saunders, ed., *North Carolina Records*, 26 vols. (1886–1905), 24:33, 158, 268; George Washington, *The Washington Papers*, ed. Saul K. Padover (New York: Harper and Brothers, 1955), 162; Nathanael Greene to Thomas Jefferson, 15 February 1781, in *Greene Papers*, William L. Clements Library, Ann Arbor, Mich.; and Greene to Joseph Reed, 4 May 1781, *Greene Papers*.

6. Lawrence D. Cress, *The Citizen in Arms: The Army and the Militia in American Society to the War of 1812* (Chapel Hill: University of North Carolina Press, 1982), 7, 53; Peter Karsten, ed., *The Military in America: From the Colonial Era to the Present* (New York: Free Press, 1986), 1; and John Shy, "A New Look at Colonial Militia," 181.

7. Saunders, *Colonial Records of North Carolina*, 3:113; Douglas E. Leach, "The Cartagena Expedition, 1740–1742, and Anglo-American Relations," in *Adapting to Conditions: War and Society in the Eighteenth Century*, ed. Maarten Ultee (University: University of Alabama Press, 1986), 43–55; Albert Harkness, Jr., "Americanism and Jenkin's Ear," *Mississippi Valley Historical Review* 37 (1950): 88–89; and E. Milton Wheeler, "Development and Organization of the North Carolina Militia," *North Carolina Historical Review* (Summer 1964): 311.

8. Saunders, "A Short Discourse of the Present State of the Colonies with Respect to the Interest of Great Britain," *Colonial Records of North Carolina*, 2:632–33; and Wheeler, "North Carolina Militia," 311–12.

9. William Clark, ed., *State Records of North Carolina*, 23:245, 25:393; Saunders, *Colonial Records of North Carolina*, 6:119–221; and Wheeler, "North Carolina Militia," 315.

10. Governor Alexander Spotswood to the Board of Trade (1716), quoted in John Shy, "A New Look at Colonial Militia," 180n.18. For a history of several compulsory and voluntary militia organizations, see Timothy H. Breen, "English Origins and New World Development: The Case of the Covenanted Militia in Seventeenth Century Massachusetts," *Past and Present* (1972): 75–96.

11. Walter Clark, ed., *State Records of North Carolina*, 26 vols. (Winston-Salem, N.C., 1895–1914), 23:940–41; and Karsten, *Military in America*, 53. Surprisingly, former military officers with the rank of captain or above were also exempted from militia service under the 1774 law, which adds weight to the argument that militia organizations had changed over the years.

12. Benjamin B. Wilborne, *The Colonial and State Political History of Hertford County, North Carolina* (Murfreesboro, N.C.: privately printed, 1906), 36–37; and Wheeler, "North Carolina Militia," 317.

13. John Shy, "A New Look at Colonial Militia," 181–82; and James Kirby Martin and Mark Lender, *A Respectable Army: The Military Origins of the Republic, 1763–1789* (Arlington Heights, Ill.: Harlan Davidson, 1982), 17. Martin and Lender also noted that militias had developed "a record of sorts [for] tracking down recalcitrant slaves, wiping out discrete Indian bands, and entertaining" the local populace with fancy drills and ceremonies and were not known as war fighters. Ibid., 17.

14. *Colonial Laws of New York from the Year 1664 to the Revolution* (Albany, 1894–96), 1:454; and John Shy, "A New Look at Colonial Militia," 182n.19.

15. George Washington to Governor Dinwiddie, 9 March 1754, *The Official Records of Robert Dinwiddie*, ed. R. A. Brock (Richmond, 1883–84), 1:92; Major General James Abercromby to Lord Loudoun, 25 February 1758, in *Loudoun Papers*, no. 5668, Henry E. Huntington Library, San Marino, Calif.; and John Shy, "A New Look at Colonial Militia," 34nn.3, 4. Drafting men for campaigns was also seen as an impolitic step. During the Revolution, both Thomas Jefferson and John Adams opposed such a measure as extraordinarily dangerous and expensive for local communities. See Thomas Jefferson to John Adams, 6 May 1777, and Adams to Jefferson, 26 May 1777, in *The Adams-Jefferson Letters: The Complete Correspondence between Thomas Jefferson and Abigail and John Adams* (Chapel Hill: University of North Carolina Press, 1959), 1:4–5.

16. Walter Millis, *Arms and Men: A Study in American Military History* (New York, 1956), 13–15; and Martin and Lender, *A Respectable Army*, 13.

17. Sylvia R. Frey, "The Common British Soldier in the Late Eighteenth Century: A Profile," *Societas: A Review of Social History* 5 (1975): 126; Sylvia R. Frey, *The British Soldier in America: A Social History of Military Life in the Revolutionary Period* (Austin: University of Texas Press, 1981), 3–21; and Martin and Lender, *A Respectable Army*, 13.

18. John Shy, *A People Numerous and Armed: Reflections on the Military Struggle for American Independence*, rev. ed. (Ann Arbor: University of Michigan Press, 1990), 122–25. For further insight into the population growth phenomenon of the eighteenth century, see J. Potter, "The Growth of Population in America, 1700–1860," in *Population in History*, ed. D. V. Glass and D. E. C. Eversley (London: E. Arnold, 1965), passim. For a contemporary observation, see Benjamin Franklin, "Observations Concerning the Increase of Mankind" (1751), in *The Papers of Benjamin Franklin*, ed. Leonard W. Larabee and William B. Willcox (New Haven, Conn.: Yale University Press, 1959), 4:255ff; and Kenneth A. Lockridge, "Social Change and the Meaning of the American Revolution," *Journal of Social History* 6 (1973): 406–9.

19. Charles S. Grant, *Democracy in the Connecticut Frontier Town of Kent* (New York: Columbia University Press, 1961), 170. Numerous New England town studies reveal the same findings. Population and decreased land availability coupled with a lack of desire by

succeeding generations to migrate caused standards of living to drop. Moreover, historians Charles Grant and Kenneth Lockridge noted that the decrease in land availability and increase of population led to the creation of a sort of agricultural "proletariat" by 1800. See Kenneth Lockridge, "Land, Population, and the Evolution of New England Society 1630–1790," *Past and Present* (April 1968): 62–80. Lockridge noted that in seventeenth-century New England, the average land holding was 210 acres in grants and purchases during a lifetime. By the eighteenth century, in almost every older New England town, the average holding was less than 50 acres (generally held as the minimum acreage necessary for a farmer to survive). In the town of Waterton, the average holding was just 17 acres, one-seventh of what it had been in the seventeenth century. See Kenneth Lockridge, "Dedham, 1636–1736: The Anatomy of a Puritan Utopia" (Ph.D. diss., Princeton University, 1965); and James Henretta, "The Social Structure of Boston, *William and Mary Quarterly*, 3d ser. (1965): 75–92.

20. "Amicus Patriae" [John Wise?], "A Word of Comfort to a Melancholy Country" (Boston, 1721), in *Colonial Currency Reprints*, ed. A. M. Davis (Boston: John Wilson and Son, 1911), 2:189; and Lockridge, "Land, Population, and the Evolution of New England Society, 1630–1790," 71. In Chester County, Pennsylvania, James T. Lemon and Gary Nash revealed a growing gap between rich and poor by the time of the Revolution. See Lemon and Nash, "The Distribution of Wealth in the Eighteenth Century America: A Century of Changes in Chester County, Pennsylvania," *Journal of Social History* (Fall 1968): 3–23.

21. Philip J. Greven, Jr., *Four Generations: Population, Land, and Family in Andover, Massachusetts* (Ithaca, N.Y.: Cornell University Press, 1970), 227–54; John J. Waters, "Patrimony, Succession, and Social Stability: Guilford, Connecticut, in the Eighteenth Century," *Perspectives in American History* (1976): 10:156; John J. Waters, "Family, Inheritance," *William and Mary Quarterly*, 3d ser., 39 (1982): 78–85; and Fred Anderson, *A People's Army* (Chapel Hill: University of North Carolina Press, 1984), 33–38.

22. Bernard Bailyn, *Voyagers to the West: A Passage in the Peopling of America on the Eve of the Revolution* (New York: Vintage Books, 1986), 25–26. Also see Peter Brunnholtz's *Reports of the United German Evangelical Lutheran Congregations in North America* (1750) and Howard B. Furer, ed., *The Germans in America, 1607–1970: A Chronology and Fact Book* (Dobbs Ferry, N.Y.: Oceana Publishers, 1973).

23. Bailyn, *Voyagers to the West*, 26.

24. Billy G. Smith, *The Lower Sort: Philadelphia's Laboring People, 1750–1800* (Ithaca, N.Y.: Cornell University Press, 1990), 26; and Application for Revolutionary War Pensions, S12602, National Archives.

25. Smith, *The Lower Sort*, 150–52; and Petitions for Revolutionary War Pensions, W15877, National Archives.

26. Muster Rolls, Ninth Massachusetts Regiment, William Watson Papers; Fourth Massachusetts Regiment, Henry Jackson Papers, Manuscripts Division, Library of Congress, Washington, D.C.; *Historical Statistics of the United States: Colonial Times to 1957* (Washington, D.C., 1960), 11; and John R. Sellers, "The Origins and Careers of the New England Soldier: Non-commissioned Officers and Privates in the Massachusetts Continental Line," Paper delivered at the American Historical Association Convention, 1972.

27. Muster Rolls, Fourth Massachusetts Regiment, Manuscript Division, Library of Congress; Orderly Books, Second Massachusetts Regiment, Manuscript Division, Library of Congress; and Sellers, "Origins and Careers of the New England Soldier," 7.

28. Pension Records of Stephen Bowen and Bristol Bennett, National Archives, Washington, D.C.; and Sellers, "Origins and Careers of the New England Soldier," 12–14.

29. John Shy, *A People Numerous and Armed*, 171–72; and Jonathan Smith, *Peterborough*,

New Hampshire, in the American Revolution (Peterborough, N.H.: Peterborough Historical Society, 1913), 165–395.

30. Smith, *Peterborough, New Hampshire,* 149; and idem, "How Massachusetts Raised Her Troops in the Revolution," *Proceedings of the Massachusetts Historical Society* (Boston, 1921–22), 365–66.

31. Smith, *Peterborough, New Hampshire,* 149–50.

32. Smith, *Peterborough, New Hampshire,* 165–337 passim. Smith researched the service records of as many of the men who were credited to the town of Peterborough that could be located in the town's historical record. He was surprised by the large number of individuals who left absolutely no trace of their existence after they ended their service. He also noted the large number of enlisted men who were not from the town but were credited to Peterborough anyway.

33. Robert A. Gross, *The Minutemen and Their World* (New York: Hill and Wang, 1976), 148–53. Before the war it was customary for the town constables to "warn out" transients or paupers so that the town would not have to support them publicly. Ezekial Brown and his entire family were habitually "warned out" of town until he ended up in the army. Another citizen, Reuben Brown, turned out for the fight at Concord but never served thereafter. Hiring a series of substitutes after being drafted by the town several times, Brown (who had been warned out of Concord in 1770) ended up in 1780 as one of the town's most active creditors. Ibid., 89–91, 149; and Douglas Lamar Jones, "The Strolling Poor: Transiency in Eighteenth-Century Massachusetts," *Journal of Social History* (Spring 1975): 28–54.

34. Douglas Lamar Jones, *Village and Seaport: Migration and Society in Eighteenth Century Massachusetts* (Boston: University of New England Press, 1981), 51–52.

35. Kruger, "Troop Life at the Champlain Valley Forest during the American Revolution," 58.

36. Mark Lender, "The Enlisted Line: The Continental Soldiers of New Jersey" (Ph.D. diss., Rutgers University, 1975), 118–23. For an analysis of the northern states, see Jackson Turner Main, *The Social Structure of Revolutionary America* (Princeton, N.J.: Princeton University Press, 1965), chap. 1.

37. Dennis P. Ryan, "Landholding, Opportunity, and Mobility in Revolutionary New Jersey," *William and Mary Quarterly,* 3d ser., 36 (1979): 575–76; and Dennis P. Ryan, "Six Towns: Continuity and Change in Revolutionary New Jersey, 1770–1792" (Ph.D. diss., New York University, 1974), 317–22.

38. Mark Lender, "The Social Structure of the New Jersey Brigade," in *The Military in America: From the Colonial Era to the Present,* ed. Peter Karsten (New York: Free Press, 1986), 67–70; and Mark Lender, "The Enlisted Line: The Continental Soldiers of New Jersey," 111–23.

39. Elliot's Recruiting Journal, 98; Role of the Men of the Second Battalion . . . May 1, 1778, New Jersey Department of Defense Manuscripts, New Jersey State Library, Trenton, N.J., MSS 3587–3706; Lender, quoted in "The Enlisted Line," 112–13; Ryan, "Landholding, Opportunity, and Mobility in Revolutionary New Jersey," 574–89.

40. Lender, "The Social Structure of the New Jersey Brigade," 73, 75.

41. Joseph Rundel, of New Fairfield, Connecticut, enlisted in the army when he was sixteen. After his second day in camp, General Israel Putnam, noting the youthfulness of the boy-soldier, took him on as his personal waiter. This later proved unfortunate for Rundel, for despite having served time as a prisoner of war, he was denied a pension in 1832 because he served as a waiter, not as a regular soldier. Deposition of Joseph Rundel, *The Revolution Remembered: Eyewitness Accounts of the War for Independence,* ed. John C. Dann (Chicago: University of Chicago Press, 1980), 65.

Edmonson, "Desertion in the American Army during the Revolutionary War" (Ph.D. diss., Louisiana State University, 1971), 156.

60. Stephen Kemble journal entry, 27 March 1777, "Kemble's Journal," *New York Historical Society Collections* (1883), 112.

61. General Pattison to Colonel Cleaveland, 1 March 1779, "Letters of General Pattison," *New York Historical Society Collections* (1875), 8:26–27, 190.

62. Pattison to Cleaveland, 5 September 1779, "Letters of General Pattison," *New York Historical Society Collections* (1875), 8:104–5.

63. Henry Clinton to George Germain, 23 October 1778, *Clinton Mss.*, in William L. Clements Library, Ann Arbor, Mich. The riots referred to by Clinton were the White-boys and Hearts of Steel unrest in Ireland in the 1760s and 1770s.

64. Ibid.; William B. Willcox, ed., *The American Rebellion: Sir Henry Clinton's Narrative of His Campaigns, 1775–1783* (New Haven, Conn.: Yale University Press, 1954), 111; and Oliver Snoddy, "The Irish Sword," *Journal of Military History of Ireland* 7, no. 27 (Winter 1965): 136–39.

65. The Irish Association for Documentation and Information Services, *Ireland, Irishmen in the American War of Independence* (Providence, R.I.: The Academy Press, 1976), document no. 4. Ambrose Serle offered evidence as to why Clinton's offer failed even though so many Irish Continental soldiers worked for meager army wages. "After 8 to 10 years," stated Serle, "they [the Irish] had become habituated to this Country [America] and estranged from their own." Serle, *The American Journal*, 259.

66. Clinton to Germain, 23 October 1778, in Serle, *The American Journal;* Snoddy, "The Irish Sword," 137–38; and Willcox, *American Rebellion*, 111.

67. Ebenezer Buck to David Kelly, Upton, Mass., 24 August 1778, *Feinstone Collection*, David Library of the American Revolution, Washington Crossing, Penn.

68. Orderly Book entry, July 1777, *The Journal and Orderly Book of Captain Robert Kirkwood* (Wilmington: Delaware Historical Society Publication, 1910), 112–13.

69. Charles Lee Papers, *New York Historical Society Collections* (1871–74), 161.

70. Joseph Galloway, *Letters to a Nobleman on the Conduct of the War in the Middle Colonies* (London, 1779, 1780), 25; and "The Examination of Joseph Galloway . . . before the House of Commons," *New York Royal Gazette*, 27 October 1779.

71. Translator note, Marquis de Chastellux, *Travels in North-America* (New York: Augustus M. Kelly, Publishers [1827]; reprint, 1970), 225 (page references are to reprint edition). The translator inserted this note with an entry by the Marquis about an Irish soldier who helped guide his unit in operations near the mountains in Virginia. The soldier stated that he had recently emigrated to North Carolina near the Catawba settlements.

72. Doyle, *Ireland*, 142.

73. Alexander Graydon, *Memoirs of His Own Time* (Harrisburg, Pa., 1811), 122.

74. The French expeditionary forces under Rochambeau included the Dillon's regiment also known as the Irish "wild geese." This regiment had served French kings since 1691. See W. S. Murphy, "The Irish Brigade at Savannah," *The Georgia Historical Quarterly* 38 (December 1954): 308–11.

75. Kraus, "Irish Revolutionary Movement," 345–48; and T. Wolfe Tone, *An Argument on Behalf of the Catholics of Ireland* (Dublin, 1792), 16. Washington's reply was reprinted in *The Massachusetts Centinel*, 22 May 1784, in *Transactions*, Colonial Society of Massachusetts, vol. 14.

CHAPTER THREE *A True Pell-Mell of Human Souls*

1. John Adams to James Warren, 6 July 1775, *Letters of the Delegates to Congress*, 1:590–91.

2. Ruth Blackwelder, "Attitude of the North Carolina Moravians toward the American Revolution," *North Carolina Historical Review* 9, no. 1 (January 1932), 10–19; and *Colonial Records of North Carolina*, 10:526.

3. Glenn Weaver, "Benjamin Franklin and the Pennsylvania Germans," *William and Mary Quarterly*, 3d ser., 14, no. 4 (October 1957): 552–54; and H. M. J. Klein, *The History of the Eastern Synod of the Reformed Church in the United States* (Lancaster, Pa., 1943), 68–69. For a more detailed breakdown of what parts of the state of Pennsylvania the various German sects inhabited, see Laura L. Becker, "The American Revolution as a Community Experience: A Case Study of Reading, Pennsylvania" (Ph.D. diss., University of Pennsylvania, 1978), 29–31, 310, 331–32.

4. Marianne S. Wokeck, "A Tide of Alien Tongues: The Flow and Ebb of German Immigration to Pennsylvania, 1683–1776" (Ph.D. diss., Temple University, 1983), 151–53. In "The Flow and Composition of German Immigrants to Philadelphia," *Pennsylvania Magazine of History and Biography* (1981), Wokeck argues that the majority of prewar German immigrants arrived during the peak years 1749–54, years that corresponded with political and economic tension in Germany. Afterward, immigration declined substantially until the Revolution, when it stopped altogether. Also see Oscar Kuhns, *The German and Swiss Settlements of Colonial Pennsylvania* (Harrisburg, Pa.: Avrand Press, 1945), 55; and Bernard Bailyn, *Voyagers to the West: A Passage in the Peopling of America on the Eve of the Revolution* (New York: Vintage Books, 1986), 25–26.

5. Gunter Moltmann, ed., *Germans to America: 300 Years of Immigration, 1683–1983* (Stuttgart, Federal Republic of Germany: Institute for Foreign Cultural Relations, 1982), 30. Germans from Salzburg also settled in Georgia. In 1733, the *Anne* brought 114 Germans to the colony. By 1736, to function in all parts of the colony a person needed to be fluent in English, French, German, and Gaelic. By 1770 the German element in Georgia was estimated at 1,200 souls, a large number considering the tiny population of the colony at the time. In fact, much of the written record of the early years of the Georgia colony survives only in German. See Harold E. Davis, *The Fledgling Province: Social and Cultural Life in Colonial Georgia, 1733–1776* (Chapel Hill: University of North Carolina Press, 1976), 14, 17.

6. Thomas Sowell, *Ethnic America: A History* (New York: Basic Books, 1981), 47–50; Carl Wittke, *The Germans in America* (New York: Columbia University Press, 1967), 1–2; and Virginia Brainard Kunz, *The Germans in America* (Minneapolis, Minn.: Lerner Publications, 1966), 9, 21–22.

7. La Vern J. Rippley, *The German-Americans: Early German Immigration to the United States* (New York: University Press of America, 1984), 28–29. Traditional estimates on the German population are attributed to the work of Albert Faust, *The German Element in the United States* (New York: Arno Press, reprinted 1969), vol. 1 passim. No study of European immigration should fail to mention the redemption system. The obligation of Germans to serve merchants in return for their seafare was part of a business agreement by which one person paid the debts of another and received, in turn, the latter's labor. More on the redemption system is found in Moltmann, *Germans to America*, 30–34.

8. Thomas J. Archdeacon, *Becoming American: An Ethnic History* (New York: Free Press, 1983), 14–15. The plight of the Germans is reminiscent of Haitian refugees in present-day Florida. Moltmann, *Germans to America*, 30; and Fritz Trautz, *Die Pfalzische Auswanderung nach Nordamerika im 18. Jahrhundert* [Emigration from the Palatine to North America in the 18th Century] (Heidelberg, Federal Republic of Germany, 1959), 17–21.

9. Chessman A. Herrick, *White Servitude in Pennsylvania* (Freeport, N.Y.: Books for Libraries Press, 1926), 171; and Archdeacon, *Becoming American*, 15.

10. Peter Brunnholtz, 21 May 1750, *Reports of the United German Evangelical Lutheran Congregations in North America* (Hallesche Nachrichten series no. 2), 412–14; and Howard B. Furer, ed., *The Germans in America, 1607–1970: A Chronology and Fact Book* (Dobbs Ferry, N.Y.: Oceana Publications, 1973), 89.

11. Furer, *Germans in America*, 89. Brunnholtz also noted the sad case of one recently arrived German immigrant who attempted to commit suicide as a result of his inability to find adequate work and the debt he had accrued as a result of their passage.

12. Ibid.

13. Johann Carl Buettner, *Narrative of Johann Carl Buettner in the American Revolution*, trans. from the original German (New York: Charles Heartman Publishers, 1915), 35–41.

14. Ibid., 41.

15. Ibid., 41–43.

16. Joseph Hewes to James Iredell, 31 October 1774, in *Letters of Members of the Continental Congress* (hereafter *LMCC*), Edmund C. Burnett (Washington, D.C.: Peter Smith, 1963), 1:83.

17. John Adams to Nathanael Greene, 10 May 1777, in *Papers of John Adams*, ed. Robert Taylor (Cambridge, Mass.: Harvard University Press, 1983), 5:190–91; and Charles Carroll of Carrollton to Benjamin Franklin, 12 August 1777, *LMCC*, 2:450–51.

18. Peter Force, *American Archives*, 4th ser., II, 1771–77.

19. Heinrich Miller, "Appeal of the Evangelical and Reformed Church Councils, as well as of the German Society in the City of Philadelphia," *Staatesbote*, 1 August 1775, pamphlet collections of the Pennsylvania-German Society Philadelphia, 34; and Executive Committee to John Hancock, 14 January 1777, *Letters of the Delegates to Congress*, 6:95–96.

20. Miller, "Appeal," 34.

21. Ibid., 35.

22. Washington to Hancock, in *The Papers of George Washington*, ed. W. W. Abbot (Charlottesville: University Press of Virginia), 5:239–40.

23. Robert K. Wright, Jr., *The Continental Army* (Washington, D.C.: Center of Military History, United States Army, 1986), 320.

24. *Archives of Maryland*, 18:261–68; and Charles F. Stein, "The German Battalion of the American Revolution," *The Report: A Journal of German-American History* 36 (1975): 43–44.

25. Stein, "The German Battalion," 43–44.

26. Ibid., 44.

27. *Papers of the Continental Congress*, reel 167, item 52, 299; and Wright, *The Continental Army*, 134, 349–50.

28. Wright, *The Continental Army*, 134. The unit also employed four men specially detailed as "executioner," a position especially detested by the rank and file of the Continental army. Washington chose to make former Prussians responsible for discipline within the army because they had little in common with native-born troops and had a fierce reputation for military order.

29. William T. Parsons, *The Pennsylvania Dutch: A Persistent Minority* (Boston: Twayne Publishers, 1976), 146.

30. Klaus Wust, *The Virginia Germans* (Charlottesville: University Press of Virginia, 1969), 80.

31. Rippley, *The German-Americans*, 34; and Henry Muhlenberg, *The Life of Major-General Peter Muhlenberg of the Revolutionary Army* (Philadelphia: Carey and Hart, 1849), 28–33, 53. The only contemporary source that mentions Muhlenberg's alleged theatrics was the war

diary of James Thacher, *Military Journal during the American Revolutionary War* (Boston, 1823), written well after Muhlenberg's death in 1809.

32. H. M. M. Richards, *The Pennsylvania-German in the Revolutionary War, 1775–1783*, originally published as part 18 of *Pennsylvania: The German Influence in Its Settlement and Development* (Philadelphia, 1908; republished by the Genealogical Publishing Co., Baltimore, 1978), 175–231 passim (page references are to reprint edition). Captain Jacob Moser was probably the same Jacob Moser who advertised in the 13 July 1773 edition of the *Staatesbote* that he was in the service of Adam Erben and sought information concerning his two sisters who had married and moved away. Thus, in a period of three years, Moser had moved from servant to Adam Erben to commissioned officer in the Continental army.

33. Robert Billigmeir, *Minorities in American Life, Americans from Germany: A Study in Cultural Diversity* (Belmont, Calif.: Wadsworth Publishers, 1974), 39.

34. Washington to the President of Congress, 11 May 1776, in W. W. Abbot, ed., *Papers of George Washington*, 4:276–81; and Lyman H. Butterfield, "Psychological Warfare in 1776: The Jefferson-Franklin Plan to Cause Hessian Desertions," *Proceedings of the American Philosophical Society* 94, no. 3 (June 1950): 233.

35. *Journals of the Continental Congress* (hereafter *JCC*), 5:640.

36. Ibid., 653–55; and Butterfield, "Psychological Warfare," 236.

37. Melodie Andrews, "Myrmidons from Abroad: The Role of the German Mercenary in the Coming of American Independence" (Ph.D. diss., University of Houston, 1986), 296; and *JCC*, 5:653–55.

38. Washington to Hancock, in *Writings of George Washington*, 5:450–51.

39. Washington to Hancock, in *Writings of George Washington*, 5:491.

40. Butterfield, "Psychological Warfare," 237. This story apparently is based on Ludwick's obituary tribute that originally appeared in the *American Daily Advertiser*, Philadelphia, 30 June 1801. Such tributes have a tendency for factual error; however, Butterfield states that "nothing is more plausible than Ludwick, at Washington's request, performed such a mission in order to convey the circulars prepared by Congress to those for whom they were meant." Ibid., 237. Another "channel" was developed by Benjamin Franklin, a later addition to the Committee to subvert the Hessians. Placing the circulars in drift-canoes that included in each a little tobacco "with some other little things," Franklin hoped that the Hessians would "divide among them as Plunder before the Officers could know the Contents of the Paper and prevent it." Benjamin Franklin to Horatio Gates, 28 August 1776, *American Archives*, 5th ser., ed. Peter Force, 1:1193. Some of the handbills were printed on the back of tobacco paper, and that is where Franklin got his idea. No copy with the "Tobacco Marks" as described by Franklin exist, however, in American or German records. Andrews, "Myrmidons from Abroad," 298. Hessian General von Heister enclosed one of the Congressional circulars in a letter to the Landgrave dated 3 September 1776. The back of the circular is blank but does prove that the bills got to the Hessian camp.

41. Dr. Julius Friedrich Wasmus, a German military surgeon, observed that Hessian prisoners of war were commonly sent out into the countryside. "A roll was put up with the name and place and of the man with whom the soldiers are working." See Gabriel Nadeau, "Julius Friedrich Wasmus: A German Military Surgeon during the Revolution," *Bulletin of the History of Medicine* 18 (October 1945): 253; and Headquarters Papers of the British Army in America, *The Sir Guy Carleton Papers*, no. 7174, letter of thirty-five Hessian prisoners of war to Lieut. Gen. von Lossberg, 20 March 1783.

42. Sir Guy Carleton Papers, no. 8236, deposition given by Jacob Peter and Valentine Landau, 27 June 1783, David Library of the American Revolution, Washington Crossing, Pa.

43. Ibid., nos. 7174, 8286. According to researchers Wayne Bodle and Linne Schenck (who have done extensive research on the Mount Hope Furnace), the Captain Dille referred to in the Hessian letter to von Lossberg was probably Captain Anthony Selin of Hazen's Second Canadian Regiment. Selin was a Swiss adventurer in the Continental army, which may explain why the Hessians thought he was German. Faesch, in an incredible circular chain of events, to cover the thirty dollar cost of the discharges from Captain Dille, simply reduced the debt still owed him by the public treasury for an unpaid iron contract. In effect, the government allowed Faesch to expropriate the labor of the Hessians to pay off its own debt.

44. Official Losses of the Hesse-Cassel Troops (Source: Preussisches Geheimes Staatsarchiv, Berlin, Heeresarchiv., Rep. 15A, Kap. 33, No. 232); and Elliot Wheelock Hoffman, "German Soldiers in the American Revolution" (Ph.D. diss., University of New Hampshire, 1982), appendix 2.

45. The average rate of desertion for both contending armies during the Revolution was around 20 to 25 percent of the total force. See James H. Edmonson, "Desertion in the American Army during the Revolutionary War" (Ph.D. diss., George Washington University, 1971), passim. For statistics on Hessian desertion, see Hoffman, "German Soldiers in the American Revolution," appendix 2.

46. William S. Cramer, "From Hessian Drummer to Maryland Ironmaker," *JSHA* 3, no. 1 (1985): 24.

47. Heinz Reuter, "Hessian Troops from Ziegenhain in America" (unpublished manuscript found in the papers of the Johannes Schwalm Historical Association, Lancaster, Pa.), 9.; and "Memoirs of a Hessian Conscript: J. G. Seume's Reluctant Voyage to America," trans. Margarete Woelfel, *William and Mary Quarterly*, 3d ser., 5 (October 1948): 556.

48. Johannes Schwalm Historical Association, ed., *Johannes Schwalm: The Hessian* (Millville, Pa.: Precision Printers, 1976), 9; and Captain Johann Ewald, *Diary of the American War: A Hessian Journal*, trans. Joseph P. Tustin (New Haven, Conn.: Yale University Press, 1979), 248.

49. Johann Conrad Dohla, *A Hessian Diary of the American Revolution*, trans. Bruce E. Burgoyne (Norman: University of Oklahoma Press, 1989), 5–6. Stephen Popp stated that the boats were so crowded that many men of both regiments had to stand all night, and that the time was passed singing hymns and praying. *A Hessian Soldier in the American Revolution: The Diary of Stephen Popp*, trans. Reinhard Pope (Racine, Wis., 1953), 27.

50. Mark Schwalm, "The True German Mercenaries," *JSHA* 3, no. 4: 19.

51. Schwalm, "The True German Mercenaries," 19. Mark Schwalm stated that previous service soldiers served in eighteen separate principalities. Twenty-four recruits served for Prussia and Holland each, and twenty for the Austrian army. These same soldiers also represented more than 12 percent of the total number of recruits who eventually deserted.

52. Rodney Atwood, *The Hessians* (London: Cambridge University Press, 1980), 189; and James Thacher, *A Military Journal during the American Revolutionary War from 1775 to 1783* (Boston, 1827), 167.

53. Ibid., 190.

54. Johannes Reuber, diary entry dated 12 January 1777, *Personal Diary*, *JSHA* 1, no. 3 (1979): 9.

55. Ibid., 10.

56. JSHA, *Johannes Schwalm*, 25.

57. Proclamation of General Israel Putnam, 16 November 1777, trans. William T. Parsons, *Deutsch-Amerikanisches Magazin* (American Antiquarian Society, Worcester, Mass.), 1:401.

58. Ibid., diary entry 8 October 1777, 10.

59. Rev. G. C. Coster, *Hessian Soldiers in the American Revolution: Records of Their Marriages and Baptisms, 1776–1783*, trans. Marie Dickore (Cincinnati, Ohio, 1959), 1–11. From 1776 to 1783, Coster married fifty-six Hessians. All the women had German surnames before marriage. About 20 percent of these women crossed the Atlantic with their unit as camp followers. The rest were of German American origin.

60. Atwood, *The Hessians*, 191; and Richard Barth, William Doernemann and Mark Schwalm, "The Trenton Prisoner List," *JSHA* 4, no. 1 (1985): 1–21. The authors noted that the Hessians were also a valuable source of exchange for American prisoners of war living in wretched conditions in New York. Therefore exchange, rather than recruitment, frequently overrode any sentiment for inducing Hessians to stay behind. American exchange commissioners were instructed not to allow, "on any pretense," Hessians to remain with American families, for if they did, it "must be after exchange, by desertion." Joseph Holmes to Ezekial Williams, ibid., 3.

61. Atwood, *The Hessians*, 201; and Kenneth S. Jones, "Karl Friedrich Fuhrer: Prisoner, Patriot, Publisher," *JSHA* 3, no. 3 (1987): 2–7.

62. *Papers of the Continental Congress* (hereafter *PCC*), reel 97, item 78, 13:479.

63. Ibid., 479–80. Fuhrer and Kleinschmitt thought it was also especially important to organize the unit on "the German footing," meaning that it should appear like the Hessian units the officers and men were used to.

64. *JCC* 12 (1778): 866–67.

65. Ibid., 866–67, 1193; *PCC*, item 147, 2:339; *PCC*, reel 157, item 147, 2:339–40. When Juliat decided to redefect back to the British, he allegedly informed the energetic British major Patrick Ferguson of Count Pulaski's lax military dispositions in the vicinity of Little Egg Harbor. Leading a raiding party ashore, Ferguson inflicted heavy casualties on the unsuspecting Americans. Pulaski, concerned about his own military reputation in the eyes of the Americans, blamed the entire disaster on Juliat's defection alone. Thus Congress quickly abandoned its plans for a deserter corps. See Franklin Kemp, *A Nest of Rebel Pirates* (Little Egg Harbor, N.J.: The Laureate Press, 1957), 37–51; and William S. Stryker, *The Affair at Little Egg Harbor* (Trenton, 1894).

66. Proclamation, *New Jersey Gazette*, 27 September 1780.

67. Ewald, *Diary*, 248; and Hoffman, "German Soldiers," 506.

68. Hoffman, "German Soldiers," 506; and Ernst Kipping, trans., *At General Howe's Side* (Monmouth Beach, N.J.: Philip Freneau Press, 1974), 48.

69. Ernst Kipping, *The Hessian View of America, 1776–1783* (Monmouth Beach, N.J.: Philip Freneau Press, 1971), 10.

70. Lord Shelburne, *Papers*, 69:117–24.

71. General von Riedesal, *Memoirs*, 2:24; *Hadden's Journal and Orderly Books* (Albany, N.Y.: J. Munsell and Sons, 1884), 328–30; and William L. Dabney, *After Saratoga: The Story of the Convention Army* (Albuquerque: University of New Mexico Press, 1954), 40–41.

72. *Johannes Schwalm Historical Association* 4, no. 3 (1991): 1–13.

73. See Clifford Neal Smith, ed., *Mercenaries from Hesse-Hanau*, ser. 26, no. 39: 93; ser. 23, no. 90, German-American Genealogical Research Monograph, no. 5 (DeKalb, Ill.: Westland Publications, 1981).

74. Lion G. Miles and Doris N. Suresch, "Two Men from Brunswick," *Johannes Schwalm Historical Association* 2, no. 2 (1982).

75. Lion G. Miles, "Johann Leibheit and the Convention Army," *Johannes Schwalm Historical Association*, vol. 2, no. 1 (1981), 35; George Washington to Moses Hazen, 25 December 1782, in *Writings of Washington*, 25:467.

76. Morristown National Historic Park, Ligerwood Collection, fiche 341, band 5, 87.

77. Ibid. Lossberg also thought that they had intentionally enlisted with the knowledge

that the frigate would probably soon fall to the British navy and that they would be free in any case. Lossberg's assertion is somewhat implausible. Eighteenth-century sea engagements were renowned for lethality. Signing aboard any man-of-war entailed great risk.

78. William L. Stone, ed., *Memoirs, Letters, and Journals of Major General Riedesal* (New York: New York Times and Arno Press, 1969), 2:4–5, 9.

79. William M. Dabney, *After Saratoga: The Story of the Convention Army* (Albuquerque: University of New Mexico Press, 1954), 39–40; and Stone, ed., *Memoirs* . . . , 2:28–29.

80. Carl Leopold Baurmeister, *Revolution in America: Confidential Letters and Journals, 1776–1784* (New Brunswick, N.J.: Rutgers University Press, 1957), 89.

81. Ibid., 541.

82. Rudolf Karl Tross, *The Zweybrucken or Royal Deux-Ponts Regiment and Yorktown* (Yorktown, Va.: York County Bicentennial Committee, 1981), 3.

83. Baron Ludwig von Closen, *The Revolutionary Journal of Baron Ludwig von Closen, 1780–1783*, trans. Evelyn M. Acomb (Chapel Hill: University of North Carolina Press, 1958), xxv.

84. Ibid., 120.

85. Mark A. Schwalm, *The Hessians: Auxiliaries to the British Crown in the American Revolution* (Mechanicsburg: Pennsylvania Chapter, Palatines to America, 1984), 14; and Jonathan Stayer, "The Hessians of Lewis Miller: Assimilation of German Soldiers in America after the Revolution" (M.A. thesis, Pennsylvania State University at Harrisburg, 1988), 9.

86. Schwalm, *The Hessians*, 32; and Stayer, "Hessians of Lewis Miller," 10.

87. Edward J. Lowell, *The Hessians and Other German Auxiliaries of Great Britain in the Revolutionary War* (originally published 1884; reprint, Williamstown, Mass.: Corner House Publishers, 1975), 288 (page references are to reprint edition); Stayer, "Hessians of Lewis Miller," 12.

88. Ibid., 22. The York County Historical Society uncovered Miller's sketches in its archives in 1966. For more information on Miller's Hessians, see Jonathan Stayer, "The Hessians of Lewis Miller," *JSHA* 4, no. 1 (1989).

89. Jonathan R. Stayer, "The Hessians of Lewis Miller," *Journal of Johannes Schwalm Historical Association* 4, no. 1 (1989): 78–79; U.S. Bureau of the Census, York Borough and Township, *Heads of Families at the First Census of the United States Taken in the Year 1790: Pennsylvania* (Washington, D.C.: Government Printing Office, 1908), 281–82; Don Yoder, "Palatine, Hessian, Dutchman: Three Images of the German in America," in *Ebbes fer Alle: Ebber Ebbes fer Dich*, Publications of the Pennsylvania German Society (Breinigsville: Pennsylvania German Society, 1980), 14:112; and Paul E. Doutrich, "The Evolution of an Early American Town: York-Town, Pennsylvania, 1740–1790" (Ph.D. diss., Department of History, University of Kentucky, 1985), 62.

90. Clifford Neal Smith, *Brunswick Deserter-Immigrants of the American Revolution*, German-American Genealogical Research Monograph no. 1 (Thomson, Ill.: Heritage House Publishers, 1973), 1.

91. Smith, *Brunswick Deserter-Immigrants*, 1–47 passim; Hans Helmuth Rimpau, "The Brunswickers in Nordamerika, 1776–1783," *Archiv fuer Sippenforschung* 43 (August 1971): 204–19; 44 (November 1971): 293–308; 45 (February 1972): 346–55. According to Smith, Rimpau did not list soldiers who were presumed dead, although it seems likely that some so listed were, in fact, deserters. The duke of Brunswick received a special indemnity from the British for every soldier killed, so that it was advantageous to report some deserters dead, when possible.

92. Clifford Neal Smith, ed., *Mercenaries from Ansbach and Bayreuth, Germany, Who Remained in America after the Revolution*, Research Monograph no. 2 (McNeal, Ariz.: West-

land Publications, 1979), 1–58; Hoffman, "German Soldiers," 373–74; and Charles W. Ingrao, *The Hessian Mercenary State: Ideas, Institutions, and Reform under Frederick II, 1760–1785* (Cambridge: Cambridge University Press, 1987), 153–63.

93. Kipping, *A Hessian View of America*, 11.

94. Ibid., 10–11.

95. Ibid., 11.

96. Ibid., 46. The consolidated lists of the men of the von Lossberg regiment are found in Robert Oakley Slagle's "The Von Lossburg Regiment" (Ph.D. diss., The American University, Washington, D.C., 1925).

97. Archivschule Marburg, Institut für Archivwissenschaft, *Hessische Truppen im amerikanischen Unabhängigkeitskrieg (HETRINA): Index nach Familiennamen*, 5 vols., passim; and Hoffman, "German Soldiers," 569.

98. John B. B. Trussell, *The Pennsylvania Line: Regimental Organization and Operations, 1776–1783* (Harrisburg: Pennsylvania Historical and Museum Commission, 1977), 222–26, 229–31, 248–56. The exact level of German participation is difficult to determine, because few soldiers, native or foreign, listed their places of birth upon enlistment. Germanic surnames abound in nearly all regiments from New York, the mid-Atlantic states, and the upper South. This trend stands to reason, because these states were areas where prewar German immigration was highest. Because record keeping by recruiting parties was lax, the level of Germanic recruitment was probably actually higher.

99. Trussell, *The Pennsylvania Line*, 253; and *Pennsylvania Archives*, 5th ser., 2:9–11. The revolt began in George Nagel's and James Ross's predominately German companies. See Nathanael Greene to George Washington, 10 September 1775, *Nathanael Greene Papers*, 1:117, William L. Clements Library, Ann Arbor, Mich.; and Fitzpatick, *Writings of Washington*, 3:490–91.

100. Horst Dippel, *Germany and the American Revolution: 1770–1800*, trans. Bernard Uhlendorf (Chapel Hill: University of North Carolina Press, 1977), 238–41.

CHAPTER FOUR *Changing One Master for Another*

1. John Chavis to Senator Willie P. Mangrum, 10 March 1832, quoted in Jeffrey J. Crow, *The Black Experience in Revolutionary North Carolina* (Raleigh: Division of Archives and History, North Carolina Department of Cultural Resources, 1989), x, 98–99; see also David Brion Davis, *The Problem of Slavery in the Age of Revolution, 1770–1823* (Ithaca, N.Y.: Cornell University Press, 1975), 398.

2. *Washington Papers*, series 3G, 30 December 1775; Peter Maslowski, "National Policy Towards the Use of Black Troops in the Revolution," *South Carolina Historical Magazine* 73 (January 1972): 5; and Alain C. White, comp., *The History of the Town of Litchfield, 1720–1920* (Litchfield, Conn.: Enquirer Print, 1920), 152. Cash Africa was allowed to reenlist in 1777 when it became obvious that African American manpower was indispensable to the army and served until the end of the war.

3. Peter Force, ed., *American Archives* (Washington, D.C., 1837–53) (hereafter *Am. Arch.*), 4th ser., 3:1161; and *Washington Papers*, series 3G, 12 November 1775, Library of Congress; *Journals of the Continental Congress*, 16 January 1776.

4. Benjamin Quarles's seminal study, *The Negro in the American Revolution* (New York: W. W. Norton, 1961), remains the most complete account of the African American in British or Continental service. It is, however, now more than thirty years old and needs to be expanded in light of new evidence and perspectives uncovered by a later generation of social, political, and military historians. See Benjamin Quarles, *The Negro in the American*

Revolution (New York: W. W. Norton, 1961). For the most recent work on black resistance in the Revolutionary period, see Sylvia Frey's excellent *Water from the Rock: Black Resistance in a Revolutionary Age* (Princeton, N.J.: Princeton University Press, 1992); Gary Nash, *Race and Revolution* (Madison, Wis.: Madison House Publishers, 1990); Peter Wood, "The Dream Deferred: Black Freedom Struggles on the Eve of White Independence," in *In Resistance: Studies in African, Caribbean, and Afro-American History*, ed. Gary Y. Okihiro (Amherst: University of Massachusetts Press, 1986); and Gary Nash, *Forging Freedom: The Formation of Philadelphia's Black Community, 1720–1840* (Cambridge, Mass.: Harvard University Press, 1988).

5. *The Colonial Laws of New York*, 2:161–62.

6. William H. Hening, ed., *The Statutes at Large: Being a Collection of All the Laws of Virginia* 4 (Richmond, Va., 1810–23), 119; and "An Agent for Carolina and Merchants Trading Thither" to the Board of Trade, 18 July 1715, in *The Colonial Records of North Carolina, 1662–1766*, ed. William Saunders (Raleigh, N.C., 1886–90), 2:197.

7. Benjamin Quarles, "The Colonial Militia and Negro Manpower," *The Mississippi Valley Historical Review*, 45, no. 4 (March 1959): 643. During the Seven Years' War, the governors of Maryland, Pennsylvania, and New Jersey all hesitated to enlist slaves and indentured servants in the provincial forces. See William H. Browne, ed., *Archives of Maryland*, vol. 6 (1883), 342; and Charles H. Lincoln, ed., *The Correspondence of William Shirley*, vol. 2 (1912), 321–22.

8. Frey, *Water from the Rock*, 45. Peter Wood noted that one reason why historians have failed to see the true role that black resistance played in defining events during the Revolution was because they have studied the Revolution colony by colony and have, therefore, failed to see the connections of prewar African American revolts. See Wood, "The Dream Deferred," 166–87. Two other recent studies that emphasized the connection between slave resistance and the Revolution are Robert A. Olwell, "Domestick Enemies: Slavery and Political Independence in South Carolina, May 1775–March 1776," *Journal of Southern History* 55 (1989): 21–48; and Richard B. Sheridan, "The Jamaican Slave Insurrection Scare of 1776 and the American Revolution," *Journal of Negro History* 61 (July 1976): 290–308.

9. Peter Linebaugh and Marcus Rediker, "The Many-Headed Hydra: Sailors, Slaves, and the Atlantic Working Class in the Eighteenth Century," *Journal of Historical Sociology* 3 (September 1990): 225–53.

10. Peter Wood, "The Dream Deferred: Black Freedom Struggles on the Eve of White Independence," 168, 169, 181.

11. Wood, "The Dream Deferred," 169. On the Somerset case, see A. Leon Higginbotham, Jr., *In the Matter of Color: Race and the American Legal Process: The Colonial Period* (New York: Oxford University Press, 1978), 333–63; and Bullock and Houston to John Adams, in *Diary and Autobiography of John Adams*, ed. L. H. Butterfield, vol. 2 (Cambridge, Mass.: Harvard University Press, 1962), 183.

12. Charles W. Akers, "Our Modern Egyptians: Phillis Wheatley and the Whig Campaign against Slavery in Revolutionary Boston," *Journal of Negro History* (1975): 406–7; Ruth Bogin, "Liberty Further Extended: A 1776 Antislavery Manuscript by Lemuel Haynes," *William and Mary Quarterly* (hereafter cited as *WMQ*), 3d ser. (1983): 85–105; and Frey, *Water from the Rock*, 49–50.

13. Abigail Adams to John Adams, 22 September 1774, in Charles F. Adams, *Familiar Letters of John Adams and His Wife Abigail Adams* (New York, 1876), 41–42.

14. Sidney Kaplan, "The Domestic Insurrections of the Declaration of Independence," *Journal of Negro History* 61 (1976): 249–50; and James Madison to William Bradford, 26 November 1774, in *The Papers of James Madison*, ed. William T. Hutchinson and William M. E. Rachal (Chicago: University of Chicago Press, 1932), 1:129–30.

15. *Georgia Gazette* (Savannah), 7 December 1774; Frey, *Water from the Rock*, 54.

16. Colonel John Simpson, Chairman of the Safety Committee in Pitt County, to Colonel Richard Cogdell, Chairman of the Safety Committee in Craven County, 15 July 1775, in Saunders, ed., *Colonial Records of North Carolina*, 10:94–95. Simpson's committee had "whipt and crapped the ears" of all slaves suspected of complicity in the conspiracy. He mentioned one "negro wench" who incited the committee with a false report of more than 250 slaves near Pometo. According to Janet Schaw, a Scottish noblewoman visiting the area at the time, the entire lower Cape Fear area of North Carolina was absolutely panicked by rumors of potential slave rebellions. See Janet Schaw, *Journal of a Lady of Quality, 1774–1776*, ed. Evangeline Walker Andrews and Charles Andrews (New Haven, Conn.: Yale University Press, 1921), 199–201.

17. *Papers of Henry Laurens*, 10:207 nn. 3, 4, 5; Wood, "The Dream Deferred," 176; and Frey, *Water from the Rock*, 61. For other incidences of slave unrest in North and South Carolina at the beginning of the war, see E. Stanley Godbolt, *Christopher Gadsden and the American Revolution* (Knoxville: University of Tennessee Press, 1982), 145; Henry Laurens to Edward Thornborough, 18 December 1775, "Journal of the Council of Safety," *Collections of the South Carolina Historical Society*, 3:94–95; Laurens journal entry, 20 December 1775, ibid., 102–3; and Henry Laurens to Captain Boykin, 20 February 1776, ibid., 263–64.

18. Alan D. Watson, "Impulse toward Independence: Resistance and Rebellion among North Carolina Slaves, 1750–1775," *Journal of Negro History*, no. 4 (1978): 325; and Saunders, *Colonial Records of North Carolina*, 10:137–39. Martin was probably not involved in the Beaufort uprising. He denied the Committee of Safety's charges against him but later added that "nothing could ever justify the design, falsely imputed to me, of giving encouragement to the negroes, but the actual and declared rebellion of the King's subjects, and the failure of all other means to maintain the King's Government." Ibid., 138. The Committee quickly declared the governor persona non grata and ordered his letter published throughout the colony.

19. Saunders, ed., *The Colonial Records of North Carolina*, 10:95.

20. Stephen Bull to Henry Laurens, 14 March 1776, in *Documentary History of the American Revolution*, ed. Robert W. Gibbes, vol. 1 (New York, 1853), 268–69.

21. *Virginia Gazette* (Williamsburg, Va.), 17, 23 November 1775.

22. Robert Honyman, *Diary*, 10 February 1776, Peter Force Collection, item 73, reel 86, Manuscripts Division, Library of Congress, Washington, D.C.

23. Force, *Am. Arch.* (1843), 5th ser., 2:160–62. African Americans who successfully made their way to Dunmore but where later recaptured by the Virginians were not returned to their former owners. Rather, the Virginia Convention ordered the recaptured slaves to be sent to work in "the Lead Mines of the County of Fincastle." In this way the Virginians felt they had contained the insurrection and frightened those who had not yet deserted. There was also an indication that the Virginians suspected Dunmore of engaging in "germ warfare." The 15 June 1776 edition of the *Virginia Gazette* reported that Dunmore "had inoculated two African Americans and sent them ashore at Norfolk to spread the smallpox." There was probably no truth to the accusation, but it is interesting to note that the first thing that Henry Laurens's raid on runaway slaves living on Sullivan's Island accomplished was to "burn the pest house" that the British had established for the sick runaway slaves. See Henry Laurens journal entry, "Journal of the Council of Safety," 20 December 1775, *Collections*, 3:102–3.

24. *Maryland Gazette*, 14 December 1775; and Quarles, "Lord Dunmore as Liberator," *The William and Mary Quarterly* (July 1958): 502–3.

25. Landon Carter diary entry, in Jack R. Greene, *The Diary of Landon Carter of Sabine Hall, 1752–1778* (Charlottesville: University Press of Virginia, 1965), 1051.

26. Ibid., 1051–52.

27. *Pennsylvania Evening Post*, 14 December 1775; and Nash, *Forging Freedom*, 45–46.

28. Charles Isham, ed., "The Papers of Silas Deane," in *Collections of the New York Historical Society* (New York, 1886), 397. *Omnia tentanda* translates, in this case, "to try everything."

29. Richard B. Sheridan, "The Jamaican Slave Insurrection Scare of 1776 and the American Revolution," *Journal of Negro History* (July 1976): 293, 300; and *Robertson-MacDonald Letters*, National Library of Scotland, MS. 3942, 259–63.

30. *Robertson-MacDonald Letters*, 260–61. The plot was apparently uncovered when a slave was caught drawing the bullets out of his overseer's pistol. More than 135 slaves were arrested by the militia; 17 were executed, 45 transported, 11 administered severe corporal punishment, and 62 acquitted. A planter who lived near Lucea stated that "some have been burnt alive, some hanged, some gibbeted, and others transported." Sheridan, "Jamaican Slave Insurrection," 298; and British Public Record Office, London, Colonial Office, 137/71, Minutes of the Privy Council, 31 July and 6 August 1776, 309, 358.

31. Sheridan, "Jamaican Slave Insurrection," 305; Governor William Mathew Burt to Lord Germaine, 28 April 1778, quoted in Elsa V. Goveia, *Slave Society in the British Leeward Islands at the End of the Eighteenth-Century* (New Haven, Conn.: Yale University Press, 1965), 95.

32. James Madison to William Bradford, 19 June 1775, in *The Papers of James Madison*, 1:153.

33. Adams diary entry, 24 September 1775, in *Letters of the Delegates to Congress*, 2:50–51; and Adams, *Works*, 2:428.

34. Extract of a letter from Charleston merchant Josiah Smith, in Force, *Am. Arch.*, 4th ser., 2:1129; John Drayton, *Memoirs of the American Revolution*, 2 vols. (Charleston, S.C.: A. E. Miller, 1821), 1:231; and Frey, *Water from the Rock*, 56–57.

35. Force, *Am. Arch.*, 4th ser., 2:762, 3:1385. Fears of African Americans' gaining knowledge of the use of weapons caused the Philadelphia Committee of Safety to send David Owen, a local recruiter, to the workhouse, "because he was suspected of enlisting Negroes" against the wishes of Congress. See *The Colonial Records of Pennsylvania, 1683–1790*, vol. 10 (Philadelphia, 1852–53), 427.

36. Gates to Massachusetts Council, 2 July 1779, Revolutionary Rolls Coll., CCI, 138–140, Mass. Arch.; and Quarles, *The Negro in the American Revolution*, 70.

37. *JCC*, 11 February 1777, 13:119; ibid., 14–15 April 1777, 262–63. In April 1777 Congress further resolved that if the states failed to forward their recruiting quotas, they should draft them from their respective militias. Language was inserted into the resolution that allowed the recruitment of servants and apprentices and prohibited the imprisonment of soldiers for debts not exceeding fifty dollars. Removed from the bill was a clause that compensated masters for the enlistment of their servants.

38. Mackenzie, *Diary*, 1:84–85.

39. William Heath to John Adams, 23 October 1775, John Adams Papers, Mass. Hist. Soc.; and Quarles, *The Negro in the American Revolution*, 12.

40. W. B. Hartgrove, "The Negro in the American Revolution," *Journal of Negro History* 1 (1916): 126.

41. Foner, *Blacks in the American Revolution*, 68.

42. David O. White, *Connecticut's Black Soldiers* (Chester, Conn.: Pequot Press, 1973), 8.

43. Lorenzo Greene, "Some Observations on the Black Regiment of Rhode Island in the American Revolution," *Journal of Negro History* 37, no. 2 (April 1952): 143.

44. Greene, "Black Regiment of Rhode Island," 143; and Philip S. Foner, *Labor and the American Revolution* (Westport, Conn.: Greenwood Press, 1976), 182.

45. *Rhode Island Archives: Records of the State of Rhode Island, December 1777–October 1779,* 10:41.

46. *Rhode Island Colonial Records,* 8:641; and Greene, "Black Regiment of Rhode Island," 149.

47. Greene, "Black Regiment," 153–55; and *Records of the State of Rhode Island,* 10:42–43. Greene points out that some whites seemingly preferred to lose the war rather than win it by arming slaves.

48. Table—Showing Name of Slave, Date of Enlistment, Place Enlisted from and Slaves Enlisted Each Month, February 25, 1778–October 14, 1778, General Treasurer's Accounts, 1761–1781, Alphabet Book No. 6, Greene, "Black Regiment," 156–57, 161; and Lorenzo Greene, *The Negro in Colonial New England, 1620–1776* (New York: Columbia University Press, 1942), 88.

49. Greene, "Black Regiment," 161–62.

50. Ibid., 164–65; *Rhode Island Archives:* Military Papers, Revolutionary War, 3:23, nos. 1, 2, 24; nos. 1, 2, 25; nos. 1, 2; General Treasurer's Accounts, 1761–81, vol. 6.

51. Greene, "Black Regiment," 171.

52. *Miscellaneous Archives of Massachusetts,* 199:80; George Livermore, *An Historical Research on Negroes as Slaves, as Citizens, and as Soldiers* (New York: Arno Press, reprinted 1969), 125–26 (page references are to reprint edition).

53. *Miscellaneous Archives of Massachusetts,* 199:80; and Livermore, *Historical Research on Negroes,* 125–26.

54. White, *Connecticut's Black Soldiers,* 32. No reason was given for the formation of the Connecticut unit. There were other African Americans in the Connecticut line who were not in this unit. Perhaps the company was formed because, as Thomas Kench suggested in 1778, it was thought that all-black units would compete with white companies in demonstrating their fighting ardor and zeal; Kaplan, *The Black Presence in the American Revolution,* 1st ed., 59. Among the black volunteers were men who were destined to become famous in the Haitian revolution. Andre Rigaud and Louis Beauvais were noncommissioned officers at the siege of Savannah in 1779. Henri Christophe earned his freedom as an infantryman in the Chasseurs and later became head of the revolutionary Haitian government.

55. E. Stanley Godbolt, Jr., and R. H. Woody, *Christopher Gadsden and the American Revolution* (Knoxville: University of Tennessee Press, 1982), 195.

56. Ibid., 195.

57. William G. Simms, ed., *The Army Correspondence of John Laurens* (New York: Bradford Club, 1867), 108–9, 114–18; and Maslowski, "National Policy toward the Use of Black Troops in the Revolution," *South Carolina Historical Magazine* 73 (January 1972): 8. Laurens, in a later letter to his father, apologized for what he termed was a "hare-brained scheme" and laid the project aside until the British army began to devastate the southern states.

58. Maslowski, "Use of Black Troops," 8.

59. Thomas Burke's Draft Committee Report, John Fell Diary, 25 March 1779, William Whipple to Josiah Bartlett, 28 March 1779, *Letters of the Delegates to Congress,* 12:242–45, 257–58.

60. Harold C. Syrett, ed., *The Papers of Alexander Hamilton* (New York: Columbia University Press, 1961–66), 2:17–19.

61. Clinton Proclamation, Clinton Papers, 30 June 1779, William L. Clements Library, Ann Arbor, Mich. The "Phillipsburg Proclamation" was published in the Rivington's Tory newspaper, *Royal Gazette,* which carried the proclamation in every issue from 3 July 1779 through 25 September 1779 and thereafter sporadically.

62. *JCC,* 18:1133. Found in the *Papers of the Continental Congress* was a report of the Board of War that directed "that arms and accoutrements together with the necessary

clothing for the said Corps" be forwarded as soon as possible. The report, however, was endorsed by the Congressional Secretary, Charles Thomson, "August 24, 1781, not to be acted upon." *PCC*, no. 20, II, folio 443.

63. *JCC*, 18:1133; and *PCC*, no. 20, II, folio 443.

64. Maslowski, "Use of Black Troops," 2.

65. Ibid., 15; and A. S. Sally, Jr., ed., *Journal of the House of Representatives of South Carolina*, 8 January 1782–26 February 1782 (Columbia, S.C: State Co., 1916), 21, 56. John Laurens was killed by Tories in late 1782. His African American battalion proposal, never having much local support, apparently died with him. Henry Laurens was captured by the British on a mission to Europe and imprisoned in the Tower of London.

66. *Washington Papers*, ser. 4, 10 July 1782.

67. Maslowski, "Use of Black Troops," 15–16.

68. Honyman Diary, 2 January 1781.

69. Donald L. Robinson, *Slavery in the Structure of American Politics* (New York: Harcourt, Brace, and Jovanovich, 1971), 124.

70. Ralph Izard letter, 10 June 1785, *Papers of Thomas Jefferson*, ed. Julian Boyd (Princeton, N.J.: Princeton University Press), 8:199; Frey, *Water from the Rock*, 142; Moore, *Historical Notes*, 15; and John Hope Franklin, *From Slavery to Freedom* (New York: Knopf, 1967), 134. For information on the formation of "maroon" communities, see Richard S. Dunn, *Sugar and Slaves* (Chapel Hill: University of North Carolina Press, 1972), 38.

71. *Journal of Henry Melchoir Muhlenberg*, vol. 3 (Philadelphia, 1958), 78; and Kaplan, *Black Presence*, rev. ed., 79.

72. *Pennsylvania Packet*, 1 January 1780.

73. Sylvia Frey, "The British and the Black: A New Perspective," *The Historian* 38, no. 2 (February 1976): 229.

74. Kaplan, *Black Presence*, rev. ed., 81.

75. Extract of a letter from Monmouth County, 12 June 1780, regarding Ty, *Pennsylvania Gazette and Weekly Advertiser*, 21 June 1780.

76. Thomas Bee to Governor John Mathews, Goose Creek, 9 December 1782, *Thomas Bee Papers*, South Carolina Library, Columbia, S.C.

77. Ibid., 233.

78. Lt. General Alexander Leslie to General Carleton, 10 August 1782, *Carleton Papers*, David Library of the American Revolution (hereafter DLAR), Washington Crossing, Pa.; and Frey, "The British and the Black," 237. Slavery had been outlawed in England and Scotland since 1772. A community of free blacks was established in Nova Scotia after the war. Some of the former slaves eventually made their way back to Africa. See James W. St. G. Walker, *The Black Loyalists: The Search for a Promised Land in Nova Scotia and Sierra Leone, 1783–1870* (New York: Dalhousie University Press, 1976).

79. John Cruden to Lord Dunmore, 5 January 1782, in Livermore, *Historical Research*, 142–45; and Frey, *Water from the Rock*, 140.

80. See Quarles, *The Negro in the American Revolution*, ix.

81. Robert Ewell Greene, *Black Courage 1775–1783: Documentation of Black Participation in the American Revolution* (Washington, D.C.: Daughters of the American Revolution, 1984), 2.

82. Charles H. Lesser, ed., *The Sinews of Independence: Monthly Strength Reports of the Continental Army* (Chicago: University of Chicago Press, 1976), 84.

83. W. B. Hartgrove, "The Negro Soldier in the American Revolution," *Journal of Negro History* 1 (1916): 127.

84. Lesser, *Sinews of Independence*, 84–85.

85. RG 93, National Archives, General Return, Main Army, 9 February 1778; and

Robert K. Wright, Jr., *The Continental Army* (Washington, D.C.: United States Army Center of Military History, 1986), 125.

86. Marquis De Chastellux, *Travels in North America in the Years 1780, 1781 and 1782*, 2 vols., ed. Howard C. Rice (Chapel Hill: University of North Carolina Press, 1963), 2:229; and White, *Connecticut's Black Soldiers*, 35.

87. Lisa Bull, "The Negro," in *The Ethnic Contribution to the American Revolution*, ed. Frederick F. Harling and Martin Kaufman (Westfield, Mass.: Historical Journal of Western Massachusetts, 1976), 72.

88. Kaplan, *The Black Presence in the American Revolution*, 19, 33, 27, 42. The watercolor of the four soldiers is from the journal of Baron von Closen, Library of Congress, Washington, D.C. See John Trumbull, *Lt. Grosvenor and His Negro Servant*, oil, 1786, Yale University Art Gallery, The Mabel Brady Garvan Collection; Jean-Baptiste Le Paon, *Lafayette at Yorktown*, oil, 1783, Art Collection, Lafayette College, gift of Mrs. John Hubbard; J. N. Gimi, *Washington Crossing the Delaware*, engraving, after painting by Thomas Sully, 1819, Library of Congress; and Paul Giradet, *Washington Crossing the Delaware*, engraving after Emanuel Leutze's painting, 1851, Miriam and D. Wallach Division of Art, Prints, and Photographs, New York Public Library, Astor, Lenox, and Tilden Foundations.

89. Kaplan, "The Black Presence in the American Revolution," 43; and William Ranney, *The Battle of Cowpens*, oil, 1845, Frederick Donhauser, Stony River, Alaska.

90. See Steven Rosswurm, *Arms, Country, and Class: The Philadelphia Militia and the Lower Sort during the American Revolution* (New Brunswick, N.J.: Rutgers University Press, 1987); extract of Continental army personnel return, Alexander Scammell, Adjutant of the Army, 24 August 1778, in Hartgrove, "The Negro Soldier in the American Revolution," 127.

91. Foner, *Blacks in the American Revolution*, 55.

92. Greene, *Black Courage*, 1775–1783, app. 8–10; National Archives, Military Pensions Files, RG 15, of the Adjutant General's Office; Special List No. 34, List of Free Black Heads of Families in the First Census of the U.S. 1790, 1973; Special List No. 36, List of Black Servicemen compiled from the War Department collection of Revolutionary War records, 1974. It should be noted that veterans who applied for pensions in 1818 had to prove that they were in need to qualify for a pension.

93. Nash, *Forging Freedom*, 57–58; and "Inspection Rolls of Negroes, Taken Onboard Sundry Vessels at Staten Island, N.Y.," Carleton Papers, document no. 10427, DLAR.

94. Special List No. 34, "List of Free Black Heads of Families in the 1790 Census" (Washington, D.C.: National Archives, 1973); and Special List No. 36, "List of Black Servicemen Compiled for War Department Records" (Washington, D.C.: National Archives, 1974).

95. Gary B. Nash, *Race and Revolution* (Madison, Wis.: Madison House, 1990), 18.

96. Berlin, *Slaves without Masters, 15; and Population of the United States in 1860* (Washington, D.C., 1864), 592–604.

97. Berlin, *Slaves without Masters*, 3–6; and Jeffrey J. Crow, *The Black Experience in Revolutionary North Carolina* (Raleigh: Division of Archives and History, North Carolina Department of Cultural Resources, 1989), 30.

98. For a similar analysis of resistance to slavery in a West African setting, see Paul E. Lovejoy, *The Ideology of Slavery in Africa* (Beverly Hills, Calif.: Sage Publications, 1981); and Frey, *Water from the Rock*, 86–87. Eugene Genovese called the tradition of African American resistance "nonrevolutionary self-assertion." See Eugene Genovese, *Roll, Jordan, Roll: The World the Slaves Made* (New York: Vintage Books, 1976), 587–97.

99. Berlin, *Slaves Without Masters*, 29.

100. Duncan J. MacLeod, *Slavery, Race, and the American Revolution* (Cambridge: Cambridge University Press, 1974), 164–65. MacLeod states that the closest modern-day paral-

lels to this kind of legislation were the pass laws formerly enforced in South Africa and the requirement in fascist Germany that Jews display the Star of David.

101. Clark, *State Records of North Carolina*, 27:385, 389, 595–96, 28:571–72, 623–25, 662–63, 680–81; Case of Harry, Dinah, and Patt, 5 April 1785, Perquimans County Slave Papers, State Archives of North Carolina; and Crow, *Black Experience*, 83.

102. Michael Mullin, "British Caribbean and North American Slaves in an Era of War and Revolution, 1775–1807," The Southern Experience in the American Revolution, ed. Jeffrey Crow and Larry Tise (Chapel Hill: University of North Carolina Press, 1978), 241–42.

103. Jackson, "Virginia Negro Soldiers and Seamen in the Revolutionary War," *Journal of Negro History*, 27 (July 1992): 253.

104. Nash, *Race and Revolution*, 54.

105. Samuel Sutphen, "Wartime Experience of a New Jersey Slave," in *New Jersey in the American Revolution, 1763–1783: A Documentary History*, ed. Larry Gerlack (Trenton: New Jersey Bicentennial Commission, 1975), 357.

106. Petition by Ned Griffen, 27 March 1784, Legislative Papers, 50, State Archives of North Carolina; and Clark, *State Records of North Carolina*, 24:639; and Crow, *The Black Experience* 65.

107. See Jesse Lemisch, "The American Revolution Seen from the Bottom Up," in *Towards a New Past: Dissenting Essays in American History*, ed. Barton J. Bernstein (New York: Pantheon Books, 1968), 3–29; Alfred F. Young, ed., *The American Revolution: Explorations in History of American Radicalism* (DeKalb: Northern Illinois University Press, 1976); Benjamin Quarles, ed., *Black Mosaic: Essays in Afro-American History and Historiography* (Amherst: University of Massachusetts Press, 1988), 49, 57–58; and Hoffman, *Slavery and Freedom*, 293.

108. Quarles, *Black Mosaic*, 57–58; see Gerald W. Mullin, *Flight and Rebellion: Slave Resistance in Eighteenth-Century Virginia* (New York: Oxford University Press, 1972), 140–63.

CHAPTER FIVE *Scalp Bounties and Truck Houses*

1. *Georgia Gazette*, 2 February 1774; Ibid., 30 March, 13 April 1774; and Edward J. Cashin, *The King's Ranger: Thomas Brown and the American Revolution* (Athens: University of Georgia Press, 1989), 11–13.

2. For a critique of how Indian culture has been traditionally portrayed in older textbooks and interpretations, see James H. Merrell, "Some Thoughts on Colonial Historians and American Indians," *William and Mary Quarterly* 46 (1989), 96; and Linda K. Kerber, "The Revolutionary Generation: Ideology, Politics, and Culture in the Early Republic," in *The New American History*, ed. Eric Foner (Philadelphia: Temple University Press, 1990), 40–41.

3. William Gordon to General Horatio Gates, 23 June 1776, *American Archives* (hereafter *Am. Arch.*), 4th ser., ed. Peter Force, 4:1041–42.

4. Bernard W. Sheehan, "The Problem of the Indian in the Revolution," in *The American Indian Experience: A Profile*, ed. Philip Weeks (Arlington Heights, Ill.: Forum Press, 1988), 66–67.

5. John Adams to Horatio Gates, 27 April 1776, *Letters of the Delegates to Congress*, 3:586–87. Adams may have had personal reasons for fearing the Indians. His grandfather had been killed in a raid years before.

6. Ibid., 433.

7. Richard Henry Lee to George Washington, 29 June 1775, *Letters of the Delegates to Congress*, 1:558–59; *Journals of the Continental Congress*, 11 July 1775, 2:1741; *The Colonial Records of North Carolina*, ed. William L. Saunders (Raleigh, N.C.: P. M. Hale, 1886–90), 10:329–31.

8. Richard Butler to Guyashusta, April 1776, *Papers of the Continental Congress* (hereafter cited as *PCC*), reel 91, item 78, 2:41.

9. *PCC*, reel 91, item 78, 2:46.

10. Albert T. Volwiler, *George Croghan and the Westward Movement, 1741–1782* (Cleveland: Arthur H. Clark, 1926), 324; Dr. John Connolly to the Continental Congress, 8 February 1776, *Am. Arch.*, 4th ser., 5:1122; and Gregory Schaff, *Wampum Belts and Peace Trees: George Morgan, Native Americans and Revolutionary Diplomacy* (Golden, Colo.: Fulcrum, 1990), 10.

11. John Stuart "anecdote" to Henry Clinton, March 1776, *The Clinton Papers*, 14:45, William L. Clements Library, Ann Arbor, Mich. Benjamin Franklin, comparing the vast number of Native-American tribes on the western frontier to Mogul hordes, warned Congress that American "security [would] not be obtained by . . . forts, unless they were connected like that of China, from one end of our settlements to the other." Benjamin Franklin, *The Interest of Great Britain Considered, with Regard to Her Colonies* (London, 1760).

12. George Washington to the President of Congress, 19 April 1776, *PCC*, reel 186, item 169, 1:291–96.

13. Daniel K. Richter and James Merrell, eds., *Beyond the Covenant Chain: The Iroquois and Their Neighbors in Indian North America, 1600–1800* (Syracuse, N.Y.: Syracuse University Press, 1987), 29–31.

14. "George Croghan's Journal, 3 April 1759 to [30] April 1763," *Pennsylvania Magazine of History and Biography* 71 (1947), 357; and John D. Barnhart, ed., *Henry Hamilton and George Rogers Clark in the American Revolution to Include the Journal of Gov. Henry Hamilton* (Crawfordsville, Ind.: R. E. Banta, 1951), 22.

15. Walter H. Mohr, *Federal Indian Relations, 1774–1788* (Philadelphia: University of Pennsylvania Press, 1933), 40.

16. William T. Hagan, *Longhouse Diplomacy and Frontier Warfare: The Iroquois Confederacy in the American Revolution*, 11.

17. Ethan Allen to the Indians of Canada, 24 May 1775, Q11, *Public Archives of Canada*, 193–94; and Barbara Graymont, *The Iroquois in the American Revolution* (Syracuse, N.Y.: Syracuse University Press, 1978), 68.

18. Graymont, *Iroquois*, 68.

19. Ibid., 95–96.

20. Ibid.

21. Martin I. J. Griffin, *The Catholic Indians and the American Revolution* (Ridley Park, Penn.: privately published, 1907), 106.

22. Graymont, *Iroquois*, 87. The Simsbury Mine was a makeshift colonial prison that had gained a notoriously unhealthy reputation among the British forces.

23. The Eastern Indians to Washington, 31 January 1776, *Washington Papers*, Library of Congress, folio 2563.

24. George Galphin was likewise appointed commissioner of the southern Indians and noted that he had lost the loyalties of half the Upper Creek Indian towns due to a shortage of trade goods. See James H. O'Donnell, *Southern Indians in the American Revolution* (Knoxville, Tenn.: University of Tennessee Press, 1973), 20–24. The best work on the activities of Morgan is Schaff, *Wampum Belts and Peace Trees*.

25. "Jonathan Elkins' Reminiscences, 1774–1783," Vermont Historical Society, MS.

774940; *Am. Arch.*, 5th ser., 3:1081; and Colin G. Calloway, "Sentinels of the Revolution: Bedel's New Hampshire Rangers and the Abenaki Indians on the Upper Connecticut," *Historical New Hampshire* (Winter 1990), 279.

26. John Allan, "An Account of Colonel John Allan: A Maine Revolutionary," *Sprague's Journal of Maine History* 2, no. 5: 12.

27. Andrew MacFarland Davis, "The Employment of Indian Auxiliaries in the American War," *English Historical Review* 2, no. 8 (October 1887): 714; and Griffin, *Catholic Indians*, 2:103.

28. Henry Mowat to Captain Barkley, 3 August 1778, *Henry Clinton Papers*, 38:76, William L. Clements Library, Ann Arbor, Mich.

29. Griffin, *Catholic Indians*, 120.

30. Thomas Gage to Lord Dartmouth, 12 January 1776, *Thomas Gage Papers*, William L. Clements Library, Ann Arbor, Mich.

31. Jack Sosin, "The Use of Indians in the War of the American Revolution," *Canadian Historical Review* 46, no. 2 (June 1965): 121; and Davis, "Indian Auxiliaries," 721.

32. *Journals of the Continental Congress* (hereafter cited as *JCC*), 17 June 1776, 5:452.

33. George Washington to Colonel David Brodhead, 23 June 1779, in Fitzpatrick, *Writings of Washington*, 15:302–3.

34. George Morgan to the Commissioners for Indian Affairs, 3 June 1776, *Morgan's Journal*, 18–19; and Schaff, *Wampum Belts and Peace Trees*, 96–98.

35. Samuel Adams to John Adams, 22 December 1775, in *Papers of John Adams*, vol. 3, ed. Robert J. Taylor (Cambridge, Mass.: Belknap Press, 1979), 374–76; and *JCC*, 3:443.

36. Deirdre Almeida, "The Stockbridge Indian in the American Revolution," *The Historical Journal of Western Massachusetts*, nos. 3–4 (1974–75): 37.

37. Provincial Congress to Jehoiakin Metoxin, *Am. Arch.*, 4th ser., 1:1347.

38. Thomas F. De Voe, "The Massacre of the Stockbridge Indians," *The Magazine of American History* 5 (September 1880): 189–90.

39. Ibid., 193.

40. Washington to the Commissioners of Indian Affairs, 13 March 1778, in Fitzpatrick, *Writings of Washington*, 11:76–77. Washington was never able to recruit more than two hundred Oneidas. There is no evidence of any Indian recruits being forwarded from the southern tribes. Later Washington retracted his efforts to procure Indian recruits, noting that he "had seen there is very little prospect of engaging a body of Indians . . . to serve with this army." Washington admitted that the scheme was an "experiment" and urged Congress to "counteract the temptations held out by the enemy, and to secure the good will of the Indians, who appear at least to be in a state of hesitancy and indecision, if nothing worse." Washington to the President of Congress, 3 May 1778, ibid., 343–44.

41. *New Hampshire Council Records*, 8:137; "Muster Roll of Captain John Vincent's Company of Indian Rangers," in *History of Newbury, Vermont, from the Discovery of the Coos Country to the Present Time*, ed. Frederick P. Wells (St. Johnsbury, Vt.: Caledonian Co., 1902), 409; and Calloway, "Sentinels of the Revolution," 291–92.

42. Colin G. Calloway, *The Western Abenakis of Vermont, 1600–1800: War, Migration, and Survival of an Indian People* (Norman: University of Oklahoma Press, 1990), 175–81, 188–92. The term "white devil" was later used in the twentieth century by minority leader Malcolm X.

43. Colin G. Calloway, "Sentinels of the Revolution," 275, 282–83; and Horatio Gates to Timothy Bedel, 15 November 1777, *Horatio Gates Papers*, 6:205, 385–87, 389–90, 393–94.

44. James Axtell, *The European and the Indian* (New York: Oxford University Press, 1981), 239.

45. Henry Hamilton to Sir Guy Carleton, 15 January 1778, *Henry Hamilton and George Rogers Clark in the American Revolution*, 32.

46. Philip Schuyler to Henry Laurens, 15 March 1778, *Indian Affairs Papers*, ed. Maryly B. Penrose (Franklin Park, N.J.: Liberty Bell Associates, 1981), 120–21.

47. *Orderly Book of the Hesse-Hanau Feldjaeger*, Ligerwood Collection, microfiche nos. 174–79, David Library of the American Revolution (hereafter cited as DLAR), Washington Crossing, Pa. There was no evidence that this gruesome threat was carried out and was promulgated for its deterrent effect on the Jaegers. Jaegers were light infantry, and the opportunity for them to desert was greater.

48. Translated from the original French quote in a letter from Governor Tryon to William Knox, 21 April 1977, *New York Colonial Documents*, ed. E. O'Callaghan, 8:707; and Sosin, "The Use of Indians in the War of the American Revolution," 120.

49. *Pennsylvania Archives*, 7:362.

50. "Scalp Bounty Proclamation," Library Company of Pennsylvania, Philadelphia; and Henry Young, "Scalp Bounties in Pennsylvania," *Pennsylvania History* 24, no. 1 (January 1957): 214.

51. Roy Harvey Pearce, *The Savages of America: A Study of the Indian and the Idea of Civilization* (Baltimore: Johns Hopkins University Press, 1953), 4; and Young, "Scalp Bounties," 208.

52. Jack M. Sosin, *The Revolutionary Frontier, 1763–1783* (New York: Holt, Rinehart, and Winston, 1967), 5–19.

53. Angie Debo, *The Road to Disappearance: A History of the Creek Indians* (Norman: University of Oklahoma Press, 1941), 35–36; and Cashin, *The King's Ranger*, 9–10.

54. Henry Stuart to John Stuart, British Public Record Office, Colonial Office Papers, ser. 5, 77:145; William L. Saunders, ed., *The Colonial Records of North Carolina*, vol. 10 (Raleigh, N.C., 1886–1890), 763–85; James H. O'Donnell III, "The Southern Indians in the War for American Independence, 1775–1783," in *Four Centuries of Southern Indians*, ed. Charles M. Hudson (Athens: University of Georgia Press, 1975), 46–64.

55. John Stuart to Thomas Gage, 15 September 1775, *PCC*, reel 65, item 51, 1:56; and Merrell, *The Catawba Trail of Tears*, 215.

56. "Journal of the Council of Safety for the Province of South Carolina, 1775," *Collections of the South Carolina Historical Society*, 2 (1858): 32–33.

57. "Journal of the Council of Safety, for the Province of South Carolina, 1775," *Collections of the South Carolina Historical Society* 2 (1858): 31–34, 63; and *Extracts from the Journal of the Provincial Congresses of South Carolina*, ed. Edwin Hemphill (Columbia: University of South Carolina Press, 1960), 56.

58. "Journal of the Second Council of Safety," 3:253, 263–64; and Douglas S. Brown, *The Catawba Indians: Allies in the Revolution* (Columbia: University of South Carolina Press, 1966), 261–62.

59. James Wright to Henry Clinton, 29 March 1776, *The Clinton Papers*, 14:42, William L. Clements Library, Ann Arbor, Mich.

60. Draper Miscellaneous Manuscripts, *Sumpter Papers*, 16:318; and Brown, *The Catawba Indians*, 267.

61. Richard Winn, "General Richard Winn's Notes—1780," ed. Samuel C. Williams, *South Carolina History and Genealogy Magazine* (January 1943), 6–7; John Henry Logan, "Extracts from the Logan Manuscript [of the Upper South]," *Historical Collections of the Joseph Habersham Chapter*, Daughters of the American Revolution, vol. 3, pt. 2, 51; and Brown, *The Catawba Indians*, 267.

62. Brown, *The Catawba Indians*, 271.

63. Homer Bast, "Creek Indian Affairs, 1775–1778," *Georgia Historical Quarterly* 33,

no. 1 (March 1949): 1–4. For a complete history of the Creeks, see Debo, *The Road to Disappearance*.

64. John Stuart to Cherokee Warriors and Headmen, January 1776, *Clinton Papers*, 13:28, William L. Clements Library, Ann Arbor, Mich.

65. 1 July 1775, *Journals of the Continental Congress*, 2:123; and Bast, "Creek Indian Affairs," 6–7.

66. "Talk Sent into the Creek Nation by George Galphin," found in letter of John Stuart to Lord Dartmouth, 17 September 1775, *Public Record Office, Colonial Office* (hereafter cited as *PRO*), 5–77; and Thomas Gage to John Stuart, *PRO*, 5–76.

67. John Stuart to Lord Dartmouth, 17 December 1775, *PRO*, 5–77; and Bast, "Creek Indian Affairs," 10.

68. "Talks at Augusta," British Public Record Office, Colonial Office, 5/94, 121; and David H. Corkran, *The Creek Frontier, 1540–1783* (Norman: University of Oklahoma Press, 1967), 297–98.

69. Archibald Henderson, "The Treaty of Long Island of Holston, July, 1777," *North Carolina Historical Review*, 8:55–116; and Robert S. Cotterill, *The Southern Indians: The Story of the Civilized Tribes Before Removal* (Norman: University of Oklahoma Press, 1954), 45.

70. *North Carolina State Records*, ed. Walter Clark, 13:90, 117, 203; and Cotterill, *Southern Indians*, 48.

71. Sheehan, "The Problem of the Indian in the Revolution," 77; and Schaff, *Wampum Belts*, 198.

72. Francis P. Prucha, *American Indian Policy in the Formative Years* (Cambridge, Mass.: Harvard University Press, 1962), 36–37; and Francis Jennings, "The Indian's Revolution," in *The American Revolution*, ed. Alfred F. Young (DeKalb: Northern Illinois University Press, 1976), 342–43.

73. Frederick Harling and Martin Kaufman, eds., *The Ethnic Contribution to the American Revolution* (Westfield: Historical Journal of Western Massachusetts, 1976), 50; and Graymont, *Iroquois*, 242, 287–88.

74. White Eyes to George Morgan, Spring 1778, *Morgan's Journal*, 2, quoted in Schaff, *Wampum Belts*, 199.

75. George Morgan to Thomas Mifflin, 12 May 1784, *PCC*, reel 180, item 163, 365; reel 91, item 78, 2:419; and Schaff, *Wampum Belts*, 199–200.

76. Jennings, "The Indian's Revolution," 321–22. For justification of comparing the situation of Indians with Irish peasants, see Francis Jennings, *The Invasion of America: Indians, Colonialism, and the Cant of Conquest* (Chapel Hill: University of North Carolina Press, 1975), chap. 5 passim. For an explanation of the American Revolution as a struggle for empire as well, see Richard W. Van Alstyne, *The Rising American Empire*, reprint ed. (New York: W. W. Norton, 1971), chap. 1.

77. Alexander Martin to the Cherokees, 25 May 1783, in Saunders, *Colonial Records of North Carolina*, 14:810; and Cornplanter to George Washington, quoted in Graymont, *Iroquois*, 192. Giving members of the conquering army portions of the defeated enemy's domain was a time-honored concept dating back to the Crusades. See Archer Jones, *The Art of War in the Western World* (New York: Oxford University Press, 1987), 145–47, 200–202, 215–20.

78. Major William Croghan, quoted in Sosin, *The Revolutionary Frontier*, 136. In 1782, frontier militia, led by William Crawford, tomahawked to death nearly ninety defenseless Delaware men, women, and children at Gnadenhutten on the east bank of the Muskingum. The following summer, Crawford and some of his men were trapped near Upper Sandusky by a band of Wyandot, Mingo, and Delawares who singled him out for special revenge. The Indians scalped him, laid hot ashes on his skull, and slowly burned him alive over an open fire. Ibid., 136.

CHAPTER SIX *To Get as Much for My Skin as I Could*

1. Joseph Plumb Martin, *Private Yankee Doodle: Being a Narrative of Some of the Adventures, Dangers and Sufferings of a Revolutionary Soldier*, ed. George F. Scheer (Boston: Little, Brown and Co., 1962), 14. For other verses sung by Revolutionary soldiers, see Oscar Brand, ed., *Songs of '76: Being a Compendium of Music and Verses, Patriotic and Treasonous Sung Both by the Rebels and the Adherents of His Royal Majesty George III* (New York: M. Evans and Co., 1972).

2. Martin, *Private Yankee Doodle*, 60–61.

3. Ibid., 61. Martin did not elaborate on the persuasive techniques used by the Lieutenant and the squad of militiamen. It is probable that they threatened him with bodily harm and impressment if he did not join; they may have, once the lieutenant received the permission of Martin's grandfather. The officer probably felt he had broad discretion with young Joseph Martin. Violence during recruitment was not unusual. Alexander Graydon, a Pennsylvania recruiting officer, was physically attacked at one tavern that served as a recruiting center. See Alexander Graydon, *Memoirs of "His Own Time" with Reminiscences of the Men and Events of the Revolution* (Philadelphia, 1846), 133–36.

4. Martin, *Private Yankee Doodle*, 15–17; and Charles K. Bolton, *The Private Soldier under Washington* (Williamstown, Mass.: Corner House Publishers, 1902; reprint, 1976), 27–31, 48–50, 78–82, 95–97 (page references are to reprint edition).

5. For information on indentured servitude in colonial society, see Abbot Smith, *Colonists in Bondage: White Servitude and Convict Labor in America* (Chapel Hill: University of North Carolina Press, 1947); Jack P. Greene, *Pursuits of Happiness: The Social Development of Early Modern British Colonies and the Formation of American Culture* (Chapel Hill: University of North Carolina Press, 1988); and Cheesman A. Herrick, *White Servitude in Pennsylvania* (Freeport, N.Y.: Books for Libraries Press, 1926).

6. William Hooper to the President of the North Carolina Convention, 16 November 1776, *Letters of the Delegates to Congress* (Washington, D.C.: Library of Congress, 1978), 5:500–503; and John Todd White, "Standing Armies in Time of War: Republican Theory and Military Practice during the American Revolution" (Ph.D. diss., George Washington University, 1978), 198–99.

7. Martin, *Private Yankee Doodle*, 43.

8. Charles Royster, *A Revolutionary People at War: The Continental Army and American Character, 1775–1783* (Chapel Hill: University of North Carolina Press, 1979), 25, 49; John Shy, *A People Numerous and Armed: Reflections on the Military Struggle for American Independence*, rev. ed. (Ann Arbor: University of Michigan Press, 1990), 21; Joseph Hodgkins to Sarah Hodgkins, 13 October 1778, in Herbert T. Wade and Robert A. Lively, *This Glorious Cause: The Adventures of Two Company Officers in Washington's Army* (Princeton, N.J.: Princeton University Press, 1958), 244; and James Duane, Notes of the Debates, 22 February 1776, *Letters of the Delegates to Congress*, 3:294–96.

9. Diary entry, 30–31 January 1776, "Caleb Haskell's Diary," *Pamphlets in American History Collection*, fiche no. B/RW14, David Library of the American Revolution, Washington Crossing, Pa. (hereafter DLAR), 16. It was the first of June before Haskell got home again.

10. Joseph Doddridge, *Notes on the Settlement and Indian Wars of the Western Parts of Virginia and Pennsylvania*, 3d ed. (Pittsburgh, Pa., 1912), 142; and John W. Chambers, *To Raise an Army: The Draft Comes to Modern America* (New York: Free Press, 1987), 17–18. A good analysis of how the colony of Virginia tried to mobilize the "lower sorts" into a long-termed force and the resistance to these designs by the soldiers is found in James R. W. Titus, "Soldiers When They Chose to Be So: Virginians at War, 1754–1763" (Ph.D. diss., Rutgers University, 1983), 154–65.

11. Otho Howard Williams to Nathanael Greene, 26 February 1781, quoted in M. F.

Treacy, *Prelude to Yorktown: The Southern Campaigns of Nathanael Greene, 1780–1781* (Chapel Hill: University of North Carolina Press, 1963), 11; George Washington to Patrick Henry, 13 April 1777, in *Writings of Washington*, vol. 7, ed. John C. Fitzpatrick (Washington, D.C., 1931–44), 408; and Royster, *Revolutionary People*, 50.

12. John Thomas to John Adams, 24 October 1775, *Papers of John Adams*, vol. 3, ed. Robert Taylor (Cambridge, Mass.: Harvard University Press, 1979), 239–41. Thomas also remarked on the diverse racial character of the soldiers. George Washington to Philip Schuyler, 28 July 1775, in *Papers of George Washington*, 1:188–90.

13. William Heath to George Washington, 19 September 1776, Heath Papers, reel 2, 42–43.

14. Fred W. Anderson, "Why Did Colonial New Englanders Make Bad Soldiers: Contractual Principles and Military Conduct during the Seven Years War," *William and Mary Quarterly* 38 (1981): 395–417. For a full treatment, see Fred W. Anderson, *A People's Army: Massachusetts Soldiers and Society in the Seven Years War* (Chapel Hill: University of North Carolina Press, 1984), passim.

15. Enoch Poor, "Enoch Poor Journal," 17 October 1759, Huntington Library; Private Gibson Clough, "Extracts from Gibson Clough's Journal, *Essex Institute Historical Collections*, 3 (1861), 99–106, 195–201; Poor and Clough, quoted in Fred Anderson, "Bad Soldiers," 407, 409.

16. Richard Buel, *Dear Liberty: Connecticut's Mobilization for the Revolutionary War* (Middletown, Conn.: Wesleyan University Press, 1980), passim. For an excellent account of how the Continental army operated under the contract system, see E. Wayne Carp, *To Starve the Army at Pleasure: Continental Army Administration and American Political Culture, 1775–1783* (Chapel Hill: University of North Carolina Press, 1984), passim.

17. Enoch Poor to Mesech Weare, 21 January 1778, Peter Force Manuscripts, series 7-E, New Hampshire Council, Library of Congress; and Wayne K. Bodle, "The Vortex of Small Fortunes: The Continental Army at Valley Forge, 1777–1778" (Ph.D. diss., University of Pennsylvania, 1987), 214–15.

18. John Adams to Joseph Reed, 7 July 1776, *Letters of the Delegates to Congress*, 4:402–3. An enlistment "during the war" meant that the soldier agreed to remain in service until the war was over. Congress not only had to compete with local jurisdictions but the British as well. Washington discovered that a Continental soldier named "John Mash, who with Six others were taken by our Guards, [and were] given Ten pounds bounty for [enlisting into the British army]." Washington to the President of Congress, 4 October 1776, in Fitzpatrick, *Writings of Washington*, 6:153; and Washington to the President of Congress, 3 May 1777, ibid., 8:6–9, 17.

19. Richard Smith Diary, 22 February 1776, *Letters to the Delegates of Congress* (Washington, D.C.: Library of Congress, 1978); and Martin, *Private Yankee Doodle*, 15.

20. *Orderly Book of the 2nd Pennsylvania Continental Line*, *Pennsylvania Magazine of History and Biography* (hereafter *PMHB*) 36 (1912): 42–43; extract from *Gaine's Paper*, 9 March 1778, *Papers of the Continental Congress* (hereafter *PCC*), reel 179, item 161, 95.

21. *New Hampshire Gazette*, 27 April 1779; and Frank Moore, ed., *Diary of the Revolution* (New York, 1858; reprint, New York: Arno Press, 1969), 152–53 (page references are to reprint edition).

22. "Recruiting Poster, Philadelphia, 1776," *Evans Collection of Early American Imprints*, no. 15163 (Washington, D.C.: Georgetown University Library); and Mark E. Lender and James Kirby Martin, *A Respectable Army: The Military Origins of the Republic, 1763–1789* (Arlington Heights, Ill.: Harlan Davidson, 1982), 88.

23. Deposition of John Claspy, 26 November 1832, *The Revolution Remembered: Eyewitness Accounts of the War for Independence*, ed. John C. Dann (Chicago: University of Chicago Press, 1980), 366.

24. Howard Applegate, "Constitutions Like Iron: The Life of American Revolutionary War Soldiers in the Middle Department, 1775–1783" (Ph.D. diss., Syracuse University, 1966), 15–22.

25. Advertisement of James Doble, *Pennsylvania Journal*, 17 April 1776. There is no evidence that Doble was ever arrested.

26. Josiah Burr to Lydia Burr, 24 January 1777; Josiah Burr to Captain Luther Stoddard, 18 July 1778, Burr Family Collection, Yale University Library, New Haven, Conn.; and Linda S. Luchowski, "Sunshine Soldiers: New Haven and the American Revolution" (Ph.D. diss., State University of New York at Buffalo, 1976), 269–70.

27. The Four Pennsylvania Companies of the German Regiment to the Continental Congress, [1780?], *PCC*, reel 49, item 41, 3:376.

28. Colonel Nathan Dennison to Roger Sherman and Samuel Huntington, 7 April 1777, Miscellaneous Manuscripts of the Revolutionary War Era, Manuscript Group 275, roll 1, Pennsylvania History and Museum Commission; and George Washington to Henry Laurens, 27 February 1778, Friedrich von Steuben Papers, reel 1, DLAR.

29. Washington to the President of Congress, 1 January 1776, in Fitzpatrick, *Writings of Washington*, 6:461. The extension of enlistment was due to Washington's plans to attack Trenton, which coincided with the expiration of enlistments of both Regular and militia soldiers.

30. James Warren to Samuel Adams, 2 February 1777, Samuel Adams Papers, New York Public Library; and Martin H. Bush, "Philip Schuyler: The Revolutionary War Years" (Ph.D. diss., Syracuse University, 1966), 128.

31. John Hancock to "Certain Colonies," 8 December 1775, *Letters of the Delegates to Congress*, 2:454. The Committee recommended that Congress decide how it was going to pay the new army in a hurry, because "Men may much more probably inlist before, than after they feel the hardships of a Winter Campaign."

32. Edward Hand to Jasper Yates, 21 February 1776, Force Collection, ser. 7E, items 57–60, Manuscript Division, Library of Congress.

33. Hancock to "Certain Colonies," 2:454; and *PCC*, item 12A, addressed "To the Council of Massachusetts Bay, President of the Convention of New Hampshire, and the governor of Rhode Island & Connecticut."

34. *Journals of the Continental Congress* (hereafter *JCC*), 3:393; and Samuel Ward to Henry Ward, 21 November 1775, *Letters of the Delegates to Congress*, 2:369–70.

35. *JCC*, 3:324, 414. And Washington to Hancock, 8 December 1775, in *Letters of the Delegates to Congress*, 2:454. As a result of the failure to attract enough soldiers to reenlist, Samuel Ward wrote that he hoped the "Difficulty of raising men without a Bounty [was] better understood." Samuel Ward to Henry Ward, 12 December 1775, in ibid., 481.

36. Washington to Hancock, 109.

37. Wind to Gates, 9 October 1776, *Horatio Gates Papers*, microfilm, reel 3, 1154; Force, *Am. Arch.*, 5th ser., 2:1274–75; and John W. Kruger, "Troop Life at the Champlain Valley during the American Revolution" (Ph.D. diss., State University of New York at Albany, 1981), 185.

38. Kruger, "Troop Life," 185.

39. Washington to the President of Congress, 6 December 1776, in Fitzpatrick, *Writings of Washington*, 6:331–32. This was a very interesting development as far as the Jersey troops were concerned, because the British were in the process of occupying and garrisoning troops throughout the state.

40. Jedidiah Huntington, "Report on the number of officers and men in the 29th Regiment of the Continental army who have consented to extend their terms of service," Roxbury, 23 October 1775, *PCC*, item 59, 2:7; Lansing to Philip Schuyler, 9 January 1777, *Schuyler Papers*, New York Public Library; and Kruger, "Troop Life," 193, 195.

41. George Washington to Robert Morris, 1 January 1777, in *General John Glover's Letterbook, 1776–1777*, ed. Russell W. Knight (Salem, Mass.: Essex Institute, 1976), 9. An entry in *The Journals of Ashley Bowen (1728–1813) of Marblehead* (Salem, Mass.: Essex Institute, 1973) dated Monday, 20 January 1777, mentioned the return of Glover and some of his men from their army service.

42. Daniel Hitchcock to John Adams, 22 July 1776, *John Adams Papers*, 4:404–6; and *JCC*, 5:483. Through campfire conversations, soldiers became aware that other jurisdictions were offering greater wages for less time in service than Congress. Hitchcock was commanding officer of the Eleventh Continental Infantry. He died of camp fever at Morristown in January 1777.

43. John E. Ferling, *A Wilderness of Miseries: War and Warriors in Early America* (Westport, Conn.: Greenwood Press, 1980), 108.

44. Lawrence Cress, *Citizens in Arms: The Army and the Militia in American Society to the War of 1812* (Chapel Hill: University of North Carolina Press, 1982), 7. For general introductions of how aggregate groups of eighteenth-century workers tried to create or defend a "moral economy," see E. P. Thompson, "The Moral Economy of the Crowd in the Eighteenth Century," *Past and Present* 50 (1971): 76–136; George Rude, *The Crowd in History, 1730–1848* (New York: Wiley, 1964); and James Kirby Martin, "A Most Undisciplined, Profligate Crew: Protest and Defiance in the Continental Ranks, 1776–1783," in *Arms and Independence: The Military Character of the American Revolution* (Charlottesville: University Press of Virginia, 1984).

45. James Sullivan to John Adams and Elbridge Gerry, 11 October 1776, in *Papers of John Adams*, vol. 5, ed. Robert J. Taylor (Cambridge, Mass.: Harvard University Press, 1979), 50–52.

46. *Papers of John Adams*, 5:51.

47. For material requirements of soldiers, see Charles K. Bolton, *The Private Soldier under Washington* (New York: Charles Scribner's Sons, 1902), 77–84; Josiah Bartlett to Anonymous, 25 November 1776, *Letters by Josiah Bartlett, William Whipple and Others* (Philadelphia, 1889), 58; Bush, "Philip Schuyler," 114; and Martin, *Private Yankee Doodle*, 100–101.

48. Graydon, *Reminiscences*, 137–38.

49. Hoadley, *Public Records of the State of Connecticut*, 1:108–9; and Luchowski, "Sunshine Soldiers," 266.

50. Connecticut Historical Society, *Collections*, vol. 7 (Hartford, 1899), 219; and "A Roll of Captain Trumbull's Company of Volunteers, January, 1777," Benjamin Trumbull Collection, Yale University Library.

51. Nathanael Greene to Samuel Ward, 16 October 1775, *Correspondence of Governor Samuel Ward, May 1775–March 1776*, ed. Bernhard Knollenberg (Providence: Rhode Island Historical Society, 1952), 104.

52. William Ledyard to Jabez Huntington, 4 February 1779, Feinstone Collection, letter no. 1957, DLAR.

53. George Washington to Patrick Henry, 13 November 1777, in Fitzpatrick, *Writings of Washington*, 10:53–56; Washington to the Committee of Congress with the Army, 29 January 1778, ibid., 362–67; and George Washington to Thomas Nelson, 8 February 1778, ibid., 431–32. Washington realized that drafting men for the duration of the war would be viewed as "disgusting and dangerous, and perhaps impracticable" by the general public. Therefore, he proposed drafting for one year's service and then offering enticements for reenlistment at the conclusion of that time. Congress evidently disagreed and continued to urge the states to fulfill their regimental quotas, which they were never able to do. By 1778 Washington flatly stated that "voluntary enlistment seemed totally out of the question." See

George Washington to the Committee of Congress with the Army, 29 January 1778, *George Washington Papers*, ser. 4, reel 47. When Washington became aware that his kinsman and manager of his Mount Vernon estate, Lund Washington, might possibly "draw a prize in the militia" (be selected for active service) and therefore be eligible for the draft, he stated that he was willing to buy him a substitute. Obviously, Washington did not think everyone should join the Continental army. See George Washington to Lund Washington, 28 February 1778, in Fitzpatrick, *Writings of Washington*, 10:530–31.

54. Washington to Thomas Burke, 5 April 1779, in Fitzpatrick, *Writings of Washington*, 14:337.

55. Benjamin Betts to Henry Clinton, 12 January 1778, Clinton MSS, 30:12, William L. Clements Library, University of Michigan, Ann Arbor.

56. Nathan Baldwin to Joshua Bigelow, Justice of the Peace, 14 October 1777, Miscellaneous Manuscripts, Revolutionary War Collection, American Antiquarian Historical Society, Worcester, Mass.

57. Ibid.

58. Benjamin Flagg to Joshua Bigelow, Justice of the Peace, 13 October 1777, ibid.

59. L. Lincoln to Major General Ward, 7 August 1777, box 2, folder 5, ibid. Lincoln wanted the militia act to be modified, because it was apparent to him that most militiamen could easily raise the money needed to avoid joining the Continental army. It stands to reason that if inflation robbed the soldiers of the true value of their wages, it also enabled others to easily raise the sum needed for fines or purchasing a substitute.

60. The best institutional study of the Continental army is Robert K. Wright, Jr., *The Continental Army* (Washington, D.C.: Center of Military History, 1986). For examples of the colonial attempt to build an army based on the bounty system, see Royster, *Revolutionary People*, 64–65; Fitzpatrick, *Writings of Washington*, 6:152–56, 186–90, 200–201; *JCC*, 5:854–56, 6:920–21, 944–45; and Shy, *A People Numerous and Armed*, 252–53. Other useful manpower studies that detail how the government struggled with staffing the army are found in John R. Sellers, "The Virginia Continental Line, 1775–1780" (Ph.D. diss., Tulane University, 1968); Mark E. Lender, "The Enlisted Line: The Continental Soldiers of New Jersey" (Ph.D. diss., Rutgers University, 1975); and John W. Chambers, *To Raise an Army: The Draft Comes to America* (New York: Free Press, 1987). For the unsuccessful congressional attempts to entice people into service with offers of a postwar land bounty, see Jean H. Vivian, "Military Land Bounties during the Revolutionary and Confederation Periods," *Maryland Historical Magazine* (September 1966), 232–51.

61. Washington to the President of Congress, 3 May, 12 May 1777, Washington to Major General Benjamin Lincoln, 25 May 1777, in Fitzpatrick, *Writings of Washington*, 8:8, 45–46, 123.

62. George Washington to the Board of War, 11 November 1778, in Fitzpatrick, *Writings of Washington*, 13:245–46.

63. "Petition for Redress, Captain Job Wright's Company," 27 June 1782, Pliney Moore Papers, in *Pamphlets in American History*, no. B/RW/44, 9–11. The soldier's letter is barely decipherable. Two of the sixteen petitioners had to make their mark in lieu of writing their own names, four men misspelled their names, and the letter writer used no punctuation whatsoever. Captain Wright apparently investigated the soldier's complaints and was told that the extra profit went toward some "carrying charges" for getting the flour/bread to and from the bakers and the men. Wright ruled that their complaint was, therefore, "groundless." There is evidence, however, that the men did not agree. One day after their complaint was ruled "groundless," the soldiers were admonished for disturbing the Sunday services of officers and civilians in the area. Sergeants were also required to visit sentinel posts more frequently during the night to deter desertion.

64. *JCC*, 2:220; and John Adams to John Winthrop, 2 October 1775, *Letters of the Delegates to Congress*, 2:96.

65. William Matthews, *American Diaries in Manuscript, 1580–1954: An Annotated Bibliography* (Athens: University of Georgia Press, 1974. For an excellent scholarly exploration of the consciousness of New England soldiers during the American Revolution, see Walter F. Wallace, "Oh Liberty! Oh Virtue! Oh, My Country: An Exploration of the Minds of New England Soldiers during the American Revolution" (M.A. thesis, Northern Illinois University, 1974), 2–106 passim.

66. John Smith diaries, September–November 1776, Miscellaneous Manuscripts, Revolutionary War Collection, box 3, folder 6, American Antiquarian Society, Worcester, Mass., 3.

67. John B. B. Trussell, *Birthplace of an Army: A Study of the Valley Forge Encampment* (Harrisburg: Pennsylvania Historical and Museum Commission, 1979), 79; and Charles K. Bolton, *The Private Soldier Under Washington*, 47–51, 130.

68. Samuel Blachley Webb to George Washington, 25 January 1777, *Correspondence and Journals of Samuel Blachley Webb*, vol. 1, ed. Worthington C. Ford (New York: New York Times & Arno Press, reprint 1969), 186 (page references are to reprint edition); and "Pennsylvania General Assembly Broadside, 12 December 1776," *Evans Collection of Early American Imprints*, no. 14986 (Washington, D.C.: Georgetown University Library).

69. George Washington to Governor Nicholas Cooke, 2 February 1777, in Fitzpatrick, *Writings of Washington*, 7:88–90. Washington was worried that states were attempting to fill their own colonial establishments at a higher rate of pay and for a shorter obligation than the Continental requirement. Ibid., 90.

70. Thomas Powell, "Thomas Powell on Inflation," *Pennsylvania Evening Post*, 16 August 1777, quoted in Larry Gerlach, ed., *New Jersey in the American Revolution, 1763–1783: A Documentary History* (Trenton: New Jersey Bicentennial Commission, 1975), 373; and James L. Abramson, *The American Home Front* (Washington, D.C.: National Defense University Press, 1983), 29.

71. George Washington to Richard Henry Lee, 23 September 1778, in Fitzpatrick, *Writings of Washington*, 12:484–85.

72. George Washington to the President of Congress, 20 August 1780, in Fitzpatrick, *Writings of Washington*, 14:403; Shy, *A People Numerous and Armed*, 252–53; and E. James Ferguson, *The Power of the Purse: A History of American Public Finance, 1776–1790* (Chapel Hill: University of North Carolina Press, 1961), 3–47.

73. *Calendar of Virginia State Papers*, 1:595, 3:630; Nathanael Greene to Jethro Sumner, 19 April 1791, to the Board of War, 18 August 1781, to George Washington, 22 April 1782, to John Hanson, 18 May 1782, *Nathanael Greene Papers*, William L. Clements Library, Ann Arbor, Mich.; and Allen Bowman, *The Morale of the American Revolutionary Army* (Washington, D.C.: American Council on Public Affairs, 1943), 23–25.

74. *Historical Statistics of the United States, Colonial Times to 1957* (Washington, D.C.: Government Printing Office, 1960), 771; Applegate, "Constitutions Like Iron," 238; and George Clinton to the Council of Safety, 31 July 1777, *Clinton Papers*, 2:142–43.

75. Joseph Hewes to Samuel Johnston, 9 November 1775, *Letters of the Delegates to Congress*, 2:323–25; and Applegate, "Constitutions Like Iron," 237–38. The *Writings of Washington*, ed. John C. Fitzpatrick, contain at least two dozen references to stoppages for which soldiers were liable; see vols. 3–20, using the key word "pay."

76. Diary entry, 10 February 1779, in *Elijah Fisher's Journal* (Augusta, Maine: Press of Badger and Manley, 1880), 14–22. By the end of the war, Fisher signed aboard a privateer and had extended his final army enlistment in "the room" of a Sergeant Whipple for one extra month in exchange for Whipple's offer to tutor Fisher to "Rite and sifer and what

other larning would be eassy &c." Ibid., 16. During the Seven Years' War, soldiers complained of the same treatment. Found tacked to a door in Fort Ontario in 1756 was a note from a man who had deserted, who reminded his officers that they should not be surprised at the level of desertion, because "now we have no Cloths & you cheatus out of our allowance of Rum & half our working money." Stanley M. Pargellis, ed., *Military Affairs in North America, 1748–1765: Selected Documents from the Cumberland Papers in Windsor Castle* (New York: Appleton-Century, 1937), 174–75.

77. Merrill Jensen, *The New Nation: A History of the United States during the Confederation, 1781–1789* (New York: Knopf, 1950), 39–41; Government currency valuation chart, 29 July 1780, *Papers of the Continental Congress*, item 12A, 2:120, item 78, 9:391–409; Washington to the Board of War, 20 December 1778, in Fitzpatrick, *Writings of Washington*, 13:437; and Applegate, "Constitutions Like Iron," 239–40.

78. For documentation of unrest in the army over wages and terms of enlistment, see Charles Carroll to William Carmichael [?], 31 May 1779, The Board of War to George Washington, 3 June 1779, *Letters to the Members of the Continental Congress*, ed. Edmund G. Burnett (Washington, D.C.: Carnegie Institution of Washington, 1928), 4:238–39, 5:513–41. This letter was not found in the more recent edition of the *Letters to the Delegates*, edited by Paul Smith.

79. *Connecticut Journal*, 14 June 1775; and Linda S. Luchowski, "Sunshine Soldiers," 264.

80. Jedediah Huntington to Jabez Huntington, 13 February 1776, Feinstone Collection, letter no. 591, DLAR.

81. Martin, *Private Yankee Doodle*, 52. Martin and his friends waited until the farmer left the area and took as much as they could carry and left him to "pull up his own share."

82. Diary entry, 10 February 1779, in *Elijah Fisher's Journal*, 11.

83. Martin, *Private Yankee Doodle*, 90. The cost of a gill of rum often exceeded the monthly wage of a private soldier and, therefore, was considered a form of payment in kind when he could get it.

84. Ibid., 90.

85. Diary entry, 5–15 June 1775, *Sergeant Samuel Bixby Diary*, MSS., Revolutionary War Collection, American Antiquarian Society, Worcester, Mass.

86. Jeremiah Greenman diary entries, 7, 12 February 1782, in *Diary of a Common Soldier in the American Revolution, 1775–1783*, ed. Robert C. Bray and Paul Bushnell (DeKalb: Northern Illinois University Press, 1978), 243–44.

87. Diary entry of Albegience Waldo, 14 December 1777, *PMHB*, vol. 21 (October 1897), 307.

88. Thomas Cartwright and James Jones to Henry Jackson, 16 May 1777, Feinstone Collection, letter no. 163, DLAR.

89. Martin, *Private Yankee Doodle*, 101–11.

90. Icabod Ward to Abraham Pierson, 19 January 1778, Pierson and Sargeant Family Papers, CSL; and Valley Forge Historical Report, Wayne K. Bodle and Jacqueline Thibaut (Valley Forge Research Project, Valley Forge Historical Park, 1980), 162–63.

91. Ward, quoted in Bodle and Thibaut, 162–63.

92. Washington to the President of Congress, 10 April 1778, in Fitzpatrick, *Writings of Washington*, 11:238–39; and Washington to Brigadier General William Smallwood, 28 January 1778, ibid., 10:360–61.

93. George Washington to the Committee of Congress with the Army, 29 January 1778, George Washington Papers, serial no. 4, reel 47, DLAR.

94. Ibid., Washington to Congress, 29 January 1778.

95. Chambers, *To Raise an Army*, 22. Chambers referred to the few militia drafts that

were conducted as "quasi-drafts" in which local militia officers "drafted" affluent militiamen, who then hired substitutes to serve for them in the Continental army. Also see Martin and Lender, *A Respectable Army*, 94. In 1778, 40 percent of the New Jersey Brigade were substitutes for wealthier militiamen who chose not to serve in the Continental army.

96. Washington to the President of Congress, 24 September 1776, in Fitzpatrick, *Writings of Washington*, 6:106–16.

CHAPTER SEVEN *Running Through the Line Like Wildfire*

1. Captain Joseph McClellan, Ninth Pennsylvania Regiment, "Diary of the Revolt," *Pennsylvania Archives*, 2d ser., vol. 11, ed. John B. Linn and William H. Egle (Harrisburg, Pa.: Lane S. Hart, 1880), 631–32. Anthony Wayne reported that during the initial outburst, "Captain Bettin [Bitting?] was shot through the body and died. Captain Tolbert was badly wounded." Ibid., 631; and "Extracts from the Letter-Books of Lieutenant Enos Reeves," *Pennsylvania Magazine of History and Biography* (hereafter *PMHB*), 21:72.

2. Enos Reeves, "Extracts," *PMHB*, 21:73. Reeves also noted that Captain Bettin was probably killed by accident when a soldier who was chasing Lieutenant Colonel William Butler between some soldier's huts ran into Bettin while in pursuit. Ibid., 74.

3. Henry Marble to B. Parkman, 7 January 1781, *Miscellaneous Manuscripts*, box 3, folder 6, U.S. Revolutionary War Collection, American Antiquarian Society, Worcester, Mass. (hereafter AAS); and Carl Van Doren, *Mutiny in January* (Clifton: Augustus M. Kelley; reprint, 1973), 54–55 (page references are to reprint edition).

4. Charles Royster claimed that soldiers plundered civilians simply because they had guns in their hands and thought they could get away with it. He argues that Washington and other senior officers hoped to check declining patriotic virtue with increased discipline. Royster thought that the "American soldier's sense of personal freedom" prevented or rendered difficult their assimilation into a system of military discipline. Charles Royster, *A Revolutionary People at War: The Continental Army and American Character, 1775–1783* (New York: W. W. Norton, 1979), 69–80.

5. Washington to Rochambeau, 20 January 1781, *Washington Papers*, ser. 3D, reel 24, David Library of the American Revolution, Washington Crossing, Pa. (hereafter DLAR); Joseph Reed to the Committee of Congress, 8 January 1781, "Diary of the Revolt," 652–53; and E. P. Thompson, "The Moral Economy of the Crowd in the Eighteenth-Century," *Past and Present* 50 (1971): 77.

6. Thompson, "The Moral Economy of the Crowd in the Eighteenth Century," 77–78; and Rudé, *The Crowd in History, 1730–1848* (New York, 1964).

7. Washington to Rochambeau, 20 January 1781, *Washington Papers;* and Rudé, *The Crowd in History*, 7–8.

8. John Shy, *A People Numerous and Armed: Reflections on the Military Struggle for American Independence*, rev. ed. (Ann Arbor: University of Michigan Press, 1990), 25–26; Charles K. Bolton, *The Private Soldier under Washington* (New York: Charles Scribner's Sons, 1902; reprint, 1976), 49, 78–80 (page references are to reprint edition); *Journal of the Continental Congress* (hereafter *JCC*), 16 September 1776, 8 October 1776; and *American Archives*, ed. Peter Force, ser. 5, vol. 2, col. 561. By late eighteenth-century standards, a soldier was generally "due" wages for this service, a stated daily ration, and an annual suit of clothes. This "contract" between the individual and the state was usually delineated in the soldier's enlistment contract. See previous chapter.

9. For a comprehensive analysis of the patterns of protest and defiance in the Continental ranks, see James Kirby Martin, "A Most Undisciplined, Profligate Crew: Protest and

Defiance in the Continental Ranks, 1776–1783," in *Arms and Independence: The Military Character of the American Revolution*, ed. Ronald Hoffman and Peter J. Albert (Charlottesville: University Press of Virginia, 1984), 119–40.

10. Douglas Edward Leach, "The Cartegena Expedition, 1740–1742," in *Adapting to Conditions: War and Society in the Eighteenth Century*, ed. Maarten Ultee (University: University of Alabama Press, 1986), 46–48. Leach noted that recruiting for the British expedition in the colonies "thrived mainly on the glittering prospect of plunder being distributed down to the lowest musket-sloper." Moreover, the men enlisted to serve under a captain they knew and were willing to obey. The soldiers all took "very seriously, the King's promise to return them home at the conclusion of the venture." Ibid., 46; see Lawrence Delbert Cress, *Citizens in Arms: The Army and Militia in American Society to the War of 1812* (Chapel Hill: University of North Carolina Press, 1982), 55, 58–60; and Bolton, *The Private Soldier under Washington*, chap. 3.

11. *Journals of the Provincial Congress*, quoted in Bolton, *The Private Soldier under Washington*, 79.

12. *JCC*, 8 October 1776; and Bolton, *The Private Soldier under Washington*, 94.

13. The Committee of Sergeants to Anthony Wayne, 4 January 1781, *Papers of the Continental Congress* (hereafter *PCC*), reel 170, 9:481; and James Thacher, *Military Journal of the American Revolution* (Hartford, Conn.: Hurlbut, Kellogg and Co., 1861), 233–34.

14. Diary entry, 30–31 January 1776, "Caleb Haskell's Diary," *Pamphlets in American History Collection*, fiche no. B/RW14, DLAR, 16. Haskell's officers, however, did not agree with his interpretation of his enlistment contract and threatened him with "39 stripes" if he did not continue to serve. Joseph Plumb Martin, *Private Yankee Doodle: Being a Narrative of Some of the Adventures, Dangers, and Sufferings of a Revolutionary Soldier*, ed. George Scheer (Boston: Little, Brown and Co., 1962), 15–17.

15. Petition to William Heath, 2 April 1776, *Heath Papers*, reel 1, DLAR.

16. William Hooper to the President of the North Carolina Convention, 16 November 1776, *Letters of the Delegates to Congress*, 5:500–503; John Todd White, "Standing Armies in the Time of War: Republican Theory and Military Practice" (Ph.D. diss., George Washington University, 1978), 198–99.

17. See *PMHB* (1908), 260, for details of the revolt at Ticonderoga; Anthony Wayne to General Philip Schuyler, 12 February 1777, quoted in Charles J. Stille, *Major General Anthony Wayne and the Pennsylvania Line in the Continental Army* (Philadelphia: J. B. Lippincott, 1893), 55–56.

18. James Kirby Martin, *In the Course of Human Events* (Arlington Heights, Ill.: Harlan Davidson, 1979), 100–101.

19. Washington to General William Maxwell, 7 May 1779, in Fitzpatrick, *Writings of Washington*, 15:13–16.

20. By the end of 1775, Washington noted that only 2,540 men out of 19,000 had reenlisted into the "new" Continental establishment. *PCC*, item 12A, addressed to "the Council of Massachusetts Bay, President of the Convention of New Hampshire, and the governor of Rhode Island and Connecticut." For an interesting analogy in which sailors struggled to extract a social wage from their merchant employers, see Marcus Rediker's *Between the Devil and the Deep Blue Sea: Merchant Seamen, Pirates, and the Anglo-American Maritime World, 1700–1750* (Cambridge: Cambridge University Press, 1987), chaps. 2 and 3 passim. Rediker noted that the admiralty courts were filled with complaints about desertion among the sailors and that the practice "was widespread among the maritime workers." Ibid., 106. Sailors habitually added to their meager or nonexistent wages through pilfering or embezzlement. Sometimes the mere threat of a mutiny or mass desertion was enough to convince some merchants to give in to the demands of the sailors. Thus wages not paid in

some form were realized through other methods. For evidence of similar methods employed by soldiers, see James H. Edmonson, "Desertion in the American Army during the Revolutionary War" (Ph.D. diss., Louisiana State University, 1971).

21. Washington to the Committee of Congress at Boston, 21 September 1775, *PCC*, reel 166, 1:119.

22. Washington to the President of Congress, 16 December 1776, in Fitzpatrick, *Writings of Washington*, 6:380; and Martin and Lender, *A Respectable Army*, 76. In a time of crisis, it appeared that even the most vehement Whigs put aside their fears of a standing army of long-term enlistees and favored one modeled after the British. "Without a well disciplined army," wrote John Hancock, "we can never expect success against veteran troops; and it is totally impossible we should have a well disciplined Army, unless our Troops are engaged to serve during the war." See Hancock to the New Hampshire Assembly, 24 September 1776, *LMCC*, 2:99; and Lyman H. Butterfield, ed., *The Adams Papers: Diary and Autobiography of John Adams*, vol. 3 (Cambridge, Mass.: Harvard University Press, 1961), 409–10, 434. For another point of view, see Shy, *A People Numerous and Armed*, 126–27.

23. William Emerson to his wife, 17 July 1775, quoted in Allen French, *The First Year of the American Revolution* (New York: Houghton-Mifflin, 1934), 301; and Royster, *Revolutionary People*, 73.

24. Edmonson, "Desertion in the American Army during the Revolutionary War," 65, 76. Besides desertion, the death penalty was provided for the following: Mutiny (sec. II, art. 3); failure of officers or noncommissioned officers to stop a mutiny (sec. II, art. 4); leaving a guard post (sec. XIII, art. 8); cowardice in battle (sec. XIII, arts. 11 and 12); plundering (sec. XIII, arts. 13 and 21); making known the watch word (sec. XIII, art. 15); and numerous other categories that dealt with aiding or providing comfort or assistance to the enemy; *JCC*, 5:788–807. The Massachusetts court liked the idea of thirty-nine lashes as the maximum penalty, because it conformed to Mosaic punishment found in biblical references. For a history of military law and its colonial development, see William L. Winthrop, *Military Law and Precedents*, 2 vols. (Boston: Little, Brown and Co., 1896).

25. James Neagles, *Summer Soldiers: A Survey and Index of Revolutionary War Courts-Martial* (Salt Lake City, Utah: Ancestry Inc., 1986), 1–285 passim. Neagles's work should not be considered exhaustive, but his collection represents the most comprehensive raw data on patterns of protest and defiance currently available. The methodology used here was to list the offense by its date of inclusion in an orderly book. The recorded dates of the offense were approximations but can be considered relatively accurate to within six months of the offense. For instance, offenses such as desertion may have occurred earlier but the individual not tried until some time after the soldier had been caught and returned to the army.

26. Neagles, *Summer Soldiers*, 16–17.

27. Daniel Barber, *The History of My Own Times*, part 3 (Frederick, Md., 1832,) 16; Daniel McCurtin, "Journal of the Times at the Siege of Boston," in vol. 12, *Papers Relating Chiefly to the Maryland Line;* ed. Balch (Philadelphia: Printed for the Seventy-Six Society, 1857); and Royster, *A Revolutionary People at War*, 71–73.

28. Martin, *Private Yankee Doodle*, 20–23. On another occasion, Martin's company had been told to scoop up as much sea bread that they could carry as they passed by some opened casks. The line was kept moving and each soldier was able to get about a handful before being forced forward by the man behind him. "As my good luck would have it," stated Martin, a "momentary halt was made" as he was in front of the casks and he literally filled his shirts and pockets with the bread. He added, "No one said anything to me and I filled my bosom [with the bread]." Ibid., 23.

29. Martin, *Private Yankee Doodle*, 82–83; Diary Entry, 28–29 September 1776, "Ser-

geant John Smith's Diary of 1776," *Mississippi Valley Historical Review*, vol. 20, ed. Louise Rau (1933–1934), 252; and Royster, *A Revolutionary People at War*, 74.

30. Rau, "Sergeant John Smith's Diary of 1776," 256–57, 266, 252; and Lender, "The Enlisted Line," 181–83. A courts-martial case of Ensign McCumber noted that the ensign was charged with plundering a house near Harlem Heights. See *PCC*, reel 71, item 58, 333. Even General Stirling's house was plundered by Continental soldiers. Stirling reported that Private Daniel Donovel of the Third New York Regiment was court-martialed and given thirty-nine lashes for breaking into his quarters. See Washington to the President of Congress, 22 September 1776, in Fitzpatrick, ed., *Writings of Washington*, 12:91.

31. Martin, *Private Yankee Doodle*, 23.

32. Neagles, *Summer Soldiers*, 1–258 passim; *JCC*, vol. 2, May 10–September 20 (Washington, D.C.: Library of Congress, 1905), 111–23; *JCC*, vol. 5, June 5–October 8, 788–808.

33. George Washington to Joseph Reed, 28 April 1780, in Fitzpatrick, ed., *Writings of Washington*, 18:310–11; Royster, *A Revolutionary People at War*, 71. People who rescued deserters may have been relatives or friends but were, most likely, potential employers who were desperate for such prospective labor.

34. Allen Bowman, *The Morale of the American Revolutionary Army* (Washington, D.C.: American Council of Public Affairs, 1943), 66–68; Fitzpatrick, ed., *Writings of Washington*, 18:77, 503; and Royster, *A Revolutionary People at War*, 71.

35. Carlos E. Godfrey, *The Commander-in-Chief's Guard* (Washington, D.C.: Stevenson-Smith Co., 1904), 120, 130–31, 152–53, 192–94, 227, 245, 264. Desertion rates were notoriously high everywhere. Various European armies had desertion rates of 40 percent. See M. S. Anderson, *Europe in the Eighteenth Century, 1713–1783* (New York: Holt, Rinehart, and Winston, 1961), 137–39. The Continental army was only slightly better than its European counterpart with an average desertion rate of around 20 to 25 percent. See Edmonson, "Desertion in the American Army during the Revolutionary War," 240. The lower rate, however, may have had as much to do with faulty American record keeping as anything else. See Enoch Anderson, *Personal Recollections of Captain Enoch Anderson* (Wilmington: Historical Society of Delaware, 1896), 58.

36. Allen Bowman, *The Morale of the American Revolutionary Army* (Washington, D.C.: American Council of Public Affairs, 1943), 66–68; Charles Lee's *Orderly Book*, entries for 1 April and 26 July 1776; William Coit's *Orderly Book*, Connecticut Historical Society *Collections*, vol. 7 (1899), 69; and Fitzpatrick, *Writings of Washington*, 18:77, 503. For an interpretation of the struggle over the mobility of labor in the eighteenth century, see Marcus Rediker, "Good Hands, Stout Heart, and Fast Feet: The History and Culture of Working People in Early America," pre-published manuscript in *Reviving the English Revolution: Reflections and Elaborations on the Work of Christopher Hill*, ed. Geoff Eley and William Hunt (London: Verso Books, 1986), 28–29.

37. James Kirby Martin and Mark E. Lender, *A Respectable Army: The Military Origins of the Republic, 1763–1789* (Arlington Heights, Ill.: Harlan Davidson, 1982), 132–33; and Bolton, *The Private Soldier under Washington*, 53.

38. Edmonson, "Desertion in the American Army during the Revolutionary War," 217–18; Enoch Anderson, a soldier of the Revolution, noted in his *Personal Recollections*, that Brigade Adjutants inflated the number of those present for duty as a matter of course. See Anderson, *Personal Recollections of Captain Enoch Anderson*. For more analysis on the problem of desertion, see Allen Bowman's "The Morale of Continental and Militia Troops in the War of the Revolution" (Ph.D. diss., University of Michigan, 1941), and Thad W. Tate, "Desertion from the American Revolutionary Army" (M.A. thesis, University of North Carolina, 1948). Both scholars have made the study of desertion an integral part of their work.

39. Edmonson, "Desertion in the American Army," chap. 8. For a useful compilation of the monthly strength reports of the army, see Charles H. Lesser's *The Sinews of Independence: Monthly Strength Reports of the Continental Army* (Chicago: University of Chicago Press, 1976).

40. John B. B. Trussell, Jr., *Birthplace of an Army: A Study of the Valley Forge Encampment* (Harrisburg: Pennsylvania Historical and Museum Commission, 1979), 66.

41. Tate, "Desertion"; Mark E. Lender, "The Enlisted Line: The Continental Soldiers of New Jersey" (Ph.D. diss., Rutgers University, 1975), 203–34; and Martin and Lender, *A Respectable Army*, 131.

42. E. B. O'Callaghan, ed., *Documents Relating to the Colonial History of the State of New York*, 15:174–244; and Bowman, *The Morale*, 72. Bowman noted that some of the officers appeared on the rolls as repeated deserters and that numbers of recruits deserted on the same day or day after they enlisted.

43. Roll of Captain Alexander Johnston's Company, Fifth Pennsylvania regiment, *Pennsylvania Archives*, 5th ser., 3:17–19.

44. Washington to Joseph Jones, 10 July 1781, in Fitzpatrick, *Writings of Washington*, 22:354, 26:123; and Edmonson, "Desertion in the American Army," 270.

45. Washington to Joseph Jones, 11 February 1783, in Fitzpatrick, *Writings of Washington*, 26:123.

46. Letter of the County Lieutenants at Salisbury, *North Carolina Records*, 16:63; and Joseph Reed and Edward Hand, quoted in Bowman, *The Morale*, 86–87.

47. Deposition of Joseph Parker, in John C. Dann, ed., *The Revolution Remembered: Eyewitness Accounts of the War for Independence* (Chicago: University of Chicago Press, 1980), 70–71.

48. David Cobb to Henry Jackson, 8 June 1780, *Fragments of Revolutionary History*, ed. Gaillard Hunt (New York: Historical Printing Club, 1892), 148.

49. John Smith Hanna, *A History and Life and Services of Captain Samuel Dewees* (Baltimore, 1844), 203–4; diary entry of Ebenezer Elmer, "Journal Kept during an Expedition to Canada in 1776," New Jersey Historical Society, *Proceedings*, 1st ser., vol. 3 (1847), 172; and Royster, *A Revolutionary People at War*, 78–79. Occasionally, floggings of one hundred lashes were delivered in four twenty-five-lash installments on successive days to heighten the pain and terror faced by the recipient. Sometimes their backs were washed with saltwater. When the cat-o'-nine tails (the lash) became clogged with blood, a new one was substituted. See Neagles, *Summer Soldiers*, 1–240; and Royster, *A Revolutionary People at War*, 79.

50. George J. Svedja, *Quartering, Disciplining, and Supplying the Army at Morristown, 1779–1780* (Washington, D.C.: U.S. Department of Interior), 105; and Neagles, *Summer Soldiers*, 25.

51. General David Cobb to Colonel Henry Jackson, 8 June 1780, Hunt, ed., *Fragments of Revolutionary History*, 148–51.

52. Diary of James Thacher, *Military Journal*, 222–23; Neagles, *Summer Soldiers*, passim; Regimental Orders, 2 July 1777, "Journal and Order Book of Captain Robert Kirkwood," Historical Society of Delaware., *Papers*, 6, no. 56, p. 95; Royster, *A Revolutionary People at War*, 78; Svejda, *Quartering*, 106. For further information, see Howard Applegate, "Constitutions Like Iron: The Life of American Revolutionary War Soldiers in the Middle Department, 1775–1783" (Ph.D. diss., Syracuse University, 1966).

53. Journal entry, 31 March 1775, Journal of Samuel Deane, in *Journals of the Rev. Thomas Smith, and the Rev. Samuel Deane, Pastors of the First Church in Portland*, ed. William Willis (Portland, Maine, 1849), 336; Anthony Wayne, Division Orders, 29 March 1778, "Orderly Book of the 2d Pennsylvania Regiment," *PMHB* (1911), 342; and Royster, *A Revolutionary People at War*, 237.

54. Diary entry, 25 July 1779, *Diary of Colonel Israel Angell* (New York: Arno Press, 1971), 67; and Royster, *A Revolutionary People at War*, 237–38.

55. Martin, *Private Yankee Doodle*, 151–52.

56. Noel Busch, *Winter Quarters: George Washington and the Continental Army at Valley Forge* (New York: Liveright Publishers, 1974), 56; Private Dennis Kennedy, quoted in Royster, *A Revolutionary People at War*, 195; and Martin, *Private Yankee Doodle*, 263–64. There were apparently personal reasons why some of the men wished to embarrass or maim their officers. The leader of the "gunpowder plot" was recently "caned" (meaning beat with a walking stick) twice by the officer for what the soldier considered insufficient cause. He now thought that some sort of humiliation was due the officer in return. Ibid., 265.

57. Nathanael Greene to George Washington, 26 August 1780, *Washington Papers*, ser. 4, reel 73, Library of Congress. Greene flatly stated that most of the officers were of the opinion by 1780 that "it was absolutely necessary for the good of the service that one of these fellows should be made an example of, and if your Excellency will give permission I will have one hung up this afternoon where the Army are to march by." Ibid., Greene to Washington, 26 August 1780.

58. Mauer Mauer, "Military Justice under General Washington," in *Military Analysis of the Revolutionary War*, editors of *Military Affairs* (1977), 60; for an excellent discussion on the British soldier in the eighteenth century, see Sylvia Frey, *The British Soldier in America: A Social History of Military Life in the Revolutionary Period* (Austin: University of Texas Press, 1981).

59. Neagles, *Summer Soldiers*, 1–258 passim.

60. Sergeant William Seymour wrote in his "Journal of the Southern Expedition" of three soldiers who met their fates after deserting to the enemy. Seymour noted that a "tory" was found guilty of desertion and piloting Indian forces against the army for which he was "hanged on a tree the same day till he was dead." Several days later Seymour recorded the demise of a cavalryman who was found guilty of desertion to the enemy and shot the same day. Months later, Seymour stated that Solomon Slocum of the Second Maryland Regiment was convicted of desertion and spying for the enemy and was "hanged on a tree by the roadside in full view of all who passed by." *PMHB*, 7, no. 3 (1883), 293, 379; and Edmonson, "Desertion in the American Army," 203.

61. Eleazer Smith Diary, Miscellaneous Manuscripts, William L. Clements Library, Ann Arbor, Mich.; and Neagles, *Summer Soldiers*, 1–258 passim.

62. Bowman, *The Morale*, passim; and Edmonson, "Desertion in the American Army during the Revolution," 345–46.

63. Thacher, *Military Journal*, 233–34; General Orders, 25 May 1780, in Fitzpatrick, *Writings of Washington*, 18:422; and Svejda, *Quartering*, 125–26.

64. Svejda, *Quartering*, 124–26; and Thacher, *Military Journal*, 233–34. The soldier not reprieved was James Coleman of the Eleventh Pennsylvania Regiment. Coleman's sentence was not lifted because he had forged "a number of discharges, by which he and more than a hundred soldiers had left the army." Ibid, 233–34. Before his execution, Coleman noted that he did not think the rope was stout enough to do the job. When the ladder was kicked from under him, the rope broke, whereupon Coleman calmly informed the hangman of his premonition and admonished him to get a stronger rope. He did and Coleman was "launched into eternity." Ibid., 233–34.

65. Thacher, *Military Journal*, 234.

66. Mathew Drury, *Orderly Book*, entries for 21 and 27 January 1780, New Jersey Historical Society; General Orders, 18 February 1780, in Fitzpatrick, *Writings of Washington*, 18:22–23, 48; and Svejda, *Quartering*, 114–15.

67. Peter Ten Broeck to Cornelius Ten Broeck, Sr., 9 July 1779, in "News from Camp," *Magazine of American History* 2:169; Washington regretted this incident and ordered the

perpetrator of the atrocity, Major Henry Lee (known later as the famous Light-Horse Harry Lee) to bury the body immediately (head and all) before the British got wind of it and used it as a propaganda tool against future American recruiting efforts. See Washington to Henry Lee, 10 July 1779, in Fitzpatrick, *Writings of Washington*, 15:388, 399.

68. For examples, see Rediker, *Between the Devil and the Deep Blue Sea*, 24–25, 27; and Samuel Dewees, *A History of the Life and Services of Captain Samuel Dewees*, in Van Doren, *Mutiny in January* (New York: Viking Books, 1943), 228–32. Thomas Jeremiah, a black slave suspected of aiding the British by the South Carolina Committee of Safety, was hanged and burned to terrorize other slaves who might harbor similar thoughts. See *Papers of Henry Laurens*, 10:207 nn. 3, 4, 5; and Peter Wood, "The Dream Deferred: Black Freedom Struggles on the Eve of White Independence," in *In Resistance: Studies in African, Caribbean, and Afro-American History*, ed. Gary Y. Okihiro (Amherst: University of Massachusetts Press, 1986), 176. Burning seemed to be the favorite white punishment for rebellious slaves. See *Georgia Gazette* (Savannah), 7 December 1774.

69. Neagles, *Summer Soldiers*, 1–258 passim.

70. Ibid. William Miller of the Second New Jersey Regiment was charged with desertion and was found to have been "an old and atrocious offender." He was sentenced to three hundred lashes and to be "sent on board a Continental Frigate, with his Crime, there to serve during the War." *Hawkins Orderly Book*, no. 1, 19 March 1780 entry, Hazen's Regiment, Historical Society of Pennsylvania (hereafter HSP); diary entry, 26 August 1780, *Diary of Colonel Israel Angell* (New York: Arno Press, 1971), 108–9. For examples of soldiers executed without recourse to a trial by courts-martial, see Henry Lee, *Memoirs of the War in the Southern Department of the United States* (New York: University Publishing Co., 1869), 546–49; Paul David Nelson, *Anthony Wayne: Soldier of the Republic* (Bloomington: Indiana University Press, 1985), 129–31; and Nathanael Greene to Robert Morris, 22 April 1782, Greene Mss., 58:58, William L. Clements Library, Ann Arbor, Mich.

71. George Washington to the Council of General Officers, 20 August 1778, in Fitzpatrick, *Writings of Washington*, 12:343–44; and Washington to the President of Congress, 3 February 1781, in ibid., vol. 21.

72. Nathanael Greene to George Washington, 10 September 1775, *Nathanael Greene Papers*, vol. 1, William L. Clements Library, 117.

73. Benedict Arnold, quoted in John William Kruger, "Troop Life at the Champlain Valley Forest during the American Revolution" (Ph.D. diss., State University of New York at Albany, 1981), 29.

74. Ibid., 29.

75. Diary entry, 25 July 1779, *Diary of Colonel Israel Angell* (New York: Arno Press, 1971), 67; and Journal entry, January 1779, Martin, *Private Yankee Doodle*, 152.

76. Petition to the General Assembly from Ann Glover, widow of Samuel Glover, 10 January 1780, *State Records of North Carolina*, vol. 15, ed. Clark, 187–88; and Royster, *A Revolutionary People at War*, 296–97.

77. The best and most comprehensive account of the "Fort Wilson" riot is found in John Alexander, "The Fort Wilson Incident of 1779: A Case Study of the Revolutionary Crowd," *William and Mary Quarterly*, 3d ser. (October 1974), 589–612; Eric Foner, "Tom Paine's Republic: Radical Ideology and Social Change," in *The American Revolution*, ed. Alfred F. Young (DeKalb: Northern Illinois University Press, 1976), 216–17; and Henry Laurens to John Adams, 4 October 1779, *Letters of the Delegates to Congress*, 14:17–19.

78. John Fell Diary, 1 October 1779; ibid., 14:3; Arnold letter attached to diary entry of Samuel Holten, 6 October 1779, ibid., 476–77. Arnold requested a bodyguard be provided him from the Continental army. He noted that he "believed a guard of 20 men with a good officer sufficient." Congress refused to respond to his request. Arnold deserted

the following year after plotting to betray the Continental citadel at West Point. See *Papers of the Continental Congress*, no. 162, 1:185, 187.

79. Diary entry of Colonel Israel Angell, 28 January 1779, in *Diary of Colonel Israel Angell*, 47–48. Angell noted that the regiment of Samuel Blanchley Webb had mutinied but dispersed "with some Difficulty." Ibid., 48; Royster, *A Revolutionary People at War*, 299.

80. Nathanael Greene to Governor William Greene of Rhode Island, 27 May 1780, *Nathanael Greene Papers*, 5:582–83; and Washington to Governor Trumbull, 26 May 1780, in Fitzpatrick, *Writings of Washington*, 18:425–26. Appeals by officers may have helped to get some soldiers back to duty, but more effective was the timely arrival of 1,000 barrels of salted meat. See *Greene Papers*, vol. 5, 584n.3; Washington to Henry Champion, 26 May 1780, in Fitzpatrick, *Writings of Washington*, 18:424; Royster, *A Revolutionary People at War*, 299; Return Meigs to George Washington, 26 May 1780, quoted in S. Sydney Bradford, "Discipline in the Morristown Winter Encampment," N.J. Historical Society, *Proceedings* 80 (1962); and Martin, *Private Yankee Doodle*, 184–87. For the New York mutiny, see Abraham Hardenbergh to Colonel Goose van Schaick, 31 May 1780, Goose van Schaick to George Washington, 1 June 1780, and 10 June 1780, *Washington Papers*, Library of Congress; Washington to the President of Congress, 20 June 1780, in *Writings of Washington*, 19:36; and T. W. Egly, Jr., *History of the First New York Regiment* (Hampton, N.H.: Peter E. Randall, 1981), 156–57.

81. Anthony Wayne to Colonel Johnstone, 16 December 1780, quoted in Stille, *Major General Anthony Wayne and the Pennsylvania Line*, 240–41.

82. "Diary of the Revolt," *Pennsylvania Archives*, ser. 2, 11:631.

83. Ibid., 631. Anthony Wayne insinuated that some of the men were forced to join the mutiny. He noted that for two days afterward, "small parties of men were still collecting [others] and marching off." Ibid., 632. This is quite likely because the personal safety of the ringleaders depended on the number of soldiers they could persuade to join the rebellion.

84. Reeves, "Extracts," 76.

85. Colonel Israel Shreve to George Washington, 8 January 1781, *Washington Papers*, ser. 4, reel 73, Library of Congress.

86. Demands delivered in conjunction by the Sergeants to General Wayne, 4 January 1781, "Diary of the Revolt," 633–34; and *PCC*, reel 170, 9:481.

87. "Diary of the Revolt," 3 January 1781, 632. Some officers suspected that the New Years' Day grog ration had something to do with the mutiny. While alcoholic drink may have given courage to some, the lack of greater destructive behavior was not evident on the march to Philadelphia. Liquor, as we shall see, had little to do with the mutinous conduct of the troops.

88. Neagles, *Summer Soldiers*, 59–60. Washington had earlier anticipated that the soldiers might contrive ways to get discharges after three years and pressed Congress to award a gratuity of one hundred dollars to those men who had earlier enlisted "for three years or during the war" for only a twenty dollar bounty. Washington noted that the award "must not be considered an admission of the construction put upon them by the soldiers" [that three years was the maximum they had to serve]. See George Washington to the Board of War, 9 June 1779, in Fitzpatrick, *Writings of Washington*, 15:248–54; and *JCC*, 22 June 1779.

89. George Washington to Philip Schuyler, 10 January 1781, in Fitzpatrick, *Writings of Washington*, 21:79–80; and President Reed to the Merchants of Philadelphia, endorsed 18 January 1781, *Pennsylvania Archives*, 8:704. For a moment-by-moment account of the mutiny, see Carl Van Doren's *Mutiny in January* (New York: Viking, 1943), passim and "Diary of the Revolt," *Pennsylvania Archives*, ser. 2, vol. 11, ed. John B. Linn and William H. Egle (Harrisburg, 1880), 631–74; and Joseph Reed to Vice-President Moore, 12 January 1781,

ibid., 671–72. For an eyewitness account, see *Military Journal of Major Ebenezer Denny: An Officer in the Revolution and Indian Wars* (Philadelphia, 1859).

90. Joseph Reed to William Henry, [date?], *Pennsylvania Magazine of History and Biography* 22 (1890): 110; and *PCC*, reel 170, item 152, 9:497.

91. Colonel Thomas Procter to Joseph Reed, 23 January 1781, *Pennsylvania Archives*, vol. 8, ed. Samuel Hazen (Philadelphia: Jos. Stevens and Co., 1853), 710. Procter recommended that after the men were discharged, two judges should certify enlistments to "prevent future complaints." Ibid., 710; and Samuel White [?] to Joseph Reed, 16 January 1781, *Joseph Reed Papers*, reel 3, p. 136, DLAR. Washington, however, was upset that the Reed commissioners so readily acceded to the mutineer's demands before he could "prosecute such measures with the Pennsylvanians as the case demanded [meaning coerce them into submission by force]." He also believed that the majority of the Pennsylvanians had fraudulently gained their discharges. See Paul David Nelson, *Anthony Wayne: Soldier of the Early Republic* (Bloomington: Indiana University Press, 1985), 123; and Washington to von Steuben, 6 February 1781, and Circular to the New England States and New York, 22 January 1781, in Fitzpatrick, *Writings of Washington*, 21:129–30, 193.

92. Anthony Wayne to George Washington, 21 January 1781, *Washington Papers*, ser. 4, reel 73, Library of Congress; and Paul David Nelson, *Anthony Wayne, Soldier of the Early Republic* (Bloomington: Indiana University Press, 1985), 123–24. Wayne strongly urged that the Pennsylvania Executive Council forward bounty money for enlistments so that New Jersey recruiters could not take advantage of the large number of former soldiers in the neighborhood of Philadelphia trying to enlist for newer, higher bounties. Moreover, he urged the Pennsylvania government to encourage Philadelphia merchants to refuse to hire the newly discharged soldiers. Ibid., 123–24. See George Nelson Diary entry for 18 January 1781, Historical Society of Pennsylvania, noting the large number of recently discharged soldiers who came to town looking for work.

93. Benjamin Stoddert to the President of Congress, 25 January 1781, *PCC*, reel 161, item 148, 1:295–96; and "Minutes of the Supreme Executive Council," *Colonial Records of Pennsylvania*, 12:624–26. Private John Bryan was one of those soldiers discharged. His certificate, signed by Anthony Wayne, established that he was duly discharged on 21 January 1781 and was entitled to five days' rations for his journey home. Bryan received 2 pounds cash and all the back clothing owed him by the government, a soldier's due under the original terms of enlistment. See Paul V. Lutz, "Rebellion among the Rebels," *Manuscripts* 19, no. 3 (Summer 1967): 12.

94. Lender, "The Enlisted Line," 241–42; van Doren, *Mutiny in January*, 215–16; Fitzpatrick, *Writings of Washington*, 21:136; and Nelson, *Anthony Wayne*, 124. On 21 January 1781, Wayne wrote Washington that he expected to have "a reclaimed and formidable Line" once again. Anthony Wayne to Washington, 21 January 1781, *Washington Papers*, ser. 4, reel 73, Library of Congress. Wayne was sadly mistaken.

95. Jonathan Sullivan, Chairman of the Committee on the Pennsylvania Mutiny, to George Washington, 10 January 1781, *Letters of the Delegates to Congress*, 16:587; William H. Denny, "Soldier of the Republic: The Life of Major Ebenezer H. Denny" (Ph.D. diss., Miami University of Ohio, 1978), 9–10.

96. Philip Schuyler to Hamilton, 25 January 1781, *Alexander Hamilton Papers*, vol. 2 (Washington, D.C.: Library of Congress), 542–43; George Washington to George Clinton, 4 January 1781, in Fitzpatrick, *Writings of Washington*, 21:58–59; Lender, "The Enlisted Line," 238–41; and Major J. N. Cumming to John Ladd Howell, New Jersey Society of Pennsylvania, *Year Book for 1930* (1931), 78–79.

97. Arthur St. Clair to George Washington, 7 January 1781, *PCC*, item 170, vol. 9, DLAR, 452.

98. Frederick Frelinghuysen to Washington, 23 January 1781, *Washington Papers*, ser. 4, reel 74, Library of Congress. Frelinghuysen noted that he thought only about 160 men actually participated in the abortive revolt. There is also evidence in his letter that the men believed that the commission would find things in their favor because of what had been recently offered to the Pennsylvanians. Also see Elias Dayton to Washington, 24 January 1781, *Washington Papers*, ser. 4, reel 74, Library of Congress. Dayton's letter sealed the fate of the mutineers when he added if the soldiers "discover they are not discharged agreeable to their wishes by the commissioners, they may again become Seditious and not consider themselves amenable to the orders of their officers." Washington was quick to write the Committee of Congress to request "no terms be made with [the Jersey mutineers]." Washington to the Committee of Congress, 21 January 1781, *Washington Papers*, ser. 4, reel 74; Washington to von Steuben, 6 February 1781, in Fitzpatrick, *Writings of Washington*, 21:193–94.

99. Washington to the President of Congress, 23 January 1781, *PCC*, reel 170, 9:515; Washington to General Robert Howe, 22 January 1781, in Fitzpatrick, *Writings of Washington*, 21:128; and Van Doren, *Mutiny in January*, 217. Lest someone interpret wrongly (in Washington's mind) that he had the Jersey soldiers at Pompton executed while under the protection of a earlier pardon offered by Elias Dayton, Washington explained to the New Jersey governor, William Livingston, that Dayton's pardon called for a full and immediate return to duty. "This condition," stated Washington, "was not performed on the part of the mutineers. . . . Besides . . . the existence of the Army called for an example." Washington to William Livingston, 27 January 1781, in Fitzpatrick, *Writings of Washington*, 21:148.

100. Robert Howe to George Washington, 27 January 1781, *Washington Papers*, ser. 4, reel 74, Library of Congress; Robert Howe to Washington, 27 January 1781, *PCC*, reel 170, 521, ibid.; and Lender, "The Enlisted Line," 242. An eyewitness to the execution was Dr. James Thacher, who observed the men who shot the Sergeants had shed tears, stated that "the condemned had neither time nor . . . power to implore the forgiveness of their God." See James Thacher, *Military Journal of Dr. James Thacher during the American Revolutionary War* (Hartford, Conn.: S. Andrus, 1854), 252–53.

101. Thacher, *Military Journal*, 252; Lieutenant Colonel Barber to Major General Robert Howe, 28 January 1781, *Washington Papers*, ser. 4, reel 74, Library of Congress; "The Journal of Ebenezer Wild (1776–1781)," *PMHB*, 2d ser., vol. 6 (1890–91), 131; Lender, "The Enlisted Line," 244; Lieutenant Benjamin Gilbert to his father, February 1781, *Winding Down: The Revolutionary War Letters of Lieutenant Benjamin Gilbert of Massachusetts, 1780–1783*, ed. John Shy (Ann Arbor: University of Michigan Press, 1989), 34–25; and van Doren, *Mutiny in January*, 231–32.

102. Arthur St. Clair to Joseph Reed, 2 April 1781, *St. Clair Papers*, reel 1, DLAR. St. Clair observed that unless the men were soon [paid], it [was] likely to end in General Desertion." Ibid., 2 April 1781.

103. Nelson, *Anthony Wayne*, 128–29; Anthony Wayne to Lafayette, 19, 20 May 1781, to Mary Wayne, 25 May 1781, *Wayne Papers*, vol. 12, HSP; and Wayne to Washington, 26 May 1781, enclosing Court Martial Proceedings, 20, 22 May 1781, *Washington Papers*, Library of Congress.

104. Dewees, *History*, 228–32, in van Doren, *Mutiny in January*, 253. Dewees was a fifer during the time of troubles in the Pennsylvania line. His account is one of the few of the York "after-mutiny" from an enlisted man's point of view. A drummer named Leonard Dubbs corroborated Dewees's account of Macaroney Jack. Macaroney Jack's wife was a camp follower who washed laundry for a number of soldiers; Dewees was one of her customers. Dewees thought she was a "very well behaved and good conditioned woman." Ibid., 228–32; and *Pennsylvania Archives*, 2d ser., 10:292.

105. Dewees, *History*, 228–32; and van Doren, *Mutiny in January*, 254–55. Van Doren noted that a number of contemporary accounts appear to diverge as to what exactly happened to cause the deaths of the soldiers and who was actually killed by firing squad. Eyewitnesses to the affair seemed to differ on the names, number, and place of execution. However, it is logical to assume that Anthony Wayne was anxious to regain some of his lost dignity after his humiliation by his own soldiers in January 1781. Therefore, it follows that Wayne would be quick to suppress any sort of mutinous conduct or perceived defiance from the men with the utmost vigor. See *Wayne Papers*, vol. 12, 20–25 May 1781, HSP; *Pennsylvania Archives*, 2d ser., 10:292; Dewees, *History*, 228–32; and *Correspondence of Samuel Blachley Webb*, 2:341. Another theory presented by Nelson in *Anthony Wayne* was the possibility that the witnesses recalled two mutinies, one on 20 and 22 May 1781, as described in Courts-martial records, and a second one on 25 May. If this is true, then the details of all witnesses have some credibility.

106. Dewees, *History*, 228–32; and van Doren, *Mutiny in January*, 255–56. Dewees noted that the soldiers at York "were afraid to say or do anything, for so trivial appeared the offenses of these men [executed by Wayne] that they knew not what in the future was to be made to constitute crime." Van Doren, *Mutiny in January*, 256.

107. Anthony Wayne to Washington, 26 May 1781, *Washington Papers*, Library of Congress; and Nelson, *Anthony Wayne*, 130–31.

108. Nathanael Greene to Robert Morris, 22 April 1782, *Greene Papers*, 58:58, William L. Clements Library, University of Michigan, Ann Arbor.

109. Ibid., Greene to Morris, 22 April 1782; Greene to William Smallwood, 22 April 1782, *Greene Papers;* and Denny, "Soldier of the Republic," 64.

110. Nathanael Greene to George Washington, 22 April 1782, *Greene Papers;* Nathanael Pendleton to Mr. Pierce, *Nathanael Pendleton Papers*, Society of the Cincinnati Papers, Manuscript Division, Library of Congress; Nathanael Greene to John Hanson, 18 May 1782, *Greene Papers;* and Henry Lee, *Memoirs of the War in the Southern Department of the United States* (New York, 1869), 546–48.

111. Nathanael Greene to George Washington, 18 May 1782, *PCC*, reel 175, item 155, 2:441. The laboratory was greatly feared by the soldiers as the work performed there was distasteful and dangerous. Moreover, it effectively isolated them from the rest of Greene's army. Icabod Burnett to Lieutenant Alexander, 29 April 1782, 59:28, *Greene Papers;* William Seymour, "A Journal of the Southern Expedition, 1780–1783, *PMHB*, vol. 7 (1883), HSP; Francis V. Greene, *General Greene* (New York: D. Appleton, 1893), 288.

112. Patrick J. Furlong, "Memoranda and Documents: A Sermon for the Mutinous Troops of the Connecticut, 1782," *The New England Quarterly* (December 1970), 621–23; William Abbott, ed., *The Memoirs of Major-General William Heath* (1798; reprint, New York, 1901), 318 (page references are to reprint edition). Washington noted the mutiny by stating that "minds soured by distress are easily rankled." See *Writings of Washington*, 24:248–49; and Washington to Robert Morris, in Fitzpatrick, *Writings of Washington*, 24:289.

113. Benjamin Lincoln to Arthur St. Clair, 12 June 1783, *St. Clair Papers*, reel 2, DLAR; Richard Humpton to the President of Congress, 24 June 1783, *PCC*, reel 45, item 38, 3–9; ibid., deposition of Sergeant James Bennett, representing the soldiers of the Pennsylvania Line, 23 June 1783; and Varnum Lansing Collins, *The Continental Congress at Princeton* (Princeton, N.J.: Princeton University Library, 1908), 9–11.

114. Elias Boudinot to Washington, 21 June 1783, *LMCC*, vol. 7, ed. Edmund C. Burnett (Washington, D.C., 1921–36), 193–94; Eugene R. Sheridan and John M. Murrin, *Congress at Princeton: Being the Letters of Charles Thomson to Hannah Thomson, June–October 1783* (Princeton, N.J.: Princeton University Library, 1985), xl; and Kenneth R. Bowling, "New Light on the Philadelphia Mutiny of 1783: Federal-State Confrontation at the Close of the War for Independence," *PMHB* (1977), 419–50.

115. J. J. Boudinot, ed., *The Life, Public Services, Addresses, and Letters of Elias Boudinot* (New York: Houghton, Mifflin, and Co., 1896), 334–37; James E. Gibson, "Benjamin Rush Terminates a Post-War Mutiny among Troops Demanding Their Discharge," *Transactions and Studies of the College of Physicians of Philadelphia*, 4th ser., 13 (December 1945): 134–38; and *PCC*, reel 45, item 38, 49, 73, "Affidavits of Sergeants Townsend and Murthwaite." Some soldiers observed Boudinot passing by when someone cried out, "There! There goes the President of Congress! Why do you let him pass?" Boudinot was seized by Private Andrew Wright and "might have fared badly" had not Sergeant Townsend intervened. See Collins, *Continental Congress at Princeton*, 21.

116. Richard Peters to von Steuben, 23 April 1783, *Letters of the Delegates to Congress*, 20:211–12; *JCC*, 24:453; Lynn Montross, *Reluctant Rebels*, 351–53; and Denny, "Soldier of the Republic," 78. Rather than facing an execution squad, Christian Nagle, after being sentenced to death for his role in the mutiny, escaped without punishment and even received 100 acres of land after the war. See "Calendar of Archival Material on Land Patents Issued by the United States," *Federal Land Series*, vol. 2, 1799–1835, ed. Clifford Neal Smith (Chicago: American Library Association, 1973).

117. Lieutenant Benjamin Gilbert to his father, late June 1783, in Shy, *Winding Down*, 108.

118. James Warren to Elbridge Gerry, 16 April 1776, in *A Study in Dissent: The Warren-Gerry Correspondence, 1776–1792*, ed. C. Harvey Gardiner (Carbondale: Southern Illinois University Press, 1962), 17; James Kirby Martin, "A Most Undisciplined, Profligate Crew: Protest and Defiance in the Continental Ranks, 1776–1783," in *Arms and Independence: The Military Character of the American Revolution*, ed. Ronald Hoffman and Peter J. Albert (Charlottesville: University of Virginia Press, 1984), 129.

119. Martin, "A Most Undisciplined, Profligate Crew," 129–30; "Sergeant John Smith's Diary of 1776," *Mississippi Valley Historical Review* (1933–34), 252–56; and Committee of Sergeants to Anthony Wayne, 4 January 1781, *PCC*, reel 170, 9:481.

120. Martin, *Private Yankee Doodle*, 287–88.

Notes to the Conclusion

1. Joseph Plumb Martin, *Private Yankee Doodle: Being a Narrative of Some of the Adventures, Dangers, and Sufferings of a Revolutionary Soldier*, ed. George F. Scheer (Boston: Little, Brown, and Co., 1962), 197–98. Loyalist Jonathan Boucher also commented on the great diversity of the American scene. He stated that this "extraordinary variety . . . always struck [him] as a thing that had a great influence on the manners and turn of thinking of the people of [America]." See Jonathan Boucher, *Reminiscences of an American Loyalist, 1738–1789* (New York: Houghton, Mifflin, and Co., 1925), 98.

2. The best compendium of recent historiography on the era is found in Don Higginbotham's "The Early American Way of War: Reconnaissance and Appraisal," *William and Mary Quarterly* 44 (April 1987), passim. Higginbotham noted that military themes have benefited from "the new social history" and cultural studies as well. The best of these "new" military/social historians are John Shy, *A People Numerous and Armed: Reflections on the Military Struggles for American Independence*, rev. ed. (Ann Arbor: University of Michigan Press, 1990); John Ferling, *A Wilderness of Miseries* (Westport, Conn.: Greenwood Press, 1980); Francis Jennings, *The Invasion of America: Indians, Colonialism, and the Cant of Conquest* (Chapel Hill: University of North Carolina Press, 1975); Fred Anderson, *A People's Army* (Chapel Hill: Univesity of North Carolina Press, 1984); James Kirby Martin and Mark E. Lender, *A Respectable Army: The Military Origins of the Republic, 1763–1789* (Arlington Heights, Ill.: Harlan Davidson, 1982); and Sylvia Frey, *Water from the Rock: Black Resistance*

in a Revolutionary Age (Princeton, N.J.: Princeton University Press, 1991). The major thrust of these new histories is to get beyond the traditional battles-and-leaders approach of past works. Indeed, many can now even be categorized as military history but include armed struggle as part of larger themes.

3. Marcus Rediker, "A Motley Crew of Rebels, Sailors, Slaves, and the Coming of the Revolution," in *The Transforming Hand of Revolution: Reconsidering the American Revolution as a Social Movement*, ed. Peter Albert and Ronald Hoffman (Charlottesville: University Press of Virginia, forthcoming). Also see comments of Hessian Colonel Dinklage's undated letter, quoted in Ernst Kipping, *The Hessian View of America, 1776–1783*, trans. B. A. Uhlendorf (Monmouth Beach, N.J.: Philip Freneau Press, 1971), 34–35; and Shy, *A People Numerous and Armed*, 11–27.

4. Martin and Lender, *A Respectable Army*, chap. 1 passim.

5. Ibid., 17; John Shy, "A New Look at Colonial Militia," *William and Mary Quarterly* 20 (April 1963): 181–82.

6. Frey, *Water from the Rock;* and Benjamin Quarles, ed., *Black Mosaic: Essays in Afro-American History and Historiography* (Amherst: University of Massachusetts Press, 1988), 49, 57–58.

7. Alfred Young, ed., "Afterword," in *The American Revolution: Explorations in the History of American Radicalism* (DeKalb: Northern Illinois University Press, 1976), 459–60; Francis Jennings, "The Indians' Revolution," in *The American Revolution*, ed. Young, 321–22; and Francis Jennings, *The Invasion of America: Indians, Colonialism, and the Cant of Conquest* (Chapel Hill: University of North Carolina Press, 1975), chap. 5 passim.

8. Thomas Jefferson to John Page, 5 August 1776, in *Papers of Thomas Jefferson*, ed. Julian C. Boyd (Princeton, N.J.: Princeton University Press, 1950), 4:622–24; and Boyd, *Papers of Thomas Jefferson*, 1:485–87.

9. Marcus Rediker, "Good Hands, Stout Heart, and Fast Feet: The History and Culture of Working People in Early America," prepublished paper in *Reviving the English Revolution: Reflections and Elaborations on the Work of Christopher Hill*, ed. Geoff Eley and William Hunt (London: Verso Books, 1986), 3–6; Mark E. Lender, "The Social Structure of the New Jersey Brigade," in *The Military in America*, ed. Peter Karsten (New York: Free Press, 1986), 67–70; John B. B. Trussell, Jr., *The Pennsylvania Line: Regimental Organization and Operation, 1776–1783* (Harrisburg: Pennsylvania Historical and Museum Commission, 1977), 244–51; Edward C. Papenfuse and Gregory A. Stiverson, "General Smallwood's Recruits: The Peacetime Career of the Revolutionary War Private," *William and Mary Quarterly* 30 (1973): 117–32; and Aubrey C. Land, "Economic Base and Social Structure," *Journal of Economic History* 25 (1965): 642.

10. See Diary entry, 30–31 January 1778, "Caleb Haskell's Diary," *Pamphlets in American History Collection*, fiche no. B/RW14, David Library of the American Revolution, Washington Crossing, Pa., 16; George Washington to Patrick Henry, 13 April 1777, in Fitzpatrick, ed., *Writings of Washington*, 7:408; and Charles Royster, *A Revolutionary People at War: The Continental Army and the American Character, 1775–1783* (Chapel Hill: University of North Carolina Press, 1979), 50.

11. E. P. Thompson, "The Moral Economy of the Crowd in the Eighteenth Century," *Past and Present* 50 (1971): 76–136; Diary of Albegience Waldo, *Pennsylvania Magazine of History and Biography* 21 (October 1897): 307; and "Diary of the Revolt," *Pennsylvania Archives*, ser. 2, 11:631–35.

12. James Kirby Martin, "A Most Undisciplined, Profligate Crew: Protest and Defiance in the Continental Ranks, 1776–1783," in *Arms and Independence: The Military Character of the American Revolution*, ed. Ronald Hoffman and Peter J. Albert (Charlottesville: University Press of Virginia, 1984), 119–40; Thompson, "The Moral Economy of the Crowd in the

Eighteenth-Century," 77–78; and Marcus Rediker, "The American Revolution and the Cycles of Rebellion in the Eighteenth-Century Atlantic" (unpublished manuscript), 11–19.

13. See James Neagles, *Summer Soldiers: A Survey and Index of Revolutionary War Courts-Martial* (Salt Lake City, Utah: Ancestry Inc., 1986), passim; and James H. Edmonson, "Desertion in the American Army during the Revolutionary War" (Ph.D. diss., Louisiana State University, 1971), 217–18.

14. Peter Linebaugh and Marcus Rediker, "The Many-Headed Hydra: Sailors, Slaves, and the Atlantic Working Class in the Eighteenth Century," *Journal of Historical Sociology* 3, no. 3 (September 1990): 225–32; Peter Wood, "The Dream Deferred: Black Freedom Struggles on the Eve of White Independence," in *Resistance: Studies in African, Caribbean, and Afro-American History*, ed. Gary Y. Okihiro (Amherst: University of Massachusetts Press, 1986), 170–75.

15. Linebaugh and Rediker, "A Many-Headed Hydra," 244–45.

Selected Bibliography

PRIMARY SOURCES

DIARIES, JOURNALS, MANUSCRIPTS, PAPERS, PERSONAL ACCOUNTS, NEWSPAPERS, AND COLONIAL RECORDS

Abbott, William, ed. *The Memoirs of Major-General William Heath*. New York: 1901.

Adams, Charles F. *Familiar Letters of John Adams and His Wife Abigail Adams*. New York: 1876.

Allan, John. "An Account of Colonel John Allan: A Maine Revolutionary." *Sprague's Journal of Maine History* 2 (1910).

Anderson, Enoch. *Personal Recollections of Enoch Anderson*. Wilmington: Historical Society of Delaware, 1896.

Angell, Israel. *Diary of Colonel Israel Angell*. New York: Arno Press, reprinted 1971.

Balderson, Marion, and David Syrett, eds. *The Lost War: Letters from British Officers during the American Revolution*. New York: Horizon Press, 1975.

Barber, Daniel. *A History of My Own Times*. Frederick, Md., 1832.

Barth, Richard, William Doernemann, and Mark Schwalm. "The Trenton Prisoner List." *Johannes Schwalm Historical Association* 4 (1985).

Bartlett, Josiah. *Letters by Josiah Bartlett, William Whipple, and Others*. Philadelphia, 1889.

Baurmeister, Carl Leopold. *Revolution in America: Confidential Letters and Journals, 1776–1784*. Translated by Bernard Uhlendorf. New Brunswick, N.J.: Rutgers University Press, 1957.

Berkenhout, John. "Journal of an Excursion from New York to Philadelphia in the Year 1778." *Pennsylvania Magazine of History and Biography*, January 1941.

Bixby, Samuel. *Sergeant Samuel Bixby Diary*. Worcester, Mass.: American Antiquarian Society.

Boucher, Jonathan. *Reminiscences of an American Loyalist, 1738–1789*. New York: Houghton, Mifflin, 1925.

Boudinout, J. J., ed. *The Life, Public Services, Addresses, and Letters of Elias Boudinout*. New York: Houghton Mifflin, 1896.

Bowen, Ashley. *The Journals of Ashley Bowen*. Salem, Mass.: Essex Institute, 1973.

Brock, R. A., ed. *The Official Records of Robert Dinwiddie*. Richmond, Va., 1883–84.

Brunnholtz, Peter. *Reports of the United German Evangelical Lutheran Congregations in North America.* Philadelphia, 1750.

Buettner, Johann Carl. *Narrative of Johann Carl Buettner in the American Revolution.* New York: Charles Heartman Publishers, 1915.

Butterfield, Lyman, ed. *Diary and Autobiography of John Adams.* Cambridge, Mass.: Harvard University Press, 1962.

Carter, Landon. *The Diary of Landon Carter of Sabine Hall, 1752–1778.* Edited by Jack R. Greene. Charlottesville: University Press of Virginia, 1965.

Chastellux, Marquis de. *Travels in North America in the Years 1780, 1781, and 1782.* Edited by Howard Rice. Chapel Hill: University of North Carolina Press, 1963.

Colden, Cadwallader. *History of the Five Indian Nations.* London, 1747.

Cook, Fred, ed. *Journals of the Military Expedition of Major General John Sullivan against the Six Nations in 1779.* Freeport, N.Y.: Books of Library Press, reprinted 1972.

Croghan, George. "George Croghan's Journal." *Pennsylvania Magazine of History and Biography* 71 (1947).

Dann, John C., ed. *The Revolution Remembered: Eyewitness Accounts of the War for Independence.* Chicago: University of Chicago Press, 1980.

Davies, K. G., ed. *Documents of the American Revolution.* Shannon, Ireland, 1976–81.

Davis, A. M., ed. *Colonial Currency Reprints.* Boston, 1911.

Denny, Ebenezer. *Military Journal of Major Ebenezer Denny: An Officer in the Revolution and Indian Wars.* Philadelphia, 1859.

Dewees, Samuel. *A History and Life and Services of Captain Samuel Dewees.* Edited by John Smith Hanna. Baltimore, Md., 1844.

Dohla, Johann Conrad. *A Hessian Diary of the American Revolution.* Translated by Bruce E. Burgoyne. Norman: University of Oklahoma Press, 1989.

Elmer, Ebenezer. "Journal Kept during an Expedition to Canada in 1776." *New Jersey Historical Society Proceedings*, 1847.

Ewald, Johann Conrad. *Diary of the American War: A Hessian Journal.* Translated by Joseph P. Tustin. New Haven, Conn.: Yale University Press, 1979.

Fisher, Elijah. *Elijah Fisher's Journal.* Augusta, Maine: Press of Badger and Manley, 1880.

Fitzpatrick, John C., ed. *The Writings of Washington.* 39 vols. Washington, D.C., 1931–44.

Force, Peter, ed. *American Archives.* Washington, D.C., 1843.

Fortesque, John W. *The Correspondence of George III.* London, 1928.

Furlong, Patrick J. "Memoranda and Documents: A Sermon for the Mutinous Troops of the Connecticut Line, 1782." *The New England Quarterly*, December 1970.

Gardiner, Harvey, ed. *A Study in Dissent: The Warren-Gerry Correspondence, 1776–1792.* Carbondale: Southern Illinois University Press, 1962.

Gerlach, Larry, ed. *New Jersey in the American Revolution, 1763–1783: A Documentary History.* Trenton: New Jersey Bicentennial Commission, 1975.

Gibbes, Robert, ed. *Documentary History of the American Revolution.* New York, 1853.

Gilbert, Benjamin. *Winding Down: The Revolutionary War Letters of Lieutenant Benjamin Gilbert of Massachusetts, 1780–1783.* Edited by John Shy. Ann Arbor: University of Michigan Press, 1989.

Glover, John. *John Glover's Letterbook, 1776–1777.* Edited by Russell Knight. Salem, Mass.: Essex Institute, 1976.

Graydon, Alexander. *Memoirs of "His Own Time" with Reminiscences of the Men and Events of the Revolution.* Philadelphia, 1846.

Greenman, Jeremiah. *Diary of a Common Soldier in the American Revolution, 1775–1783.* Edited by Robert C. Bray and Paul Bushnell. DeKalb: Northern Illinois University Press, 1978.

Hawkins Orderly Book. Hazen's Regiment. Philadelphia: Historical Society of Pennsylvania, 1782.

Heinrichs, Johann. "Journal." *Pennsylvania Magazine of History and Biography* (1898).

Hooker, Richard, ed. *The Carolina Backcountry on the Eve of the Revolution: The Journal and Other Writings of Charles Woodmason, Anglican Itinerant*. Chapel Hill: University of North Carolina Press, 1953.

Hutchinson, William T., and William M. E. Rachel, eds. *The Papers of James Madison*. Chicago, 1932.

Isham, Charles, ed. "The Papers of Silas Deane." *Collections of the New York Historical Society*. New York, 1886.

Journals of the Reverend Thomas Smith, and the Reverend Samuel Deane, Pastors of the First Church in Portland. Portland, Maine, 1849.

Kemble, Stephen. "Kemble's Journal." *New York State Historical Society Collections*, 1883.

Kirkwood, Robert. *The Journal and Orderly Book of Captain Robert Kirkwood*. Wilmington: Delaware Historical Society, 1910.

Lamb, Roger. *Diary of Sergeant Roger Lamb, Royal Welch Fuzileers: Occurences [sic] during the Late American War*. Dublin: Wilkinson and Courtney Publishers, 1809.

Larabee, Leonard W., and William B. Willcox. *The Papers of Benjamin Franklin*. New Haven, Conn.: Yale University Press, 1959.

Laurens, John. *The Army Correspondence of John Laurens*. Edited by William G. Simms. New York: The Bradford Club, 1867.

Lee, Henry. *Memoirs of the War in the Southern Department of the United States*. New York, 1869.

Lesser, Charles H., ed. *The Sinews of Independence: Monthly Strength Reports of the Continental Army*. Chicago: University of Chicago Press, 1976.

MacKenzie, Frederick. *Diary of Frederick MacKenzie as an Officer of the Regiment of Royal Welch Fusileers during the Years 1775–1781*. Cambridge, U.K., 1930.

Marshall, Christopher. *Diary of Christopher Marshall, 1774–1781*. Edited by William Duane. New York: Arno Press, 1969.

Martin, Joseph Plumb. *Private Yankee Doodle: Being a Narrative of Some of the Adventures, Dangers, and Sufferings of a Revolutionary Soldier*. Edited by George Scheer. Boston: Little, Brown and Co., 1962.

Moore, Frank, ed. *Diary of the Revolution*. New York: Arno Press, reprinted 1969.

Muhlenberg, Henry Melchoir. *The Journal of Henry Melchoir Muhlenberg*. Philadelphia, 1958.

Neagles, James. *Summer Soldiers: A Survey and Index of Revolutionary War Courts-Martial*. Salt Lake City, Utah: Ancestry Inc., 1986.

Orderly Book of the 2nd Pennsylvania Continental Line. Pennsylvania Magazine of History and Biography 36 (1912).

Pargellis, Stanley M. *Military Affairs in North America, 1748–1765: Selected Documents from the Cumberland Papers in Windsor Castle*. New York: Appleton-Century, 1937.

Popp, Stephen. *A Hessian Soldier in the American Revolution: The Diary of Stephen Popp*. Translated by Reinhard Pope. Racine, Wis., 1953.

Powell, William S., Jame K. Huhta, and Thomas J. Farnharm, eds. *The Regulators in North Carolina: A Documentary History*. Raleigh, N.C.: State Department of Archives and History, 1971.

Reeves, Enos. "Extracts from the Letter-Books of Lieutenant Enos Reeves." *Pennsylvania Magazine of History and Biography* 21 (1898).

Reuber, Johannes. "Diary." *Johannes Schwalm Historical Association* 1 (1979).

Richardson, John. "Letters of Lieutenant John Richardson, 1776." *Pennsylvania Magazine of History and Biography* 16 (1892).

Schaw, Janet. *Journal of a Lady of Quality*. Edited by Evangeline Walker Andrews and Charles Andrews. New Haven, Conn.: Yale University Press, 1921.

Schoepf, Johann David. *Travels in the Confederation, 1783–1784*. Translated by Alfred J. Morrison. Philadelphia, 1911.

Serle, Ambrose. *American Journal of Ambrose Serle*. New York: Arno Press, 1969.

Seume, J. G. "Memoirs of a Hessian Transcript: J. G. Seume's Reluctant Voyage to America." Translated by Margarete Woelfel. *William and Mary Quarterly* (1948).

Seymour, William. "The Journal of the Southern Expedition." *Pennsylvania Magazine of History and Biography* 7 (1883).

Sheridan, Eugene R., and John M. Murrin, eds. *Congress at Princeton: Being the Letters of Charles Thomson to Hannah Thomson*. Princeton, N.J.: Princeton University Press, 1985.

Smith, Eleazer. *Eleazer Smith Diary*. Miscellaneous Manuscripts. Ann Arbor, Mich.: William L. Clements Library.

Smith, John. "John Smith's Diary of 1776." *Mississippi Valley Historical Review* 20 (1933–34).

Smith, Peter, ed. *Letters to the Members of the Continental Congress*. 8 vols. Washington, D.C.: Carnegie Institution of Washington, reprinted 1963.

Stevens, Benjamin F., ed. *Facsimiles of Manuscripts in European Archives Relating to America*. 25 vols. New York, 1889–98.

Stone, William L., ed. *Memoirs, Letters, and Journals of Major General von Riedesal*. New York, 1969.

Thacher, James. *Military Journal of Dr. James Thacher during the American Revolutionary War*. Hartford, Conn.: S. Andrus, 1854.

Tilghman, Tench. *Memoir of Lieutenant Colonel Tench Tilghman*. Edited by Samuel A. Harrison. 1876.

Valley Forge Orderly Book of General George Weedon of the Continental Army. New York: Liveright Publishers, reprinted 1971.

von Closen, Baron Ludwig. *The Revolutionary Journal of Baron Ludwig von Closen, 1780–1783*. Translated by Evelyn M. Acomb. Chapel Hill: University of North Carolina Press, 1958.

Wade, Herbert T., and Robert A. Lively, eds. *This Glorious Cause: The Adventures of Two Company Grade Officers in Washington's Army*. Princeton, N.J.: Princeton University Press, 1958.

Ward, Samuel. *Correspondence of Governor Samuel Ward*. Edited by Bernhard Knollenburg. Providence: Rhode Island Historical Society, 1952.

Wasmus, Julius Friedrich. "Julius Friedrich Wasmus, A German Military Surgeon during the Revolution." *Bulletin of the History of Medicine* 18 (October 1945).

Webb, Samuel Blachley. *The Correspondence and Journals of Samuel Blachley Webb*. Edited by Worthington C. Ford. New York: New York Times and Arno Press, reprinted 1969.

Willard, Margaret Wheeler, ed. *Letters on the American Revolution, 1774–1776*. Boston: Houghton Mifflin, 1925.

Willcox, William B. *The American Rebellion: Sir Henry Clinton's Narrative of his Campaigns, 1775–1783*. New Haven, Conn.: Yale University Press, 1954.

Winn, Richard. "General Winn's Notes—1780." Edited by Samuel C. Williams. *South Carolina History and Genealogy Magazine*, January 1943.

NEWSPAPERS

American Daily Advertiser (Philadelphia), 30 June 1801

Boston Evening-Post, 1 November 1773

Connecticut Journal, 14 June 1775

Deutsch-Amerikanisches Magazin, 16 November 1777
Freeman's Journal, 2, 12 July 1774
Gaine's Paper, 9 March 1778
Georgia Gazette (Savannah), 2 February, 7 December 1774
Limerick Chronicle, 20 October 1768
Maryland Gazette, 14 December 1775
Massachusetts Centinel, 22 May 1784
New Hampshire Gazette, 27 April 1779
New Jersey Gazette, 17 June 1778; 27 September 1780
New York Gazette, 22 June 1772
New York Royal Gazette, 27 October 1779
Pennsylvania Evening Post, 14 December 1775; 16 August 1777
Pennsylvania Journal (Philadelphia), 17 April 1776
Pennsylvania Packet, 26 February 1778
Rivington's Royal Gazette, 3 July 1779
Royal Georgia Gazette, 11 February 1779
Scot's Magazine, October 1772
Staatesbote (Philadelphia), 1 August 1775
Virginia Gazette (Williamsburg), 17, 23 November, 2 December 1775; 26 January 1776

MANUSCRIPTS, PAPERS, AND COLLECTIONS

Adams, John. *The John Adams Papers*. Boston, Mass.: Massachusetts Historical Society.
Adams, Samuel. Papers. New York Public Library, New York.
Benjamin Trumbull Collection. Yale University Library, New Haven, Conn.
Boyd, Julian C., ed. *Papers of Thomas Jefferson*. Princeton, N.J.: Princeton University Press, 1950.
British Public Record Office Papers. David Library of the American Revolution, Washington Crossing, Pa.
Burr Family Collection. Yale University Library, New Haven, Conn.
"Calendar of Archival Material on Land Patents Issued by the United States." *Federal Land Series*. Vol. 2. Chicago, 1973.
Carleton, Guy. Papers. David Library of the American Revolution, Washington Crossing, Pa.
Clinton, Henry. Manuscript Papers. William L. Clements Library, Ann Arbor, Mich.
Dartmouth Manuscripts Calendar. London: Historical Manuscripts Commission, 1895.
Elizabeth Furnace Manuscripts. Pig Iron Book. Historical Society of Pennsylvania.
Evans Collection of Early American Imprints, Georgetown University Library, Washington, D.C.
Feinstone Collection. David Library of the American Revolution, Washington Crossing, Pa.
Force, Peter. Manuscript Collection. Library of Congress, Washington, D.C.
Gage, Thomas. Manuscript Papers. William L. Clements Library, Ann Arbor, Mich.
Gates, Horatio. *Horatio Gates Papers*. New York Public Library, New York.
Greene, Nathanael. Manuscript Papers. William L. Clements Library, Ann Arbor, Mich.
Heath, William. Manuscript Papers. David Library of the American Revolution, Washington Crossing, Pa.
Huntington, Samuel. Manuscript Papers. *Collections*. Connecticut Historical Society.
Johannes Schwalm Historical Association Papers. Lancaster Historical Society, Lancaster, Pa.

Laurens, Henry. *Papers of Henry Laurens.* David Library of the American Revolution, Washington Crossing, Pa.

Lee, Charles. "Charles Lee Papers." *New York Historical Society Collections.* New York, 1878.

Ligerwood Manuscript Collection. Morristown National Historic Park, Morristown, N.J.

Logan, John Henry. "Extracts from the Logan Manuscript [of the Upper South]." *Historical Collections of the Joseph Habersham Chapter.* Daughters of the American Revolution.

Loudoun Papers. Henry E. Huntington Library, San Marino, Calif.

Miscellaneous Manuscripts. Pennsylvania Historical and Museum Commission, Harrisburg, Pa.

Miscellaneous Manuscripts. U.S. Revolutionary War Collection, American Antiquarian Society, Worcester, Mass.

Nelson, George. Manuscript Papers. Historical Society of Pennsylvania, Philadelphia.

Pamphlets. American History Collection, David Library of the American Revolution, Washington Crossing, Pa.

Pendleton, Nathanael. Manuscript Papers. Society of the Cincinnati Collection, Library of Congress, Washington, D.C.

Penrose, Maryly B. *Indian Affairs Papers.* Franklin Park, N.J.: Liberty Bell Associates, 1981.

Pinckney, Thomas. Pinckney Family Papers. South Carolina Historical Society, Charleston, S.C.

Powell, Leven. Manuscript Papers. Swem Memorial Library, College of William and Mary, Williamsburg, Va.

Reed, Joseph. Manuscript Papers. David Library of the American Revolution, Washington Crossing, Pa.

Rimpau, Hans Helmuth, ed. "The Brunswickers in Nordamerika, 1776–1783." *Archiv fuer Sippenforschung.* Federal Republic of Germany.

St. Clair, Arthur. Manuscript Papers. David Library of the American Revolution, Washington Crossing, Pa.

Schuyler, Philip. *Philip Schuyler Papers.* New York Public Library, New York.

Selections from the Correspondence of the Executive of New Jersey, from 1776 to 1786. Newark, N.J., 1849.

Smith, Clifford Neal, ed. *Brunswick Deserter-Immigrants of the American Revolution.* Thomson, Ill.: Heritage House Publishers, 1973.

Syrett, Howard, ed. *The Papers of Alexander Hamilton.* New York: Columbia University Press, 1961.

Taylor, Robert J. *The Papers of John Adams.* Cambridge, Mass.: Belknap Press, 1979.

Vermont Historical Society. Miscellaneous Manuscripts. Montpelier, Vt.

von Steuben, Friedrich. Papers. David Library of the American Revolution, Washington Crossing, Pa.

Waldo, Albegience. "Diary of Albegience Waldo." *Pennsylvania Magazine of History and Biography* 21 (October 1897).

Washington, George. Washington Papers. Library of Congress, Washington, D.C.

Wayne, Anthony. Manuscript Papers. Historical Society of Pennsylvania, Philadelphia.

ARCHIVES

Clark, Walter, ed. *State Records of North Carolina.*

Colonial Laws of New York from the Year 1664 to the Revolution. Albany, N.Y., 1894–96.

Colonial Records of Pennsylvania, 1683–1790. Philadelphia, 1852–53.

Connecticut Historical Society Collections. Hartford, Conn., 1899.

Delaware Archives, Military. Wilmington, Del.

Hemphill, Edwin, ed. *Extracts from the Journal of the Provincial Congresses of South Carolina.* Columbia, S.C., 1960.

Hening, William H., ed. *The Statutes at Large: Being a Collection of All the Laws of Virginia.* Richmond, Va., 1810–23.

Historical Statistics of the United States, Colonial Times to 1957. Washington, D.C.: Government Printing Office, 1960.

Journals of the Continental Congress. Washington, D.C.: Government Printing Office.

Kilty, William, ed. *The Laws of Maryland.* Annapolis, Md., 1799.

New Hampshire Council Records. Concord, N.H.

New Jersey Department of Defense Manuscripts. New Jersey State Library, Trenton, N.J.

New York Archives. *The American Revolution in New York: Its Political, Social, and Economic Significance.* Albany, N.Y., 1926.

O'Callaghan, E., ed. *New York Colonial Documents.* New York.

Papers of the Continental Congress. Washington, D.C., Library of Congress.

Pennsylvania Archives. Harrisburg, Pa.

Public Records of the State of Connecticut.

Revolutionary War Pension Records. Washington, D.C., National Archives.

Rhode Island Archives: Records of the State of Rhode Island. Providence, R.I.

Saunders, William, ed. *The Colonial Records of North Carolina.* 26 vols. Raleigh, N.C.: P. M. Hale, 1886–90.

South Carolina Historical Society Collections. Columbia, S.C.

Steiner, Bernard, et al., eds. *Archives of Maryland.*

United States Bureau of Census. *Heads of Families at the First Census of the United States Taken in the Year 1790: Pennsylvania.* Washington, D.C.: Government Printing Office, 1908.

Secondary Sources

BOOKS

Abramson, James L. *The American Home Front.* Washington, D.C.: National Defense University Press, 1983.

Anderson, Fred. *A People's Army: Massachusetts Soldiers and Society in the Seven Years War.* Chapel Hill: University of North Carolina Press, 1984.

Aptheker, Herbert. *American Negro Slave Revolts.* New York: Columbia University Press, 1943.

Archdeacon, Thomas J. *Becoming American: An Ethnic History.* New York: The Free Press, 1983.

Atwood, Rodney. *The Hessians.* London: Cambridge University Press, 1980.

Axtell, James. *The European and the Indian.* New York: Oxford University Press, 1981.

———. *The Invasion Within: The Contest of Cultures in Colonial North America.* New York: Oxford University Press, 1985.

Bailyn, Bernard. *Voyagers to the West: A Passage in the Peopling of America on the Eve of the Revolution.* New York: Vintage Books, 1986.

Barnhart, John D., ed. *Henry Hamilton and George Rogers Clark in the American Revolution to Include the Journal of Governor Henry Hamilton.* Crawfordsville, Ind.: R. E. Banta, 1951.

Berger, Carl. *Broadsides and Bayonets: The Propaganda War of the Revolution.* Philadelphia: University of Pennsylvania Press, 1961.

Berlin, Ira. *Slaves without Masters: The Free Negro in the Antebellum South.* New York: Pantheon Books, 1974.

Bernstein, Barton J., ed. *Towards a New Past: Dissenting Essays in American History*. New York: Knopf, 1968.
Billigmeir, Robert. *Minorities in American Life, Americans from Germany: A Study in Cultural Diversity*. Belmont, Calif.: Wadsworth Publishers, 1974.
Billington, Ray Allen. *Westward Expansion: A History of the American Frontier*. New York: Macmillan, 1974.
Bodle, Wayne K., and Jacqueline Thibaut. *Valley Forge Research Project*. Valley Forge, Pa., 1980.
Bolton, Charles K. *The Private Soldier under Washington*. Williamstown, Mass.: Corner House Publishers, reprinted 1976.
Bowman, Allen. *The Morale of the American Revolutionary Army*. Washington, D.C.: American Council on Public Affairs, 1943.
Boyer, Charles S. *Early Forges and Furnaces in New Jersey*. Philadelphia: University of Pennsylvania Press, 1931.
Brand, Oscar, ed. *Songs of '76: Being a Compendium of Music and Verses, Patriotic and Treasonous Sung Both by the Rebels and the Adherents of His Royal Majesty George III*. New York: M. Evans & Co., 1972.
Bridenbaugh, Carl. *Myths and Realities*. Westport, Conn.: Greenwood Press, 1952.
Brooks, Noah. *Henry Knox, A Soldier of the Revolution*. New York, 1900.
Brown, Douglas S. *The Catawba Indians: Allies in the Revolution*. Columbia: University of South Carolina Press, 1966.
Brunhouse, Robert H. *The Counter-Revolution in Pennsylvania, 1776–1790*. Harrisburg: Pennsylvania Historical and Museum Commission, 1971.
Buel, Richard. *Dear Liberty: Connecticut's Mobilization for the Revolutionary War*. Middletown, Conn.: Wesleyan University Press, 1980.
Burton, William L. *Melting Pot Soldiers: The Union's Ethnic Regiments*. Ames: Iowa State University Press, 1988.
Busch, Noel. *Winter Quarters: George Washington and the Continental Army at Valley Forge*. New York: Liveright, 1974.
Calloway, Colin G. *The Western Abenakis of Vermont, 1600–1800: War, Migration, and Survival of an Indian People*. Norman: University of Oklahoma Press, 1990.
Carp, E. Wayne. *To Starve an Army at Pleasure: Continental Army Administrators and American Political Culture, 1775–1783*. Chapel Hill: University of North Carolina Press, 1984.
Cary, John. *Joseph Warren: Physician, Politician, Patriot*. Urbana: University of Illinois Press, 1961.
Cashin, Edward J. *The King's Ranger: Thomas Brown and the American Revolution on the Southern Frontier*. Athens: University of Georgia Press, 1989.
Chambers, John W. *To Raise an Army: The Draft Comes to Modern America*. New York: Free Press, 1987.
Cockran, David H. *The Creek Frontier, 1540–1783*. Norman: University of Oklahoma Press, 1967.
Collins, Varnum Lansing. *The Continental Congress at Princeton*. Princeton, N.J.: Princeton University Library, 1908.
Cotterill, Robert S. *The Southern Indians: The Story of the Civilized Tribes before Removal*. Norman: University of Oklahoma Press, 1954.
Countryman, Edward. *A People in Revolution: The American Revolution and Political Society in New York, 1760–1790*. Baltimore: Johns Hopkins University Press, 1981.
Cress, Lawrence Delbert. *Citizens in Arms: The Army and the Militia in American Society to the War of 1812*. Chapel Hill: University of North Carolina Press, 1982.
Crow, Jeffrey, and Larry Tise, eds. *The Southern Experience in the American Revolution*. Chapel Hill: University of North Carolina Press, 1978.

Cunliffe, Marcus. *Soldiers and Civilians: The Martial Spirit in America, 1775–1865*. Boston: Little, Brown and Co., 1968.

Cunz, Dieter. *The Maryland Germans*. Princeton, N.J.: Princeton University Press, 1948.

Dabney, William M. *After Saratoga: The Story of the Convention Army*. Albuquerque: University of New Mexico Press, 1954.

Davidson, Philip G. *Propaganda and the American Revolution, 1763–1783*. New York: W. W. Norton, 1941.

Davis, David Brion. *The Problem of Slavery in the Age of Revolution, 1770–1823*. New York: Cornell University Press, 1975.

———. *The Problem of Slavery in Western Culture*. Ithaca, N.Y.: Cornell University Press, 1966.

Debo, Angie. *The Road to Disappearance: A History of the Creek Indians*. Norman: University of Oklahoma Press, 1941.

Dickson, R. J. *Ulster Emigration to America, 1718–1775*. London: Routledge and Kegan Paul, 1966.

Dippel, Horst. *Germany and the American Revolution, 1770–1800*. Chapel Hill: University of North Carolina Press, 1977.

Doddridge, Joseph. *Notes on the Settlement and Indian Wars of the Western Parts of Virginia and Pennsylvania*. Pittsburgh, Pa.: privately published, 1912.

Downey, Fairfax. *Indian Wars of the United States Army, 1776–1865*. Garden City, N.Y.: Doubleday, 1963.

Doyle, David Noel. *Ireland, Irishmen, and Revolutionary America, 1760–1820*. Dublin: Mercier Press, 1981.

Dunaway, Wayland. *The Scotch-Irish of Colonial Pennsylvania*. Chapel Hill: University of North Carolina Press, 1944.

Dunn, Richard. *Sugar and Slaves*. Chapel Hill: University of North Carolina Press, 1972.

Everest, Allan S. *Moses Hazen and the Canadian Refugees in the American Revolution*. Syracuse, N.Y.: Syracuse University Press, 1976.

Ferguson, E. James. *The Power of the Purse: A History of American Public Finance, 1776–1790*. Chapel Hill: University of North Carolina Press, 1961.

Ferling, John E. *A Wilderness of Misery: War and Warriors in Early America*. Westport, Conn.: Greenwood Press, 1980.

Fischer, David Hackett. *Historian's Fallacies*. New York: Harper and Row, 1970.

Fitch, William E. *Some Neglected History of North Carolina*. New York: Neale Publishing Co., 1905.

Foner, Eric, ed. *The New American History*. Philadelphia: Temple University Press, 1990.

———. *Tom Paine and Revolutionary America*. London: Oxford University Press, 1976.

Foner, Philip S. *Labor and the American Revolution*. Westport, Conn.: Greenwood Press, 1976.

———. *Blacks in the American Revolution*. Westport, Conn.: Greenwood Press, 1981.

Franklin, John Hope. *From Slavery to Freedom*. New York: Knopf, 1967.

French, Allen. *The First Year of the American Revolution*. New York: Houghton Mifflin, 1934.

Frey, Sylvia. *The British Soldier in America: A Social History of Military Life in the Revolutionary Period*. Austin: University of Texas Press, 1981.

———. *Water from the Rock: Black Resistance in a Revolutionary Age*. Princeton, N.J.: Princeton University Press, 1991.

Furer, Howard B., ed. *The Germans in America, 1607–1970: A Chronology and Fact Book*. Dobbs Ferry, N.Y.: Oceana Publications, 1973.

Genovese, Eugene. *Roll, Jordan, Roll: The World the Slaves Made*. New York: Vintage Books, 1976.

Glass, D. V., and D. E. C. Eversley, eds. *Population in History*. London: E. Arnold, 1965.

Godbolt, E. Stanley. *Christopher Gadsden and the American Revolution.* Knoxville: University of Tennessee Press, 1982.

Godfrey, Carlos E. *The Commander-in-Chief's Guard: The Revolutionary War.* Baltimore: Genealogical Publishing Co., 1972.

Gold, Philip. *Evasions: The American Way of Service.* New York: Paragon House, 1985.

Grant, Charles S. *Democracy in the Connecticut Frontier Town of Kent.* New York: Columbia University Press, 1961.

Graymont, Barbara. *The Iroquois in the American Revolution.* Syracuse, N.Y.: Syracuse University Press, 1978.

Greene, Jack P. *Pursuits of Happiness.* Chapel Hill: University of North Carolina Press, 1988.

Greene, Lorenzo. *The Negro in Colonial New England, 1620–1776.* New York: Columbia University Press, 1942.

Greene, Robert Ewell. *Black Courage.* Washington, D.C.: Daughters of the American Revolution, 1984.

Greven, Philip J., Jr. *Four Generations: Population, Land, and Family in Andover, Massachusetts.* Ithaca, N.Y.: Cornell University Press, 1970.

Griffin, Martin I. J. *Catholics and Revolutionary America.* Ridley Park, Pa.: privately published, 1907.

———. *The Catholic Indians and the American Revolution.* Ridley Park, Pa.: privately published, 1907.

Gross, Robert A. *The Minutemen and Their World.* New York: Hill and Wang, 1976.

Guilday, Peter. *The Life and Times of John England.* New York: America Press, 1927.

Hagan, William T. *Longhouse Diplomacy and Frontier Warfare: The Iroquois Confederacy in the American Revolution.* Albany: New York State Bicentennial Commission, 1976.

Harling, Frederick, and Martin Kaufman, eds. *The Ethnic Contribution to the American Revolution.* Westfield, Mass.: Historical Journal of Western Massachusetts, 1976.

Harvey, Oscar, ed. *The History of Wilkes-Barre, Pennsylvania.* Wilkes-Barre, Pa.: Wilkes-Barre Historical Society, 1910.

Herrick, Cheesman A. *White Servitude in Pennsylvania.* Freeport, N.Y.: Books for Libraries Press, 1926.

Higginbotham, A. Leon. *In the Matter of Color: Race and the American Military Tradition.* New York: Oxford University Press, 1978.

Higginbotham, Don. *Reconsiderations on the Revolutionary War.* Westport, Conn.: Greenwood Press, 1978.

———. *George Washington and the American Military Tradition.* Athens: University of Georgia Press, 1985.

———. *The War of American Independence: Military Attitudes, Policies, and Practice, 1763–1789.* New York: Macmillan, 1971.

———. *War and Society in Revolutionary America.* Columbia: University of South Carolina Press, 1988.

Hocker, Edward W. *German Settlers of Pennsylvania and Adjacent Territory: From Advertisements Published in Philadelphia and Germantown.* Baltimore: Genealogical Publishing Co., 1980.

Hoffman, Ronald, and Peter J. Albert, eds. *Arms and Independence.* Charlottesville: University Press of Virginia, 1984.

Jackson, John W. *With the British Army in Philadelphia, 1777–1778.* San Rafael, Calif.: Presidio Press, 1979.

Jennings, Francis. *The Invasion of America: Indians, Colonialism, and the Cant of Conquest.* Chapel Hill: University of North Carolina Press, 1975.

Jensen, Merrill. *The New Nation: A History of the United States during the Confederation, 1781–1789.* New York: Knopf, 1950.

Johannes Schwalm Historical Association. *Johannes Schwalm: The Hessian*. Millville, Pa.: Precision Printers, 1976.

Jones, Douglas Lamar. *Village and Seaport: Migration and Society in Eighteenth Century Massachusetts*. Boston: University of New England Press, 1981.

Jones, Maldwyn Allen. *American Immigration*. Chicago: University of Chicago Press, 1967.

Jordan, Winthrop. *White over Black*. Chapel Hill: University of North Carolina Press, 1967.

Kaplan, Sidney. *The Black Presence in the Era of the American Revolution, 1770–1800*. Washington, D.C.: Smithsonian Institution, revised edition 1980.

Karsten, Peter, ed. *The Military in America: From the Colonial Era to the Present*. New York: Free Press, 1986.

Kipping, Ernst. *At General Howe's Side*. Monmouth Beach, N.J.: Philip Freneau Press, 1974.

———. *The Hessian View of America, 1776–1783*. Monmouth Beach, N.J.: Philip Freneau Press, 1971.

Klein, H. M. J. *The History of the Eastern Synod of the Reformed Church in the United States*. Lancaster, Pa.: Lancaster Historical Society, 1943.

Kuhns, Oscar. *German and Swiss Settlements*. New York: Abingdon Press, 1900.

Kurtz, Stephen G., and James H. Hutson, eds. *Essays on the American Revolution*. Chapel Hill: University of North Carolina Press, 1973.

Leyburn, James G. *The Scotch-Irish: A Social History*. Chapel Hill: University of North Carolina Press, 1962.

Livermore, George. *On Negroes: As Slaves, As Citizens, and Soldiers*. New York: Arno Press, reprinted 1969.

Lockhart, Audrey. *Emigration from Ireland to the North American Colonies, 1660–1783*. New York: Arno Press, 1976.

Lovejoy, Paul E. *The Ideology of Slavery in Africa*. Beverly Hills, Calif.: Sage Publications, 1981.

Lowell, Edward. *The Hessians*. Williamstown, Mass.: Cornerstone Publishing House, reprinted 1975.

MacLeod, Duncan. *Slavery, Race, and the American Revolution*. Cambridge: Cambridge University Press, 1974.

Main, Jackson Turner. *The Social Structure of Revolutionary America*. Princeton, N.J.: Princeton University Press, 1965.

———. *The Sovereign States, 1775–1783*. New York: Franklin Waters, 1973.

Marshall, W. F. *Ulster Sails West*. Belfast: Genealogical Publishing Co., 1984.

Martin, James Kirby. *In the Course of Human Events*. Arlington Heights, Ill.: Harlan Davidson, 1979.

Martin, James Kirby, and Mark E. Lender. *A Respectable Army: The Military Origins of the Republic, 1763–1789*. Arlington Heights, Ill.: Harlan Davidson, 1982.

Matthews, William. *American Diaries in Manuscript, 1580–1954: An Annotated Bibliography*. Athens: University of Georgia Press, 1974.

Mayo, Bernard, ed. *Myths and Men*. Athens: University of Georgia Press, 1959.

McCusker, John J., and Russell R. Menard, eds. *The Economy of British America, 1607–1789*. Chapel Hill: University of North Carolina Press, 1985.

Meginness, John F. *Biography of Frances Slocum: The Lost Sister of Wyoming*. Williamsport, Pa., 1891.

Merrell, James H. *The Indian's New World: Catawbas and Their Neighbors from European Contact through the Removal Era*. Chapel Hill: University of North Carolina Press, 1989.

Miles, Lion. *The Hessians of Lewis Miller*. Harrisburg: Pennsylvania-German Tricentennial Project, 1983.

Miller, Kerby A. *Emigrants and Exiles: Ireland and the Irish Exodus to North America*. New York: Oxford University Press, 1985.

Millis, Walter. *Arms and Men: A Study in American Military History*. New York: Putnam, 1956.

Moltmann, Gunter, ed. *Germans to America: 300 Years of Immigration, 1683–1983*. Stuttgart, Federal Republic of Germany: Institute for Foreign Cultural Relations, 1982.

Mohr, Walter H. *Federal Indian Relations, 1774–1788*. Philadelphia: University of Pennsylvania Press, 1933.

Moore, George. *Historical Notes*. Boston, 1862.

Morris, Richard B., ed. *The Era of the American Revolution*. Gloucester, Mass.: Peter Smith Publishers, 1971.

Muhlenberg, Henry. *The Life of Major-General Peter Muhlenberg of the Revolutionary Army*. Philadelphia: Carey and Hart Publishers, 1849.

Mullin, Gerald W. *Flight and Rebellion: Slave Resistance in the Eighteenth-Century*. New York: Oxford University Press, 1972.

Nash, Gary. *Forging Freedom: The Foundation of Philadelphia's Black Community, 1720–1840*. Cambridge, Mass.: Harvard University Press, 1988.

———. *Race and Revolution*. Madison, Wis.: Madison House, 1990.

Nell, William C. *Colored Patriots of the American Revolution*. Boston, Mass.: Walcott Publishers, 1855.

Nelson, Paul David. *Anthony Wayne: Soldier of the Early Republic*. Bloomington: Indiana University Press, 1985.

O'Brien, Michael. *A Hidden Phase of American History*. New York: Devin-Adair, 1919.

O'Connell, Maurice R. *Irish Politics and Social Conflict in the Age of the American Revolution*. Westport, Conn.: Greenwood Press, 1976.

O'Donnell, James H. *Southern Indians in the American Revolution*. Knoxville: University of Tennessee Press, 1973.

Okihiro, Gary Y., ed. *In Resistance: Studies in African, Caribbean, and Afro-American History*. Amherst: University of Massachusetts Press, 1986.

Paine, Thomas. *Common Sense and the Crisis*. New York: Anchor Press, reprinted 1973.

Pancake, John S. *1777: The Year of the Hangman*. University: University of Alabama Press, 1977.

Parsons, William T. *The Pennsylvania Dutch: A Persistent Minority*. Boston: Twayne Publishers, 1976.

Pearce, Roy Harvey. *The Savages of America: A Study of the Indian and the Idea of Civilization*. Baltimore: Johns Hopkins University Press, 1953.

Pollard, H. B. C. *The Secret Societies of Ireland*. London: P. Allan, 1922.

Prucha, Francis P. *American Indian Policy in the Formative Years*. Cambridge, Mass.: Harvard University Press, 1962.

Quarles, Benjamin, ed. *Black Mosaic: Essays in Afro-American History and Historiography*. Amherst: University of Massachusetts Press, 1988.

———. *The Negro in the American Revolution*. New York: W. W. Norton, 1961.

Ramsey, David. *The History of the American Revolution*. London, 1793.

Rediker, Marcus. *Between the Devil and the Deep Blue Sea: Merchant Seamen, Pirates, and the Anglo-American Maritime World, 1700–1750*. Cambridge: Cambridge University Press, 1987.

Reid, John Philip. *In a Defiant Stance*. University Park: Pennsylvania State University Press, 1977.

Richards, H. M. M. *The Pennsylvania-German in the Revolutionary War, 1775–1783*. Baltimore: Genealogical Publishing Co., reprinted 1978.

Richter, Daniel K., and James Merrell, eds. *Beyond the Covenant Chain: The Iroquois and Their Neighbors in Indian North America, 1600–1800*. Syracuse, N.Y.: Syracuse University Press, 1987.

Rippley, La Vern J. *The German-Americans: Early German Immigration to the United States.* New York: University Press of America, 1984.
Robinson, Donald L. *Slavery in the Structure of American Politics.* New York: Harcourt, Brace, Jovanovich, 1971.
Rosswurm, Steven. *Arms, Country, and Class: The Philadelphia Militia and the Lower Sort during the American Revolution.* New Brunswick, N.J.: Rutgers University Press, 1987.
Royster, Charles. *A Revolutionary People at War: The Continental Army and the American Character, 1775–1783.* Chapel Hill: University of North Carolina Press, 1979.
Rude, George. *The Crowd in History, 1730–1848.* New York: Wiley, 1964.
Schaff, Gregory. *Wampum Belts and Peace Trees: George Morgan, Native Americans, and Revolutionary Diplomacy.* Golden, Colo.: Fulcrum Publishing Co., 1990.
Scheer, George, and Hugh Rankin, eds. *Rebels and Redcoats: The American Revolution through the Eyes of Those Who Fought It and Lived It.* New York: Da Capo Press, 1957.
Schrader, Frederick F. *The Germans in the Making of America.* Boston: Stratford Co., 1924.
Schwalm, Mark. *The Hessian: Auxiliaries to the British Crown in the American Revolution.* Mechanicsburg, Pa.: Pennsylvania Chapter, Palatines to America, 1984.
Shy, John. *A People Numerous and Armed: Reflections on the Military Struggle for American Independence.* Ann Arbor: University of Michigan Press, 1990.
Smith, Abbot Emerson. *Colonists in Bondage: White Servitude and Convict Labor in America, 1607–1776.* Chapel Hill: University of North Carolina Press, 1947.
Smith, Adam. *The Wealth of Nations.* London, 1776.
Smith, Billy G. *The Lower Sort: Philadelphia's Laboring People, 1750–1800.* Ithaca, N.Y.: Cornell University Press, 1990.
Smith, Jonathan. *Peterborough, New Hampshire, in the American Revolution.* Peterborough, N.H.: Peterborough Historical Society, 1913.
Sosin, Jack. *The Revolutionary Frontier, 1763–1783.* New York: Holt, Rinehart, and Winston, 1967.
Sowell, Thomas. *Ethnic America: A History.* New York: Basic Books, 1981.
Stille, Charles J. *Major-General Anthony Wayne and the Pennsylvania Line in the Continental Army.* Philadelphia, 1893.
Stone, William L. *Border Wars of the American Revolution.* New York, 1874.
Svedja, George J. *Quartering, Disciplining, and Supplying the Army at Morristown, 1779–1780.* Washington, D.C.: U.S. Department of the Interior, 1970.
Trautz, Fritz. *Die Pfalzische Auswanderung nach Nordamerika im 18. Jarhhundert.* [Emigration from the Palatine to North America in the 18th Century]. Heidelberg, Federal Republic of Germany, 1959.
Treacy, M. F. *Prelude to Yorktown: The Southern Campaigns of Nathanael Greene, 1780–1781.* Chapel Hill: University of North Carolina Press, 1963.
Tross, Rudolf Karl. *The Zweybrucken or Royal Deux-Ponts Regiment and Yorktown.* Yorktown, Va.: York County Bicentennial Committee, 1981.
Trussell, John B. B. *Birthplace of an Army: A Study of the Valley Forge Encampment.* Harrisburg: Pennsylvania Historical and Museum Commission, 1979.
———. *The Pennsylvania Line: Regimental Organization and Operation, 1776–1783.* Harrisburg: Pennsylvania Historical and Museum Commission, 1977.
Truxes, Thomas M. *Irish-American Trade, 1660–1783.* Cambridge: Cambridge University Press, 1988.
Ultee, Maarten, ed. *Adapting to Conditions: War and Society in the Eighteenth Century.* University: University of Alabama Press, 1986.
van Alstyne, Richard W. *The Rising American Empire.* New York: W. W. Norton, reprinted 1974.
Van Doren, Carl. *Mutiny in January.* New York: Viking, 1943.

Voltaire. *Candide*. Edited by John Butt. New York: Penguin Books, 1947.

Votwiler, Albert T. *George Croghan and the Westward Movement, 1741–1782*. Cleveland, Ohio: Arthur H. Clark Co., 1926.

Walker, James W. St. G. *The Black Loyalists: The Search for a Promised Land in Nova Scotia and Sierra Leone, 1783–1870*. New York: Dalhousie University Press, 1976.

Weeks, Philip, ed. *The American Indian Experience: A Profile*. Arlington Heights, Ill.: Forum Press, 1988.

Wells, Frederick P. *History of Newbury, Vermont, from the Discovery of the Coos Country to the Present Time*. St. Johnsbury, Vt.: Caledonian Co., 1902.

White, Alain C. *The History of the Town of Litchfield, Connecticut, 1720–1920*. Litchfield, Conn., 1920.

White, David O. *Connecticut's Black Soldiers*. Chester, Conn.: Pequot Press, 1973.

Wilborne, Benjamin B. *The Colonial and State Political History of Hertford County, North Carolina*. Murfreesboro, Tenn., 1906.

Winthrop, William L. *Military Law and Precedents*. Boston: Little, Brown and Co., 1896.

Wittke, Carl. *We Who Built America*. New York: Prentice-Hall, 1939.

Wolf, George D. *The Fair Play Settlers of the West Branch Valley, 1769–1784: A Study of Frontier Ethnography*. Harrisburg: Pennsylvania Historical and Museum Commission, 1969.

Wright, Robert K., Jr. *The Continental Army*. Washington, D.C.: U.S. Army Center of Military History, 1986.

Wust, Klaus. *The Virginia Germans*. Charlottesville: University Press of Virginia, 1969.

Young, Alfred F., ed. *The American Revolution: Explorations in the History of American Radicalism*. DeKalb: Northern Illinois University Press, 1976.

ARTICLES

Akers, Charles W. "Our Modern Egyptians: Phillis Wheatley and the Whig Campaign against Slavery in Revolutionary Boston." *Journal of Negro History* (1975).

Alexander, Arthur J. "How Maryland Tried to Raise Her Continental Quotas." *Maryland Historical Magazine* (1947).

Anderson, Fred. "A People's Army: Provincial Military Service in Massachusetts during the Seven Years War." *William and Mary Quarterly* (1983).

———. "Why Did Colonial New Englanders Make Bad Soldiers? Contractual Principles and Military Conduct during the Seven Years War." *William and Mary Quarterly* 38 (1981).

Bast, Homer. "Creek Indian Affairs, 1775–1778." *Georgia Historical Quarterly* 33 (March 1949).

Blackwelder, Ruth. "Attitude of the North Carolina Moravians toward the American Revolution." *North Carolina Historical Review* 9 (January 1932).

Bogin, Ruth. "Liberty Further Extended: A 1776 Antislavery Manuscript by Lemuel Haynes." *William and Mary Quarterly* (1983).

Bowling, Kenneth R. "New Light on the Philadelphia Mutiny of 1783: Federal-State Confrontation at the Close of the War for Independence." *Pennsylvania Magazine of History and Biography* (1977).

Bradford, S. Sydney. "Discipline in the Morristown Winter Encampment." *New Jersey Historical Society Proceedings* 80 (1962).

Breen, Timothy H. "English Origins and New World Development: The Case of the Covanented Militia in Seventeenth Century Massachusetts." *Past and Present* (1972).

Butterfield, Lyman H. "Psychological Warfare in 1776: The Jefferson-Franklin Plan to Cause Hessian Desertions." *Proceedings of the American Philosophy Society* 94 (June 1950).

Calloway, Colin G. "Sentinels of the Revolution: Bedel's New Hampshire Rangers and the Abenaki Indians on the Upper Connecticut." *Historical New Hampshire* (Winter 1990).

Cramer, William S. "From Hessian Drummer to Maryland Ironmaker." *Johannes Schwalm Historical Association* 3 (1985).

Davis, Andrew MacFarland. "The Employment of Indian Auxiliaries in the American War." *English Historical Review* (October 1887).

De Voe, Thomas F. "The Massacre of the Stockbridge Indians." *The Magazine of American History* 5 (September 1880).

Douglass, Elisha P. "A Three-Fold American Revolution." *The American Revolution: A Heritage of Change*. Minneapolis, Minn.: John Ford Bell Library, 1975.

Edwards, Owen. "The American Image of Ireland." *Perspectives in American History* 4 (1970).

Egly, T. W., Jr. *History of the First New York Regiment*. Hampton, N.H.: Peter E. Randall, 1981.

Ferling, John. "Oh That I Was a Soldier: John Adams and the Anguish of War." *American Quarterly* (Summer 1984).

Frey, Sylvia. "The British and the Black: A New Perspective." *Historian* 38 (1976).

———. "Between Slavery and Freedom: The Virginia Blacks in the American Revolution." *Journal of Southern History* 49 (August 1983).

———. "The Common British Soldier in the Late Eighteenth Century: A Profile." *Societas* 5 (Spring 1975).

Gibson, James E. "Benjamin Rush Terminates a Post-War Mutiny among the Troops Demanding Their Discharge." *Transactions and Studies of the College of Physicians of Philadelphia* 13 (December 1945).

Green, E. R. R. "The Scotch-Irish and the Coming of the Revolution in North Carolina." *Irish Historical Studies* 7 (1950).

Greene, Lorenzo. "Some Observations on the Black Regiment of Rhode Island in the American Revolution." *Journal of Negro History* 37 (April 1952).

Harkness, Albert, Jr. "Americanism and Jenkin's Ear." *Mississippi Valley Historical Review* 37 (1950).

Hartgrove, W. B. "The Negro in the American Revolution." *Journal of Negro History* 1 (1916).

Henretta, James. "The Social Structure of Boston." *William and Mary Quarterly* (1965).

Higginbotham, Don. "The Early American Way of War: Reconnaissance and Appraisal." *William and Mary Quarterly* 44 (April 1987).

Jackson, Luther P. "Virginia Negro Soldiers and Seamen in the American Revolution." *Journal of Negro History* 27 (July 1942).

Jones, Douglas Lamar. "The Strolling Poor: Transciency in Eighteenth-Century Massachusetts." *Journal of Social History* (Spring 1975).

Jones, E. Alfred. "English Convicts in the American Army." *Proceedings of the New Jersey Historical Society* 7 (1922).

Jones, Kenneth S. "Karl Friedrich Fuhrer: Prisoner, Patriot, Publisher." *Johannes Schwalm Historical Association* 3 (1987).

Kaplan, Sidney. "The Domestic Insurrections of the Declaration of Independence." *Journal of Negro History* 61 (1976).

Land, Aubrey C. "Economic Base and Social Structure: The Northern Chesapeake in the Eighteenth Century." *Journal of Economic History* 25 (1965).

Lemisch, Jesse. "Jack Tar in the Streets: Merchant Seamen in the Politics of Revolutionary America." *William and Mary Quarterly* (1968).

Linebaugh, Peter, and Marcus Rediker. "The Many-Headed Hydra: Sailors, Slaves, and the Atlantic Working Class in the Eighteenth Century." *Journal of Historical Sociology* 3 (September 1990).

Lockridge, Kenneth A. "Land, Population, and the Evolution of New England Society, 1630–1790." *Past and Present* (April 1968).

———. "Social Change and the Meaning of the American Revolution." *Journal of Social History* 6 (1973).

Maslowski, Peter. "National Policy towards the Use of Black Troops in the Revolution." *South Carolina Historical Magazine* 73 (January 1972).

Mauer, Mauer. "Military Justice under General Washington." *Military Analysis of the Revolutionary War, Military Affairs* (1977).

McAdams, Donald R. "The Sullivan Expedition: Success or Failure?" *New York Historical Society Quarterly* 54 (January 1970).

McDonald, Forrest, and Ellen Shapiro McDonald. "The Ethnic Origins of the American People, 1790." *William and Mary Quarterly* 37 (1980).

Merrell, James H. "Some Thoughts on Colonial Historians and American Indians." *William and Mary Quarterly* 46 (1989).

Miles, Lion. "The Ironmaster and the Hessians." *Johannes Schwalm Historical Association* 2 (1981).

Papenfuse, Edward C., and Gregory Stiverson. "Smallwood's Recruits." *William and Mary Quarterly* 30 (January 1973).

Pocock, J. G. A. "British History: A Plea for a New Subject." *New Zealand Journal of History* 8 (1974).

Quarles, Benjamin. "Lord Dunmore as Liberator." *William and Mary Quarterly* (July 1958).

———. "The Colonial Militia and Negro Manpower." *Mississippi Valley Historical Review* 45 (1959).

Rediker, Marcus. "Good Hands, Stout Heart, and Fast Feet: The History and Culture of Working People in Early America." In *Reviving the English Revolution: Reflections and Elaborations on the Work of Christopher Hill*, ed. Geoff Eley and William Hunt. London: Verso Books, 1986.

———. "The American Revolution and the Cycles of Rebellion in the Eighteenth-Century Atlantic." United States Capitol Historical Society Symposium, March 1989.

Ryan, Dennis P. "Landholding, Opportunity, and Mobility in Revolutionary New Jersey." *William and Mary Quarterly* 36 (1979).

Salay, David L. "The Production of War Material in New Jersey during the Revolution." In *New Jersey in the American Revolution*, vol. 3 (1976).

Schwalm, Mark. "The True Hessian Mercenaries." *Johannes Schwalm Historical Association* 3.

Sellers, John R. "The Common Soldier in the American Revolution." In *Proceedings of the 6th Military History Symposium*, edited by Stanley J. Underdal. Colorado Springs, Colo.: U.S. Air Force Academy.

Snoddy, Oliver. "The Irish Sword." *Journal of Military History Society of Ireland* 7 (Winter 1965).

Sosin, Jack. "The Use of Indians in the War of the American Revolution: A Re-Assessment of Responsibility." *Canadian Historical Review* 46 (June 1965).

Stayer, Jonathan. "The Hessians of Lewis Miller." *Johannes Schwalm Historical Association* 4 (1989).

Stein, Charles F. "The German Battalion of the American Revolution." *The Report: A Journal of German-American History* 36 (1975).

Thedore, Tappert. "Henry Melchoir Muhlenberg and the American Revolution." *Church History* 11 (December 1942).

Thompson, E. P. "The Moral Economy of the English Crowd in the Eighteenth Century." *Past and Present* 50 (1971).

Torok, C. H. "The Tyendinaga Mohawks: The Village as a Basic Factor in Mohawk Social Structure." *Ontario History* 57.

Vivian, Jean H. "Military Land Bounties during the Revolutionary and Confederation Periods." *Maryland Historical Magazine* (September 1966).

Waters, John J. "Family, Inheritance." *William and Mary Quarterly* 39 (1982).

———. "Patrimony, Succession, and Social Stability: Guilford Connecticut in the Eighteenth Century." *Perspectives in American History* 10 (1976).

Watson, Alan D. "Impulse toward Independence: Resistance and Rebellion among North Carolina Slaves, 1750–1775." *Journal of Negro History* (1978).

Weaver, Glenn. "Benjamin Franklin and the Pennsylvania Germans." *William and Mary Quarterly* (October 1957).

Wheeler, E. Milton. "Development and Organization of the North Carolina Militia." *North Carolina Historical Review* (Summer 1964).

Yoder, Don. "Palatine, Hessian, Dutchman: Three Images of the German in America." *Ebbes fer Alle—Ebber Ebbes fer Dich.* Breinigsvilles, Pa.: Pennsylvania German Society, 1980.

Young, Henry. "Scalp Bounties in Pennsylvania." *Pennsylvania History* 24 (January 1957).

DISSERTATIONS AND THESES

Andrews, Melodie. "Myrmidons from Abroad: The Role of the German Mercenary in the Coming of American Independence." Ph.D. diss., University of Houston, 1986.

Applegate, Howard. "Constitutions Like Iron: The Life of American Revolutionary War Soldiers in the Middle Department, 1775–1783." Ph.D. diss., Syracuse University, 1966.

Bodle, Wayne K. "The Vortex of Small Fortunes: The Continental Army at Valley Forge, 1777–1778." Ph.D. diss., University of Pennsylvania, 1987.

Bowman, Allen. "The Morale of the Continental and Militia Troops in the War of the Revolution." Ph.D. diss., University of Michigan, 1941.

Bush, Martin H. "Philip Schuyler: The Revolutionary War Years." Ph.D. diss., Syracuse University, 1966.

Denny, William H. "Soldier of the Republic: The Life of Major Ebenezer H. Denny." Ph.D. diss., Miami University of Ohio, 1978.

Doutrich, Paul E. "The Evolution of an Early American Town: York-Town, Pennsylvania, 1740–1790." Ph.D. diss., University of Kentucky, 1985.

Edmonson, James H. "Desertion in the American Army during the Revolutionary War." Ph.D. diss., Louisiana State University, 1971.

Fingerhut, Eugene R. "Assimilation of Immigrants of the Frontier of New York, 1764–1776." Ph.D. diss., Columbia University, 1962.

Hoffman, Eliot Wheelock. "German Soldiers in the American Revolution." Ph.D. diss., University of New Hampshire, 1982.

Kruger, John William. "Troop Life at the Champlain Valley Forest During the American Revolution." Ph.D. diss., State University of New York at Albany, 1981.

Lender, Mark E. "The Enlisted Line: The Continental Soldiers of New Jersey." Ph.D. diss., Rutgers University, 1975.

Lockridge, Kenneth A. "Dedham, 1636–1736: The Anatomy of a Puritan Utopia." Ph.D. diss., Princeton University, 1965.

Luchowski, Linda S. "Sunshine Soldiers: New Haven and the American Revolution." Ph.D. diss., State University of New York at Buffalo, 1976.

Ryan, Dennis P. "Six Towns: Continuity and Change in Revolutionary New Jersey, 1770–1792." Ph.D. diss., New York University, 1974.

Sellers, John R. "The Virginia Continental Line, 1775–1780." Ph.D. diss., Tulane University, 1968.

Slagle, Robert O. "The von Lossberg Regiment." Ph.D. diss., American University, 1925.

Stayer, Jonathan. "The Hessians of Lewis Miller: Assimilation of German Soldiers in America after the Revolution." M.A. thesis, Pennsylvania State University at Harrisburg, 1988.

Tate, Thad. "Desertion from the American Revolutionary Army." M.A. thesis, University of North Carolina, 1948.

Titus, James R. W. "Soldiers When They Chose to Be So: Virginians at War, 1754–1763." Ph.D. diss., Rutgers University, 1983.

Wallace, Walter F. "Oh Liberty! Oh Virtue! Oh, My Country: An Exploration of the Minds of New England Soldiers during the American Revolution." M.A. thesis, Northern Illinois University, 1974.

Wokeck, Marianne S. "A Tide of Alien Tongues: The Flow and Ebb of German Immigration to Pennsylvania, 1683–1776." Ph.D. diss., Temple University, 1983.

Index

Printed in the United States
6505